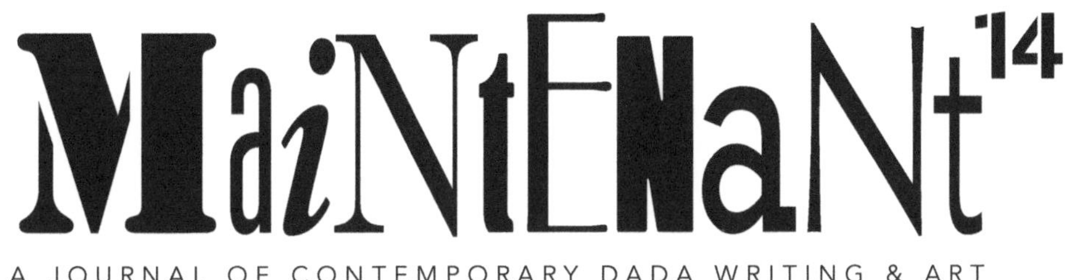MaiNtENaNt ⁴¹⁴

A JOURNAL OF CONTEMPORARY DADA WRITING & ART

PETER CARLAFTES & KAT GEORGES

EDITORS

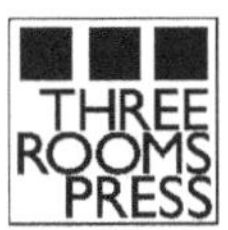

THREE ROOMS PRESS

NEW YORK

WWW.THREEROOMSPRESS.COM

EACH BOOK BORN IN GREENWICH VILLAGE

MAINTENANT: A JOURNAL OF CONTEMPORARY DADA WRITING & ART
ISSUE 13

Editors
Peter Carlaftes & Kat Georges

Contemporary Adviser
Roger Conover

Design & Production
KG Design International

Inspiration
Arthur Cravan

ON THE COVER:

"THESE ARE OUR CHILDREN"
WALTER ROBINSON

A five-painting composite; acrylic paint on canvas

©Copyright Walter Robinson | New York, NY

An American painter and art critic based in New York. As the founding editor-in-chief of *artnet Magazine* from 1996 to 2012, Robinson applies his critical voice as a writer to contemporary culture and consumerism. Often considered a post-modernist painter, Robinson's subject matter ranges from pulp-fiction book covers and fashion advertising to banal objects such as hamburgers, donuts, and Vaseline jars.

This issue is published in memory of the dada artists and poets we lost in the past year, including Steve Dalachinsky, Ronald Sauer, and Dobrica Kamperelic.

Special thanks to Mary Manspeaker, all the contributors, and everyone who supports this journal.

ISBN: 978-1-941110-91-1   ISSN 2333-2034   TRP-082

MAINTENANT: A JOURNAL OF CONTEMPORARY DADA WRITING & ART
is published annually by Three Rooms Press, New York, NY
Back issues available at www.threeroomspress.com.

For submission details, visit www.threeroomspress.com.

For inquiries about obtaining the MAINTENANT series for your educational or cultural institution archives, shop, or classroom, please email editor@threeroomspress.com.

Distributed by PGW/Ingram (www.pgw.com)

INTRODUCTION:
UN-SUSTAIN-A-BULL-SH*T

Dada was born as an artistic protest. An unfettered reclamation of the trenches flowing blood. Along came influenza which couldn't choose sides. And now, here we sit in isolation—100 years later—still creating. Revolutionaries facing a new form of plague accompanied by demagogic projections.

Each page to follow is a physical conviction. Each spread relates an intimate correspondence. The entire volume is a familial tree of leaves and shapes and buds of thoughts to be.

Our theme might be UN-SUSTAIN-A-BULL-SH*T, but here as one soul, the moment is sustainable.

Peter Carlaftes, NYC
May 2020

CONTENTS

MaiNtENaNt ^14

SUSAN SHUP

PARIS, FRANCE

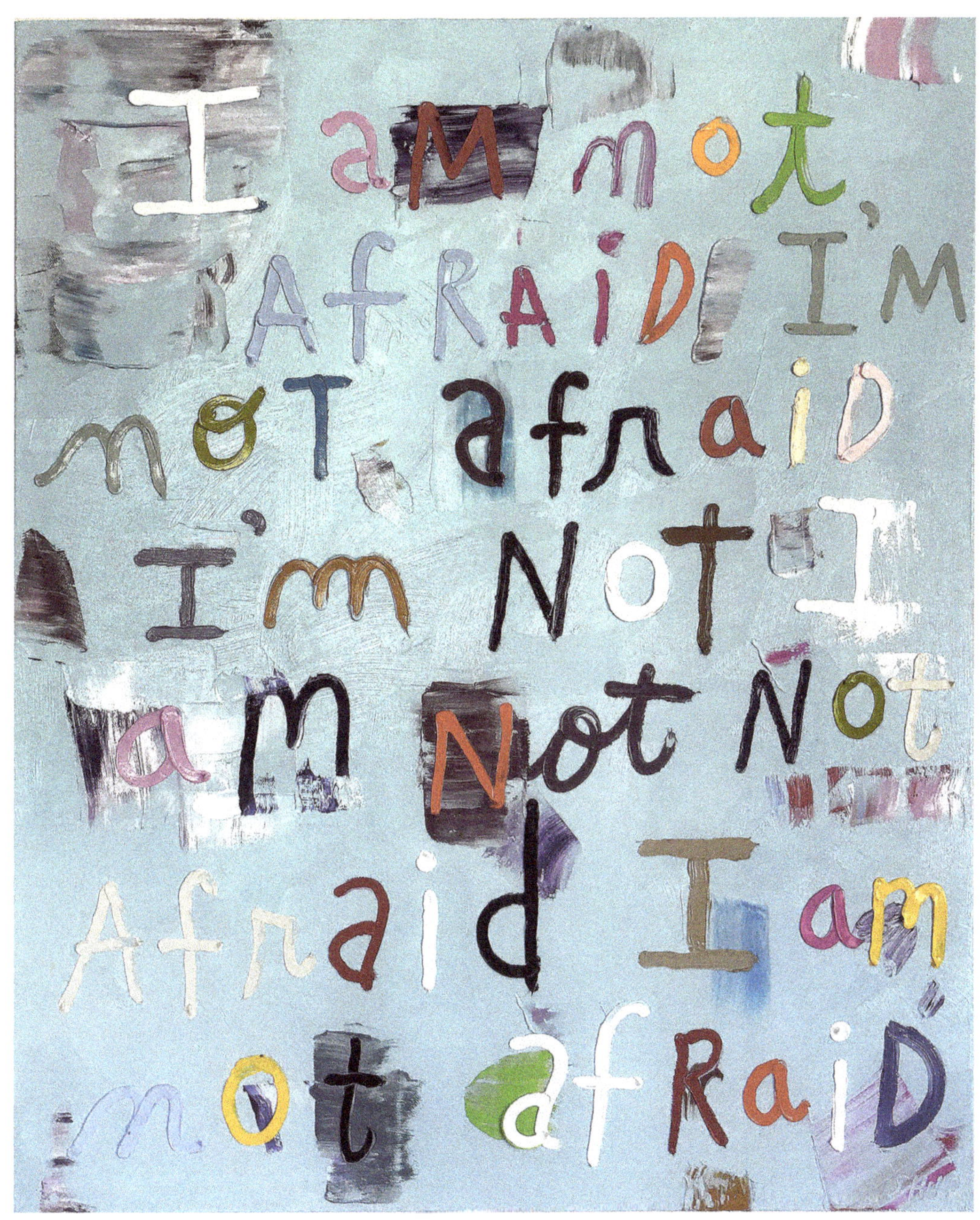

I AM NOT AFRAID

Oil on Canvas

RAFAEL CRUZ

LISBOA, PORTUGAL

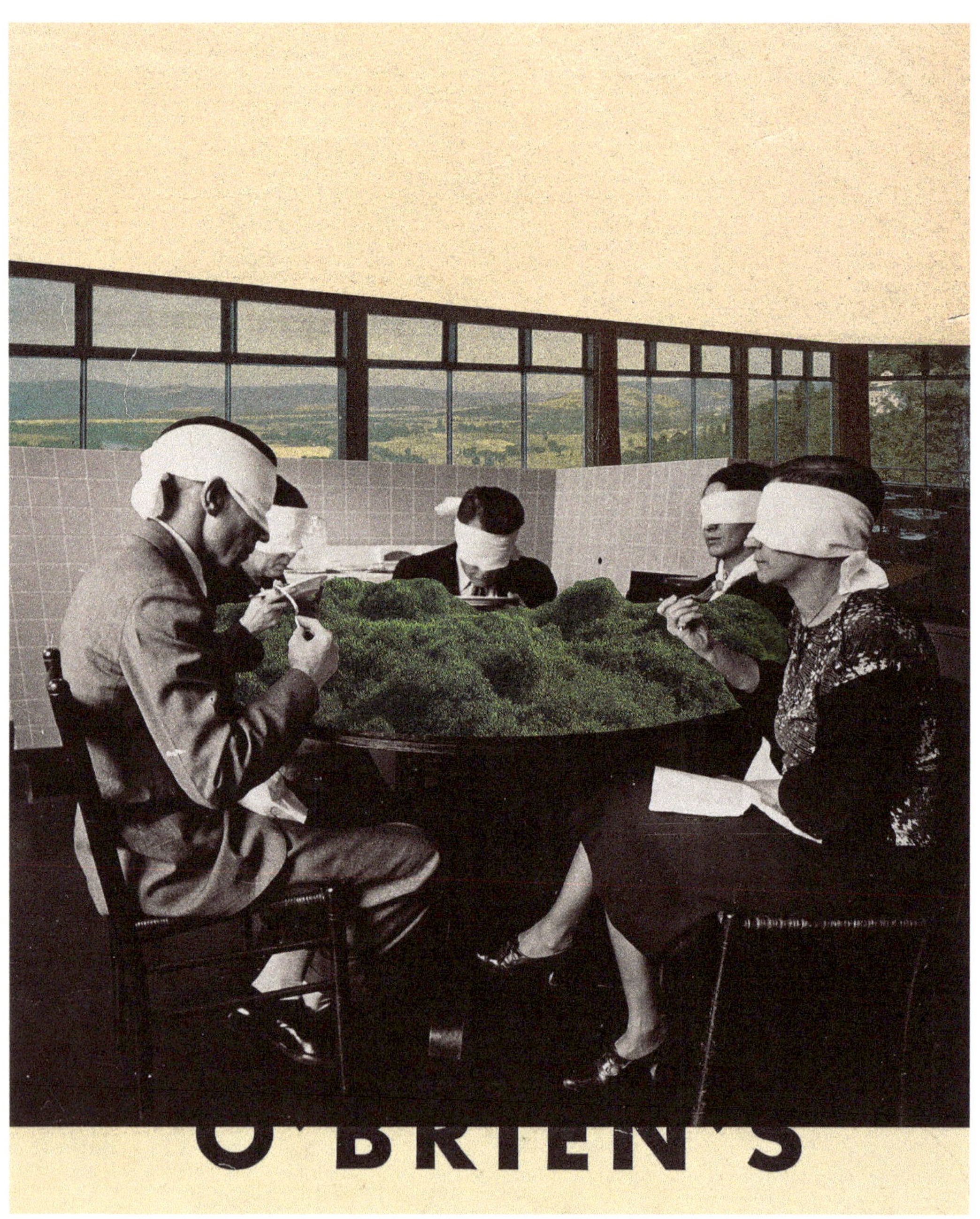

SCENIC RESTAURANT

Collage

TRACEY JACKSON
NEW YORK, NEW YORK

MY RELIGION IS KINDNESS.

It doesn't matter where you pray, what you wear, what bumper sticker you
have on your car

if we are not kind if we do not look out for each other, embrace the other in
each other . . .

If we do not take care of our planet, and the burning Koalas, of the
homeless in our streets,

if we don't stop the anti-Semitism, the racism and the hatred, the abuse of
women, and the insane killings,

if we lose more of our young men to a senseless war in the Gulf

we have not moved one step from where it all started.
And it doesn't make any difference if Mary was a virgin or not.

No one is coming to save us. We have to save ourselves. And we have to
get moving.

IRENE CAESAR

MOSCOW, RUSSIA

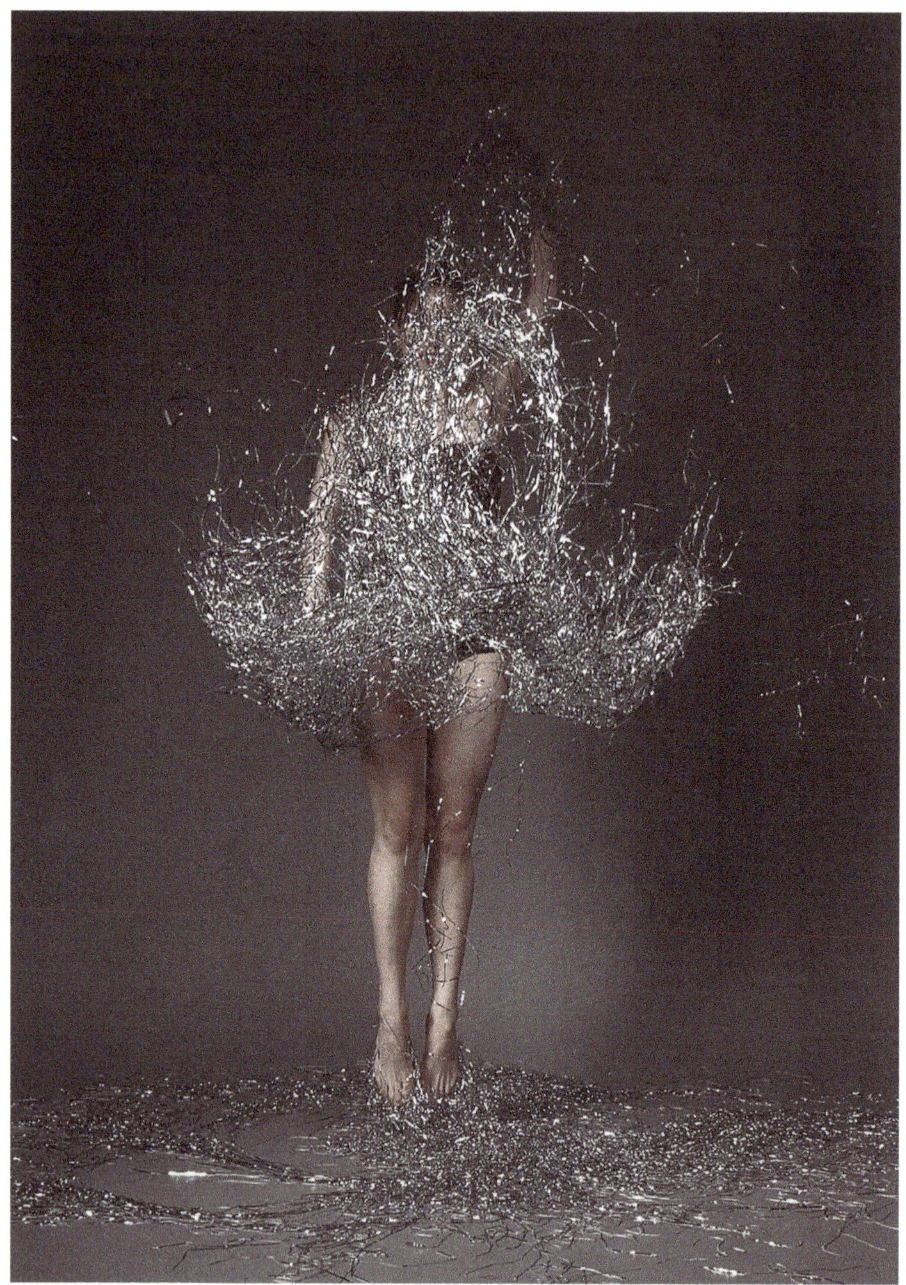

BALLERINA

Photograph

BRUCE ROBINSON

BROOKLYN, NEW YORK

VESTIGES OF THE FLOATING WORLD

They didn't see it coming, how could they?
And then it rained, rained
and we weren't witness,

but it did rain, you know, poured,

so we can only surmise
although we weren't witness
that the days grew in upon themselves

or so we might surmise

despite the unavailable clocks
and our inability to witness
for there were no clocks to set the tone

and the odd nights and even days foreshortened

there dawned nothing perhaps
because we mistrusted the clocks
who seemed to us ever unavailable

to point the way and . . . look, there was nothing

they could do about it, I mean,
how could they, we too, we
never saw it coming.

GIUSEPPE COLARUSSO

BOTTICINO, ITALY

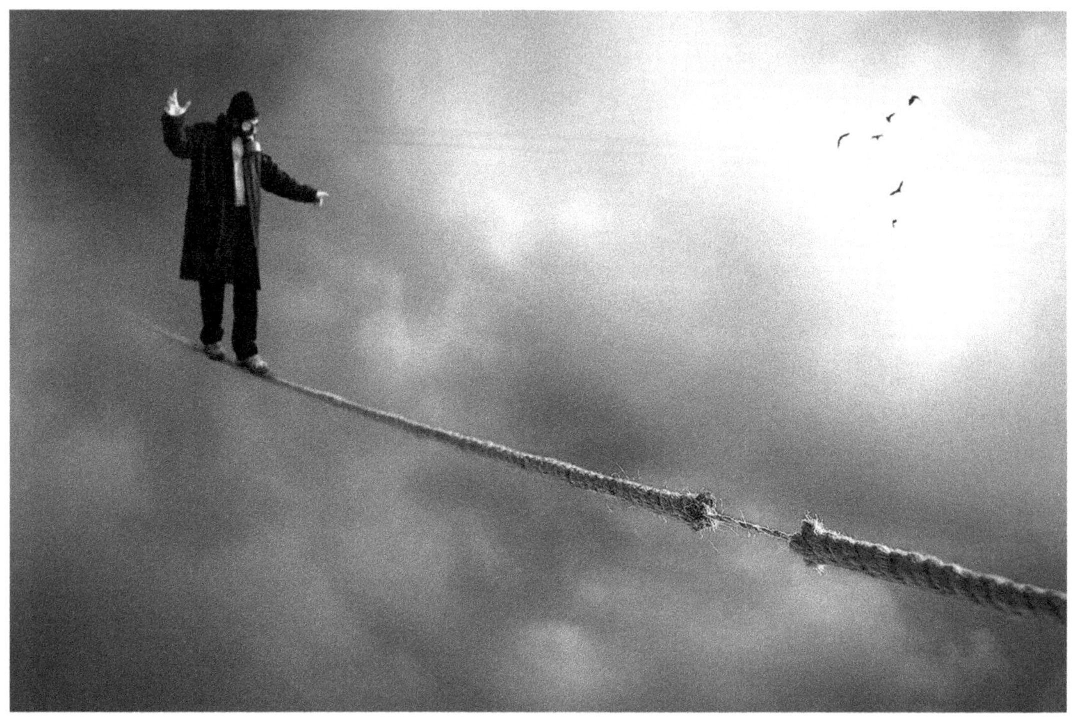

MANUFACTURING DEFECT

Photo Collage

ANDREI CODRESCU

QUEENS, NEW YORK

WALK ON ALL FOURS

I remember walking out of the ocean. What struggle!

Millions of mollusk years and shell games that hurt.

I remember getting up from all fours and looking down

on all my astonished variously shaped former friends.

Not one of them wanted to look up at me now I was up.

Bipedal and lonely until there were a bunch of others.

I remember the first scene in 2001 where I killed another.

I remember that every time I bent down to be closer

to the busy world of things that crawled loped or burrowed

I was condescending and they moved away from me.

I remember towering over everything that wasn't me.

I remember the day I howled in pain because my back gave out.

That was the day I knew my body was weakly hinged

at the place where it first stood up, and I wanted down again.

Lord, help me walk on all fours again. I know that it's late.

We only grow taller now like the towers we can't stop building.

Since we got language not one nonhuman creature deigns

to speak to us though we pretend in vain to understand them.

Animals find it more understandable when we shoot them

then when we kneel down and pretend we are their friends.

We do kneel down often to pray not to commune but pray

that we won't suffer from the back pain that is our sign of Cain.

continued

I remember that I can still return to water and do flips

but I'm in charge now of all the things I covered over.

I remember kneeling to gods who were so tall I couldn't see them.

Their heads were in the clouds, we barely reached their sandals.

Even the mono god was so tall he dropped the tablets on Moses

and made lightning to scare us all to the death we knew was coming.

In the little world I live in I sell diminishment at one dollar an inch

and practice quadrupedal yoga every morning in my living room

hoping to walk one day into the street with my quadripedal brood.

It will be the day of no pain and of trading language for nuzzling.

If we succeed it won't be so hard to hope that learning screens hurts

less than when we first left the ocean, equally pushed by hubris.

Our new weak spot is memory. A bad back and a lousy memory

may smooth our way to becoming humble and wild again and good.

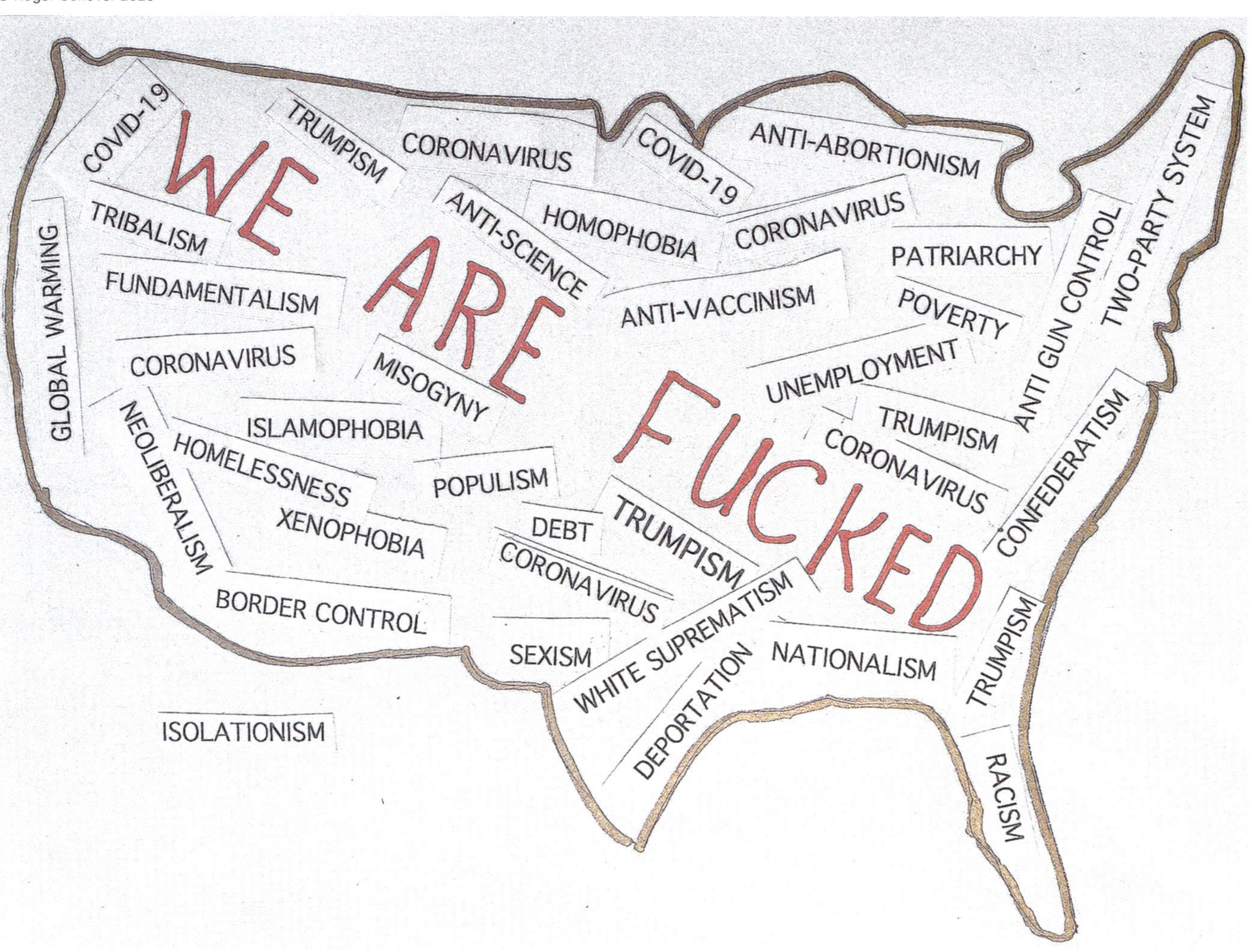

END OF STORY INC.

Collage; Paper and Ink

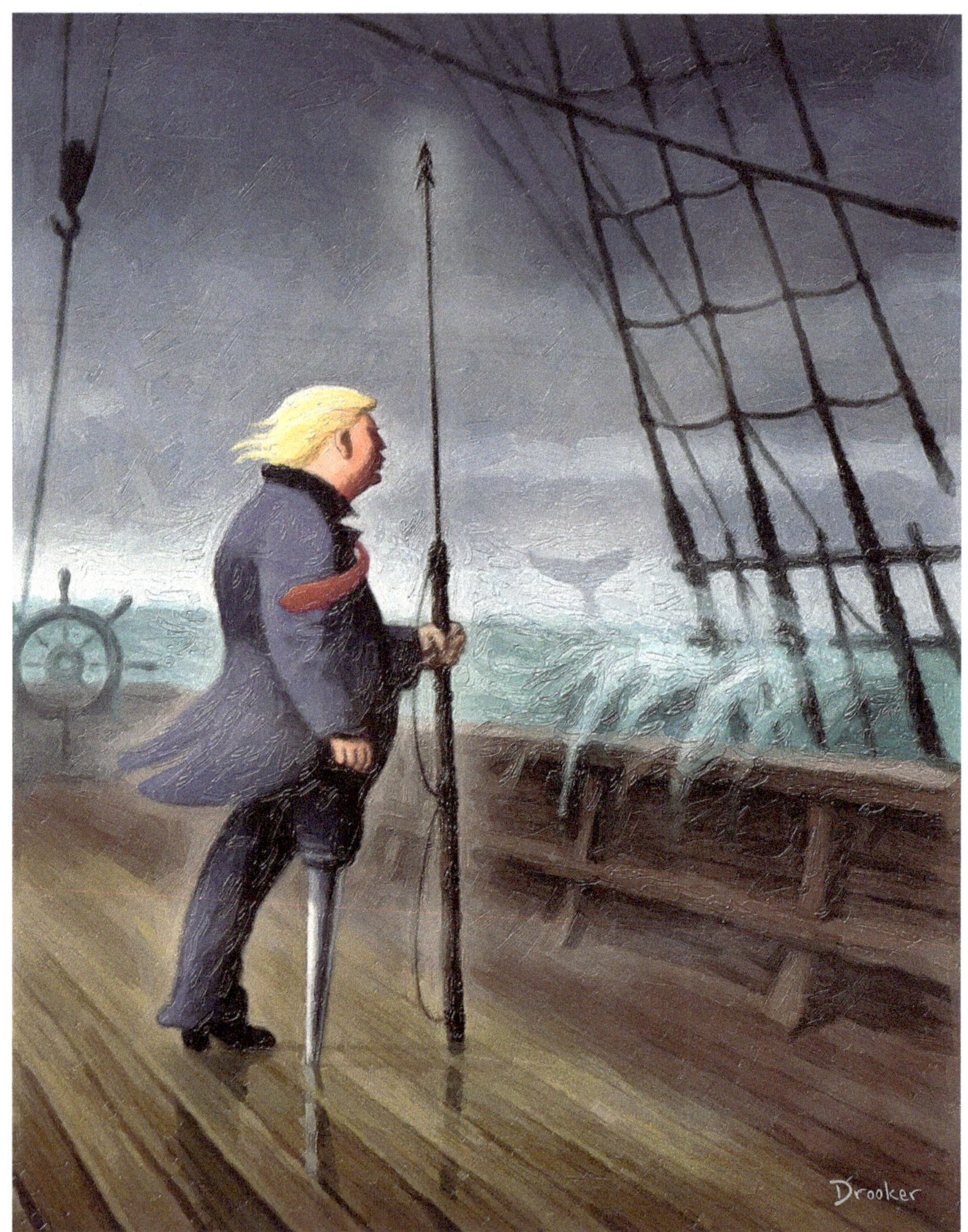

PRESIDENT AHAB

Watercolor; 11" x 8"

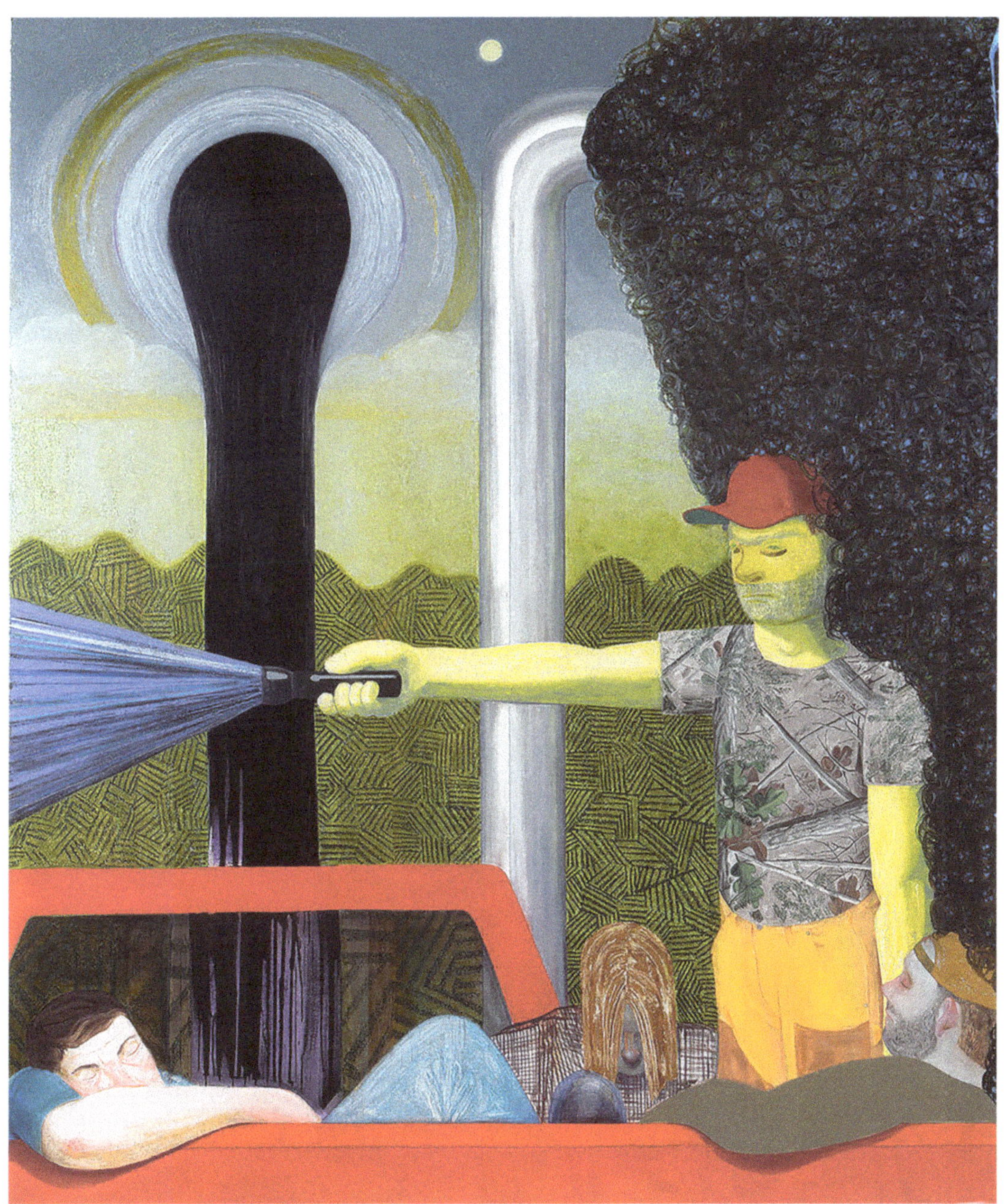

DARK LIGHT

Painting

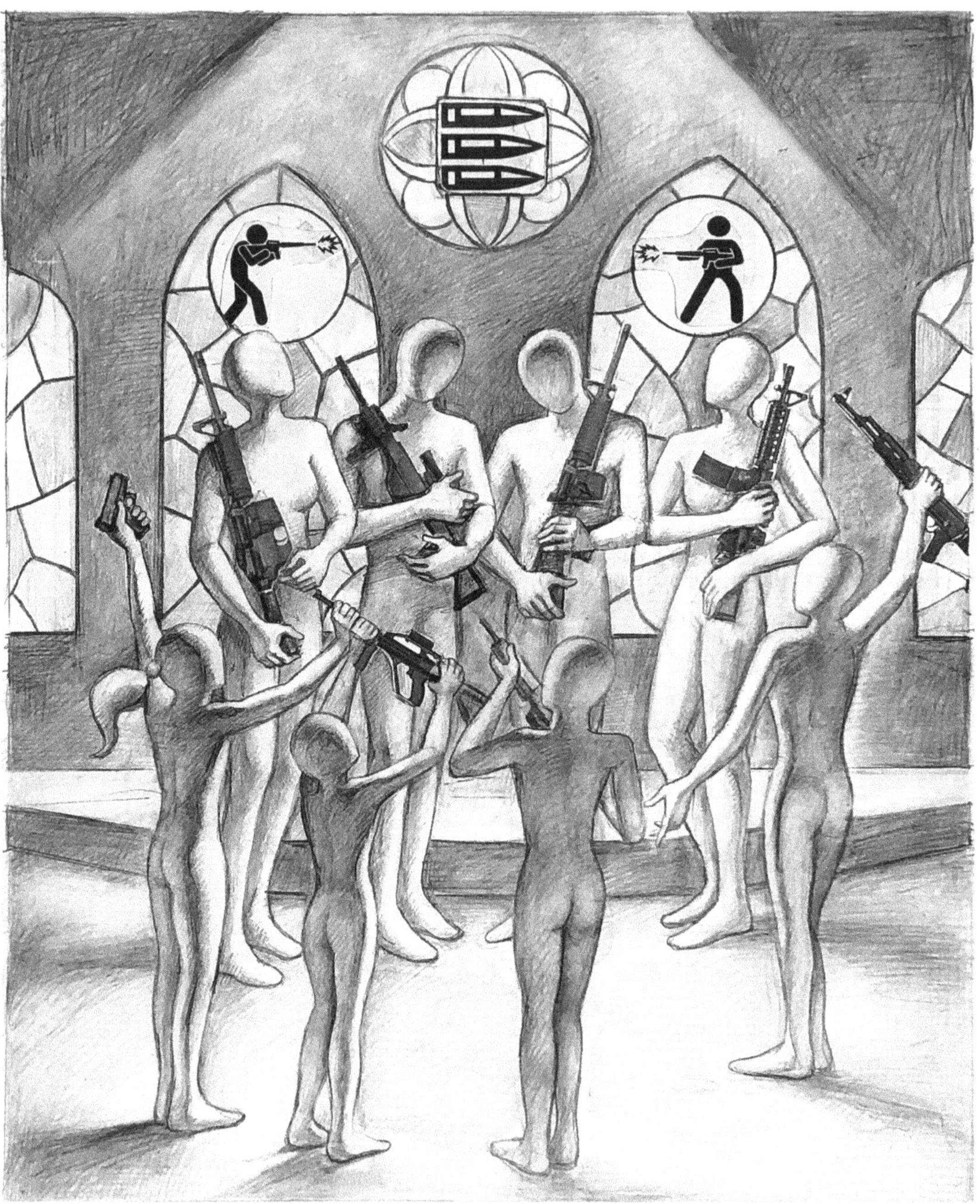

CHURCH GUNS

INGRID WENDT
EUGENE, OREGON

SINGLE MINDED

Take Salmon
    the way it navigates ocean

river   dam   boulder   creek   hundreds of miles
    to spawn in the very same spot it hatched from

Take Oystercatcher
    somehow building baby bird comfort

thirty years in a row on the same Seal Rock rock
    Take Swallow

returning to Capistrano   and featherbrained
    Spotted Towhee who raises its young each year in grasses

so close to the edge of the narrow dirt road   a wheel
    too far to the left might crush it

Take some People   crossing the line between single
    and simple

minded   doing
    what they've always done   and their parents

before them   supporting
    a leader who's rough and tough and gets by with it

leader who never
    lies   no matter what anyone says or conscience

or evidence   look
    they voted for him last time

dammit
    they'll vote for him again

FRED TOMASELLI

NEW YORK, NEW YORK

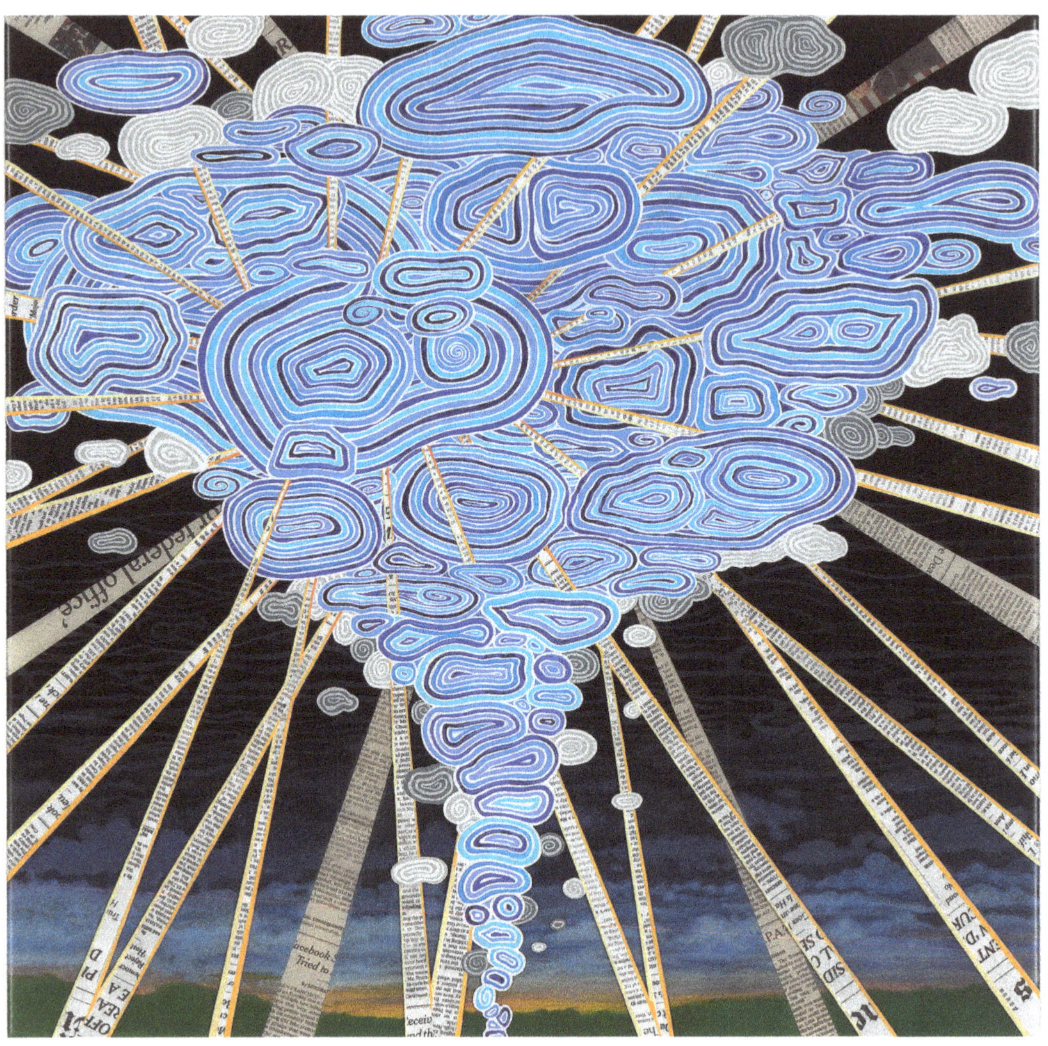

UNTITLED (CLOUD)

Collage

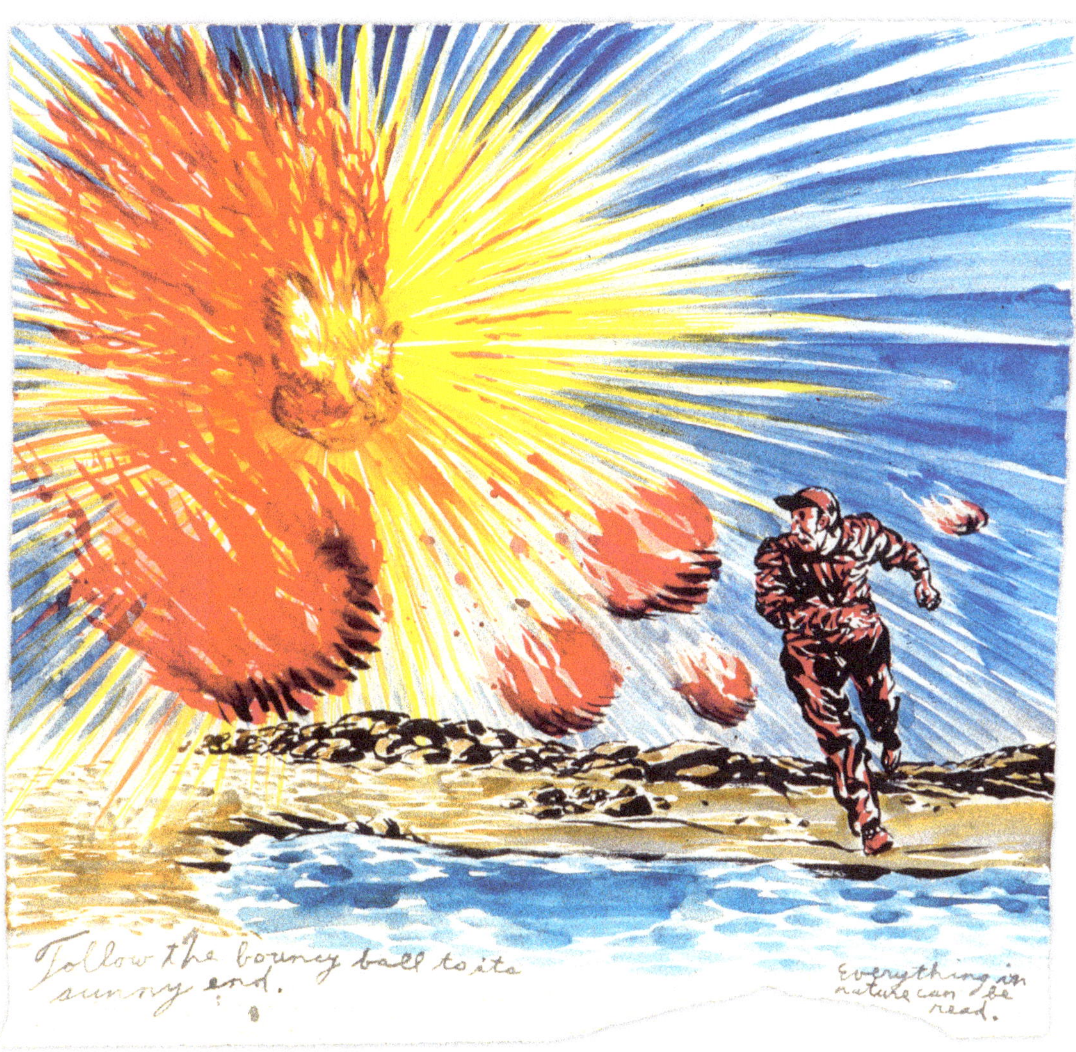

No Title (Follow the bouncy . . .)

Pen and Ink on Paper, 2002, 15 x 15-3/8 inches; 38.1 x 39.1 cm

MIKE WATT

SAN PEDRO, CALIFORNIA

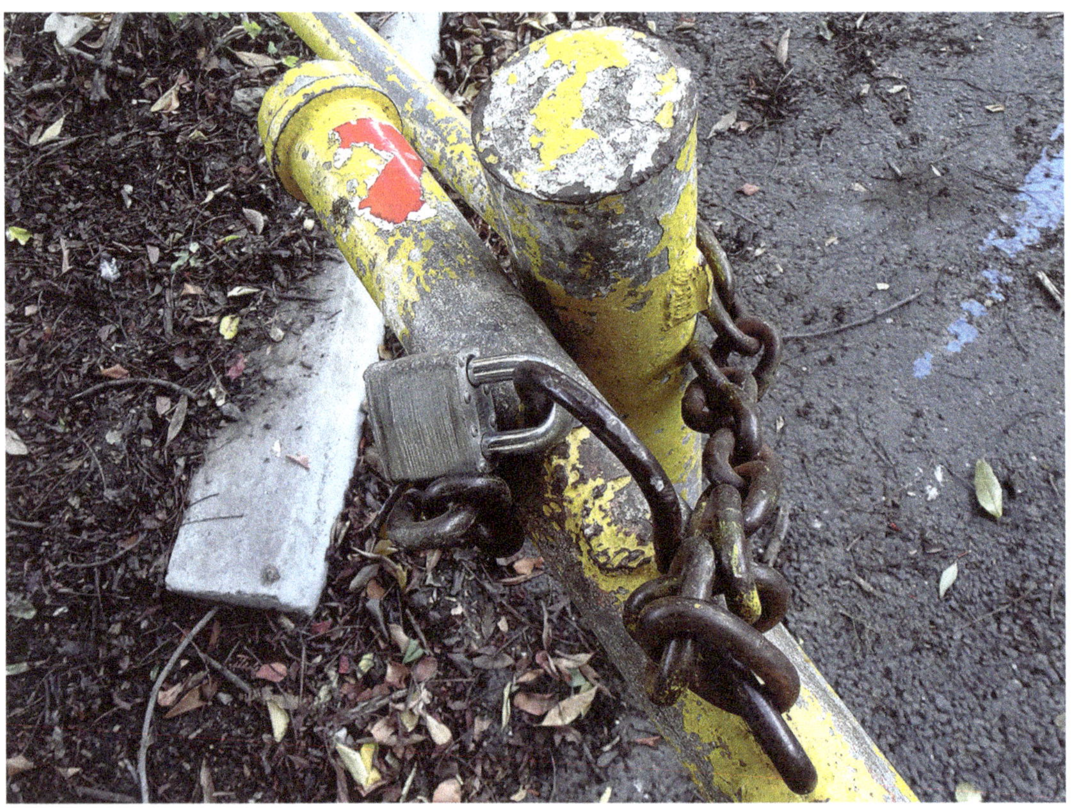

GATE AT PECK PARK

Digital Photograph

THURSTON MOORE

LONDON, UNITED KINGDOM

GONG

Disempowerment

Of no money

In travel is charity

Language inspired by meditation

Creativity the open field

Energized by happiness

People are not the enemy

There is no enemy

Only the word, the name

Yes is the answer

There's a huge castle coming up

Friends play music together

Free poems among friends

He brought him tea in the bathtub

Money comes to shape the dynamic

Marc Bolan helped fund

Ed Blackwell's hospice expense

Expensive things look bad

Wealth is the disregard of money

The flying teapot is how we travel

Rest your love in modest community

Welcome the day

Pockets empty, you're in luck

DONALD BATTERSHALL

RHINECLIFF, NEW YORK

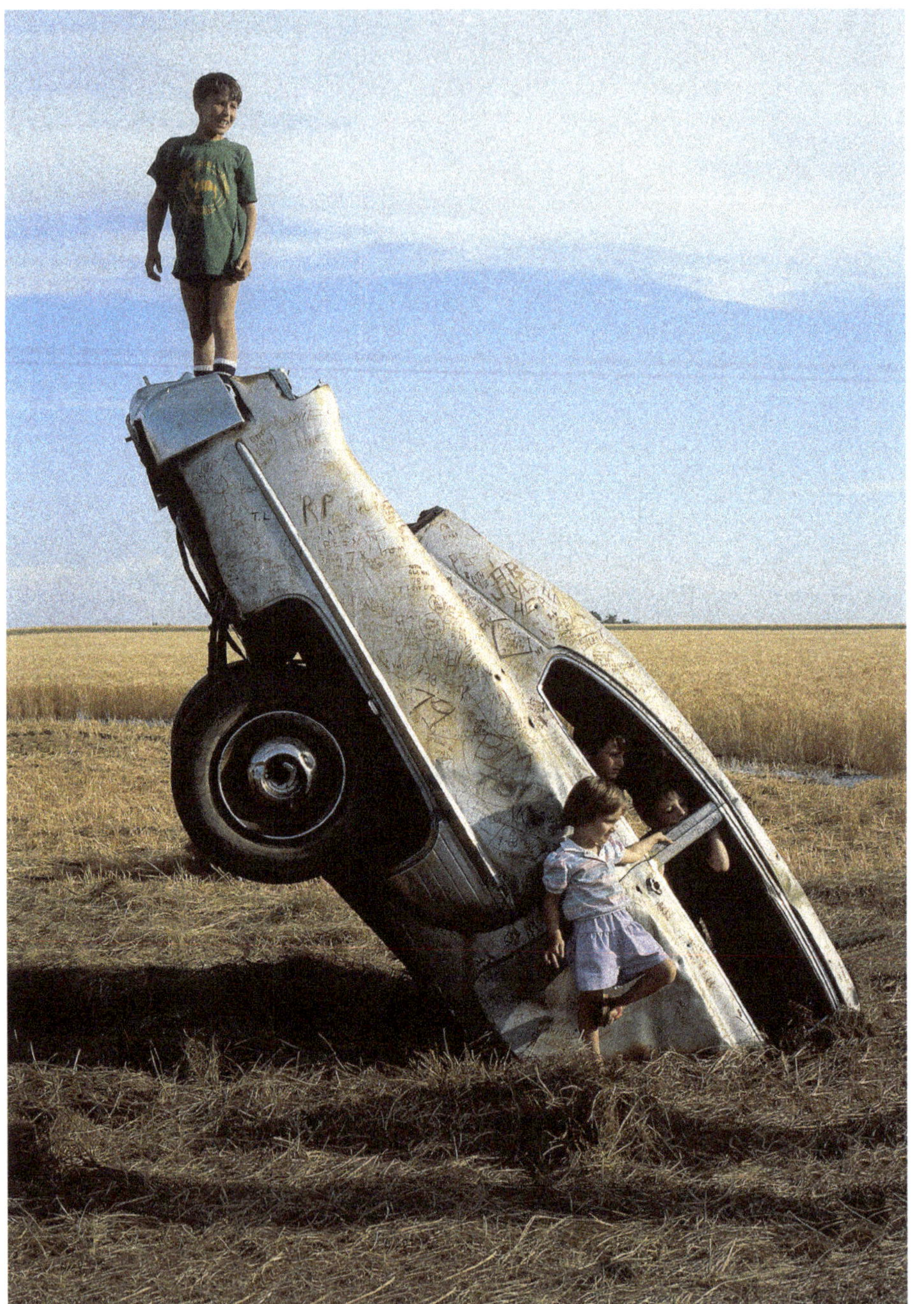

CADILLAC

Photograph

CHARLES PLYMELL

CHERRY VALLEY, NEW YORK

THEY DON'T TEACH THAT IN DRIVING CLASSES

My pop always made me keep a firm grip on steering wheel of our trucks.
It was made of carbon, not plastic, which was produced then.
The seats were always made of cow hide. I don't know what Lear invented.
That was just told to me by a friend of his in Wichita.

The radio in my '49 Caddy had an automatic selector, which was hot stuff in those days.
The hand selector knob is still the best. It's o.k. on a long stretch
to take one hand off wheel to find a radio station.

Of course our trucks didn't have radio.

My dad wouldn't even have heater because it cost extra.
It would have been nice to have in the Dakotas!

I'm thinking of selling my Subaru because it has too many distractions.
It started talking to me & I had to pull over & shut it off
because I didn't know what I pressed.

Also that damn TV thing on dash had a green line crawling across it.
I had just put in my *Rocket 88* cd by Jackie Brenston to check out player,
(The Youtube has picture of my 1950 Olds 88 convertible in it).

I asked Pam what was the line crawling across the TV dash. She said
it indicates how much volume. I said that would only help if I was deaf,
and if I was deaf I wouldn't be listing to cd anyway!!

Now who the hell wants to be distracted looking at the green line on dash??

Everyone knew if you leave radio on in old cars,
YOU WOULD RUN THE BATTERY DOWN,
The first time I left keys in Subaru the other night—it ran the battery down!
It says everything else, but not a peep! Big words display all the time on dash
that "PASSENGER SEAT BELT IS ON"

Now why the hell do I care?

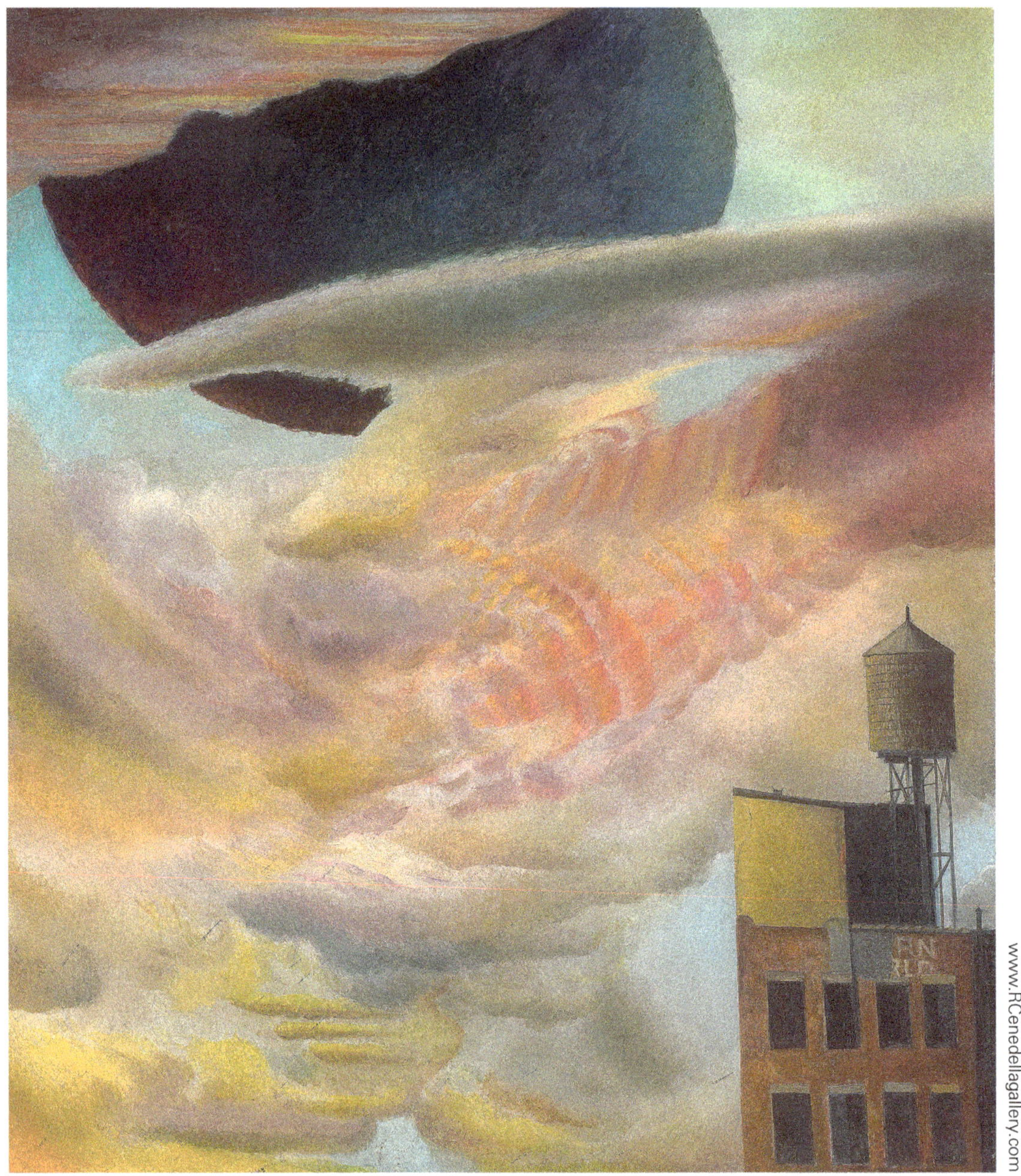

MANHATTAN PROJECT

Oil Painting on Primed Linen, 48" x 40", 2019

AIMEE HERMAN

BROOKLYN, NEW YORK

I AM AN UNSUSTAINABLE POLLUTANT![1]

We cannot see each other more.

My eyes burn from the fog of war that has collapsed the bones holding my sight in place because all the cows have collapsed from over-breeding and I cannot achieve my daily calcium intake.

Our teeth crumble each time we kiss; is it worth it?

You taught me how to eat newspapers, cut into the commentary like communism and gristle. All this red is confusing my blood where to go. I bathe in the puddles that have become like oceans wrapping around houses and huts.

Do you remember when you taught me how to hold my breath? Without your prompting, I cut each breast from my undeclared chest to float you back home. You arrived months later, wearing anemia, convulsions in your comments, and when you smiled all that blue on your gums attracted the birds toward your smile, which was flimsy and haunted.

This is all to say: I miss you.

Did you know some of them have stopped sucking on straws; the rich ones bring their own. They are burning all the leftover Styrofoam, but its styrene stops our lungs from breathing in and in.

When you held my hand all those times, we'd stretch our necks toward the rain and drink the sky's waterfalls. We drank lightning and forest fires, corrosion of bridges, and volcanic temper tantrums. We drank hyperventilating lightning bugs and radioactive pelicans.

My organs are an alphabet of William S. Burroughs.

Does your tongue even know what it is meant for?

In conclusion, there is nothing left. The landfills have become our supermarkets. Our wombs are secrets that used to hold beings of light. Soon, dusk will replace everything else, but we will all glow-in-the-dark from our persistent denial of unsustainability. All that will be remembered will no longer remember   will no longer know how will no longer have anyone or anything left

to be heard.

---

1 a found letter of dissolution

ARAM SAROYAN

LOS ANGELES, CALIFORNIA

I wanted the intermission to last forever.

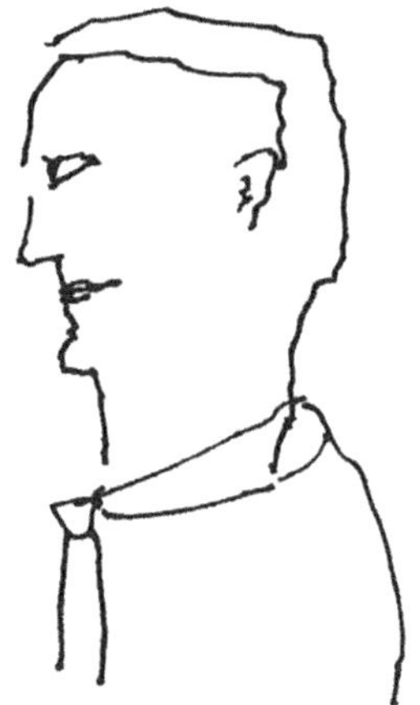

UNTITLED

Ink on Paper

GERARD MALANGA

HUDSON, NEW YORK

ROMAIN GARY, NOVELIST, 1914–1980

Romain,

      I've missed the centennial of your birth by nearly 5 years.

Am I forgiven?

I've had you on my shelf for decades now.

My memory doesn't serve me right. Your *Roots of Heaven*,

a Hollywood spectacular,

yet I never saw it.

A movie much missed. Where was I

when it played the RKO Palace?

I was home alone in the Bronx, laid up with an earache. I was 15.

Your marriage to Jean Seberg,

remarkable for an unlikely duo . . . I take it back.

The perfecto you & you,

veiled in the imaginary.

You & Jean now legendary.

It's how to measure Time when time is all we have and staying happy.

Elusive to the touch, what's left?

Always the smart suit & tie, fitted to perfection in Oxford Street,

& vivid in the tabloid photographs.

I imagine much. *Imaginaire*

still takes me far & wide,

these separate *réalités*, separate still.

Those "spots of time," as Wordsworth marked them

in his nature wanderings.

To our lives before us, there are many.

Our parting words, there are few.

Our greetings passing through the Paris dusks in dream time,

we keep it loose, we keep it dreamy.

Your dreamy voice: "I had a lot of fun, thank you."

Your forever lasting, parting note.

A true gentleman & warrior.

      Adieu, adieu.

BARBARA VOS

BRISBANE, CALIFORNIA

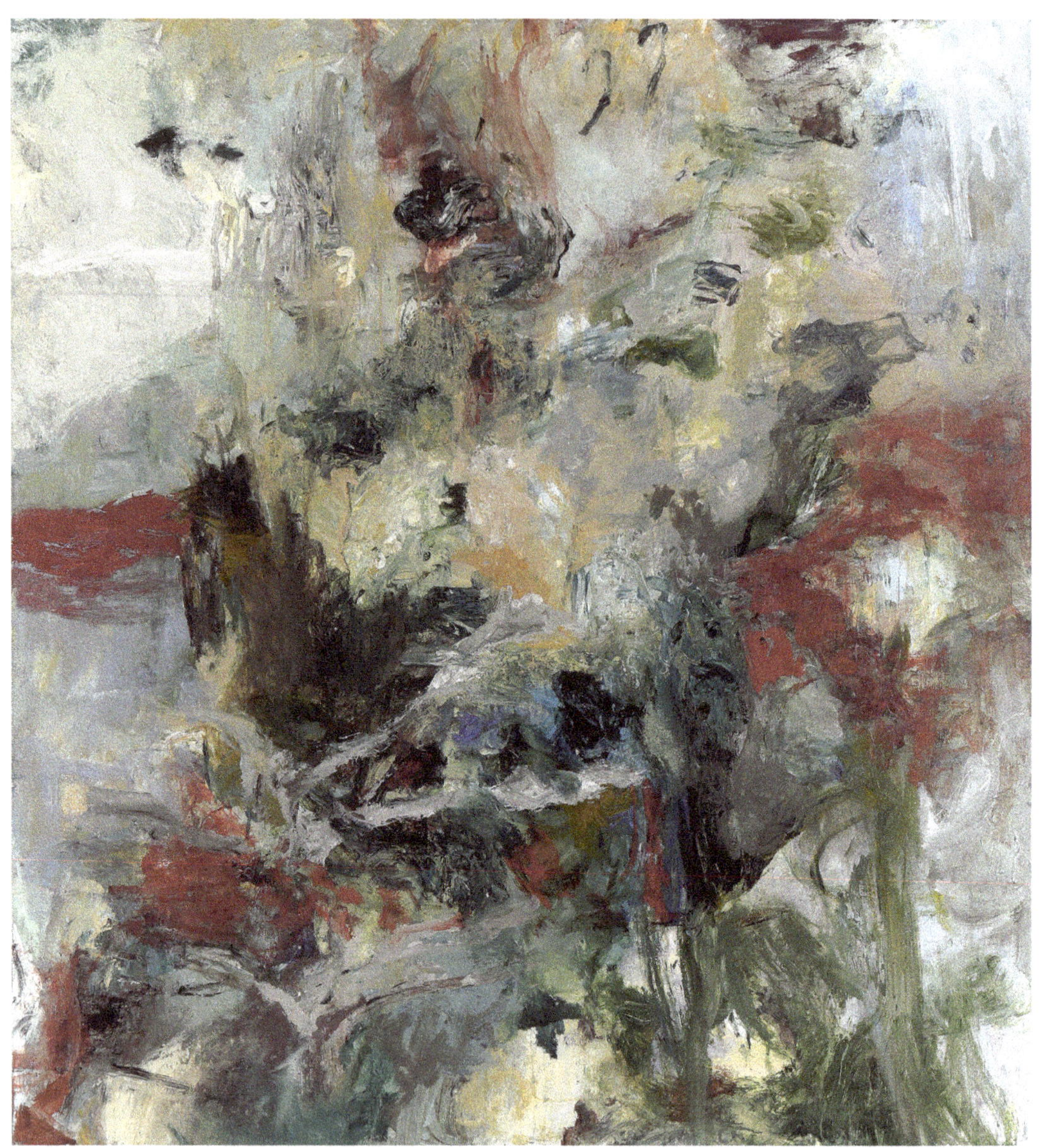

BIRCH

Acrylic on Canvas, 2017, 54" x 60"

FRED MARCHANT

ARLINGTON, MASSACHUSETTS

WHAT

It was a time of mid-level feelings,
>with mid-level degrees of authenticity.
We all got along well, and yet we were
>troubled by the direction we were taking.
We had a leader, one might say a Dear Leader,
>but that would be too ironic for our taste.
Still we had a leader, and there were troops
>overseas. We couldn't remember the name
of the language of the people we fought,
>but it was more or less a difficult tongue,
with a strange tribal history, the words
>mostly like a secret handshake. We still
had enough fuel then to face the winters,
>which we all agreed were getting milder.
My beloved and I calculated we had about
>twenty years to go. We had no children.
We planned on getting a dog to see us
>through. Outside the window of the room
where we spoke, a brilliant azure sky
>and the deep, shadowy green of the maple
thriving beneath it. The temperature was
>perfect. Nothing felt so complicated we
would not eventually come to terms with it.
>What—I now see the legitimacy and depth
of the question—were we afraid of? What
>were we trying so hard not to think about?
What looping snare inside held us back,
>froze us, tightened, then broke us at the neck?

BOB BRANAMAN

SANTA MONICA, CALIFORNIA

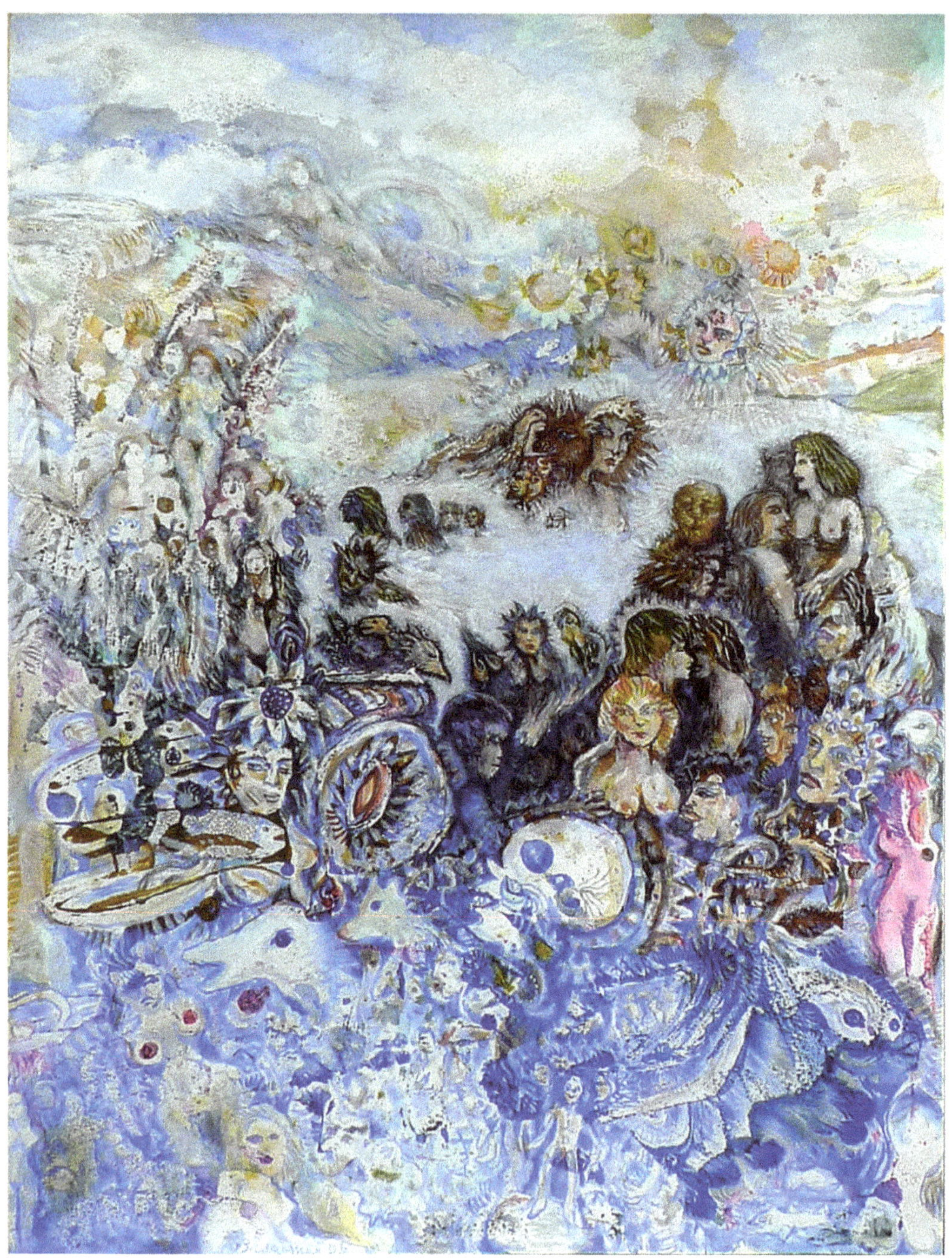

UNTITLED

Painting

HALA ALYAN
BROOKLYN, NEW YORK

BORDER :: LAND

If I knew what to miss
I'd miss it. Lipstick. Low
light. The moon

is drowning between winters;
it is midnight. The lavender clock
tells the time of another city—

where the children are.
The moon is under smog.
The moon is a calla lily.

The earth says her name
twice. It is midnight. The earth
smuggles her languages like

a dragon egg, tucked in suitcases
of olive jars and rugs.
We didn't choose this house,

the blackbirds tattling on the rain,
but we'll burn it brick by nail.
The flowers are extinct:

silphium. Cry violet.
The comeliest flower
is the last to bloom. If it does.

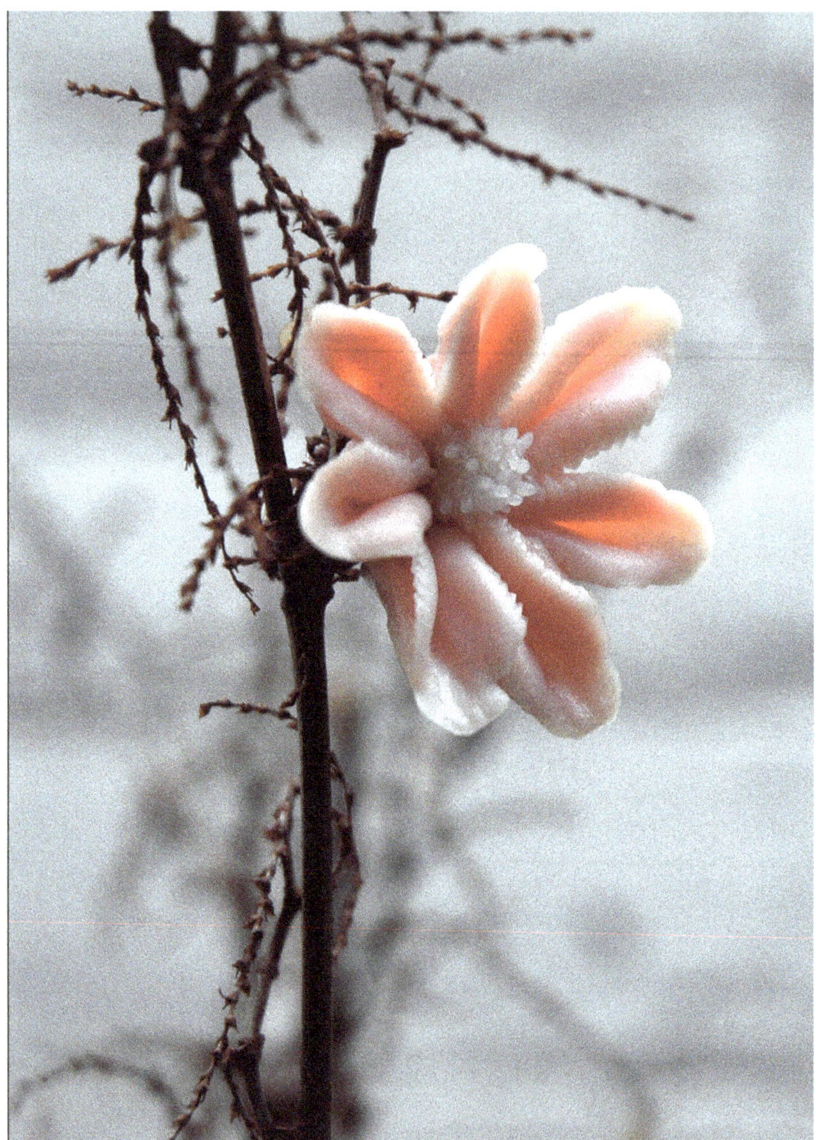

MOO MOO MOO MOO MOO MOO MOO MOO MOO MOO MOO MOO MOO MOO MOO MOOO
QUACK QUACK QUACK QUACK QUACK QUACK QUACK QUACK QUACK QUACK QUAACK QUAACK
MOOOO MOOOOO MOOOOOO MOOOOO MOOOOOOO MOOOOO MOOOOO MOOOOOOOOO
QUAAACK QUAAAACK QUAAAAACK QUAAAAAACK QUAAAAACK QUAAAAAACK QUAAAAAAAACK
MOOOOOOOOOOOOOOOOOOOOOOOOOOOOOOOOOOOOOOOOOOOOOOOOOOOOOOOOOOOOOO
QUAAAAAAAAAAAAAAAAAAAAAAAAAAAAAAAAAAAAAAAAAAAAAAAAAAAAAAAAAAAAAACK

UNSUSTAINABULLANDDUCKSHIT

Sculpture / Photograph

GERALD NICOSIA
CORTE MADERA, CALIFORNIA

DID SHAKESPEARE FORESEE GLOBAL WARMING?

Persimmon tree in my yard
That's like an old friend
Growing old with me
Has started dropping its fruit
A day or two earlier each year
Now those squishy orange missiles come hurling down
End of November, not end of December
How much longer can people
Keep rushing the world like that?
A tree can't bear fruit before it flowers
You can't drive a car before turning on the ignition
You can't grow old before you're young
Shakespeare couldn't write Hamlet
Before he was born
Global warming means
Leaving out parts of life
More than 400 years ago he wrote
"The time is out of joint"
But now the whole skeleton has nearly come
Unjointed
What nobody wants to see
Heating the world is like running a race
And if you run fast enough
You run right past life
And into your own grave.

HARRY E. NORTHUP
WOODLAND HILLS, CALIFORNIA

TO DAMPEN FIRE

Each night I dwell on the flower
The darkness recompenses petals
Falling faster than golden light
Fades into the winds' fires

But the roundness never ceases
Fire like a fish struggles upward
Its feet like seahorses jumping
Fences, ridges, a hand reaching upward

Where are you going in such a hurry
Why can't you sleep, put things to rest
Why have you so much work to do
But the roundess continues sweeping
Won't let us sleep, won't let words die
A hand reaches to pick up broken states
Keys from a circle ready to open
The circle moves upward like a jeallyfish

Death of white fences, evergreen trees
Is the whiteness really an angel in water
Does darkness make too much of color
When a country burns do we sleep

Each moment the water crashes
A divide ceases, a twirling churns
Dark waves with moonlight to settle
Needed water a morality bridge: light
Circle, hands, bridge, heart, awake

AMY BARONE
NEW YORK, NEW YORK

EXOPLANET K2

Scientists found another earth-sized planet.
New discoveries give me hope
that our days aren't numbered

on numbing earth—with its too
many people, problems, waste.
I could start over 339 light years away

at peace among the Virgo constellation.
But they say it's unlivable; sits too close to its star.

Atmosphere's metallic, hot, dense like Mercury.
How can that be, it sounds like the perfect spot for me.

DEREK ADAMS
SUDBURY, SUFFOLK, UNITED KINGDOM

ABANDON HOPE

The bonfire's flames
spit
at the grey February sky

nostrils seared
by the sickly sweet stench
of burning flesh.

At the gates a sign,
bright yellow, black letters—
Infected Area.

MALAK MATTAR
ISTANBUL, TURKEY

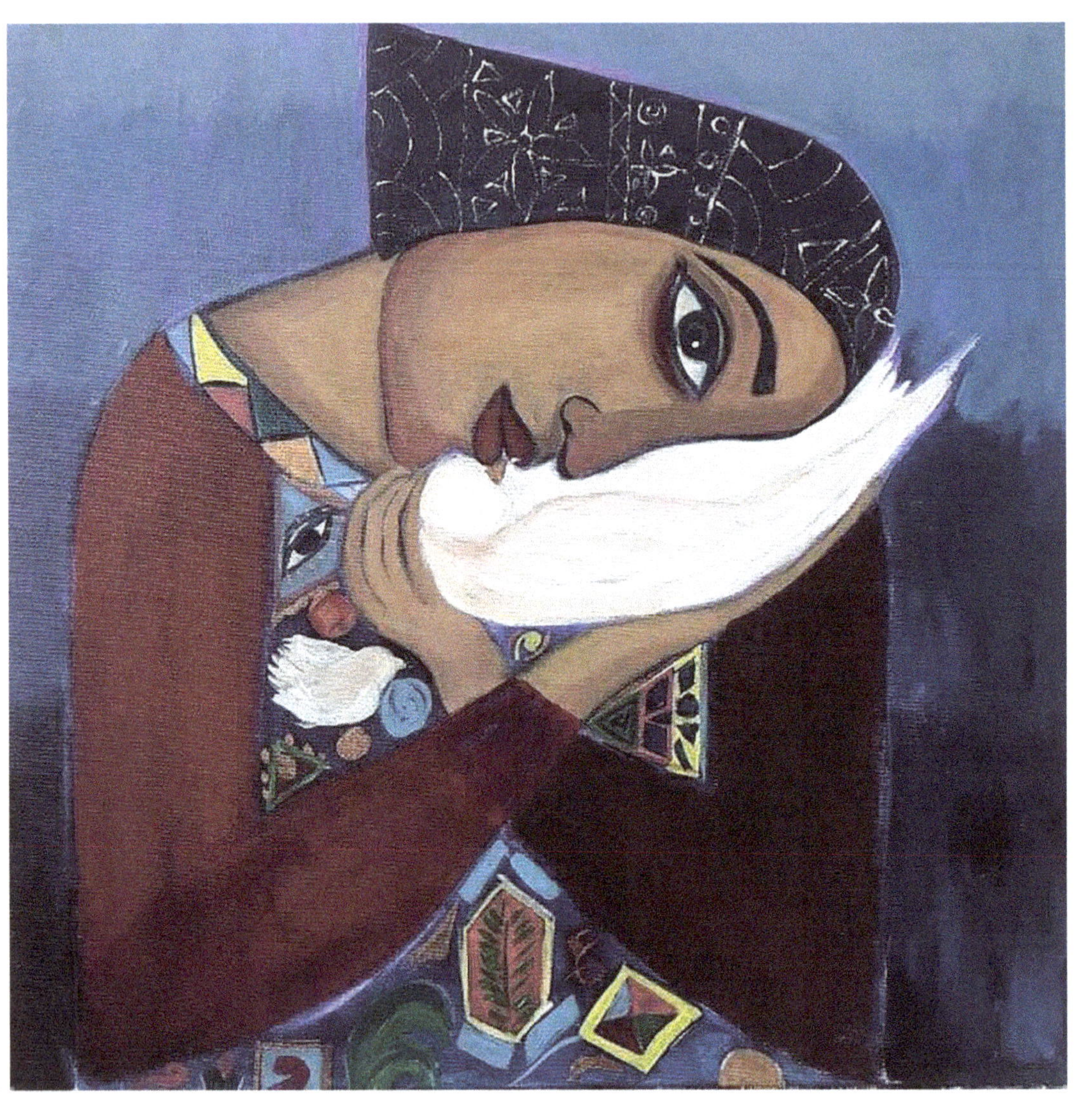

WHEN PEACE DIES, EMBRACE IT—IT WILL LIVE AGAIN

Painting

FAITHFULL BAANA ENONO ARNUAD

YAOUNDÉ, CAMEROON

MA LAIDE

Le mariage tant refusé aura bel et bien lieu

Les cieux ne pleureront plus de joies

Le sol même avec l'engrais ne sera plus fertile

Les mammifères seront obligés d'être herbivores

Et les Carnivores omnivores

Les poissons quitteront l'eau pour je ne sais où

Puisque les africains veulent séjourner en mer pour rejoindre le paradis sur terre

j'aperçois le soleil, il n'est plus loin bientôt il atterrit sur terre

Personne n'osera aller l'accueillir

Mais ils sont nombreux qui ont oeuvrés pour sa venue

Je comprends pourquoi ma faune et ma flore sont en larme

Ma forêt ne danse plus au rythme du son des animaux

C'est le sauve qui peut

D'ailleurs dès lors en toute saison il pleut

Tout ceci à cause de quelques billets d'euro

Bientôt on finira par tuer le beau

Paraît il la planète Mars est en chantier

Vois êtes avertis, d'ailleurs moi je commence à préparer mes papiers

Le passport se font où ? Et ça coûte combien ?

Même le pasteur n'y peut rien

Je doute fort que tout le monde soit de ce voyage

Puisqu'un visa il faut déjà pour visiter certains endroits du monde

Nos usines lâchent des fumées de chanvre que l'humain hume sans gène en
    plein centre ville

Au nom de l'industrialisation l'environnement est sous assistance respiratoire

Le médecin ne sait plus quoi prescrire,

tout sauf L'Afrique, elle si pauvre mais riche en air pure

Tout mais d'abord son sous sol,

grâce à ses ressources naturelles, on ne perdra pas le Nord.

JOHN BOWMAN

NEW YORK, NEW YORK

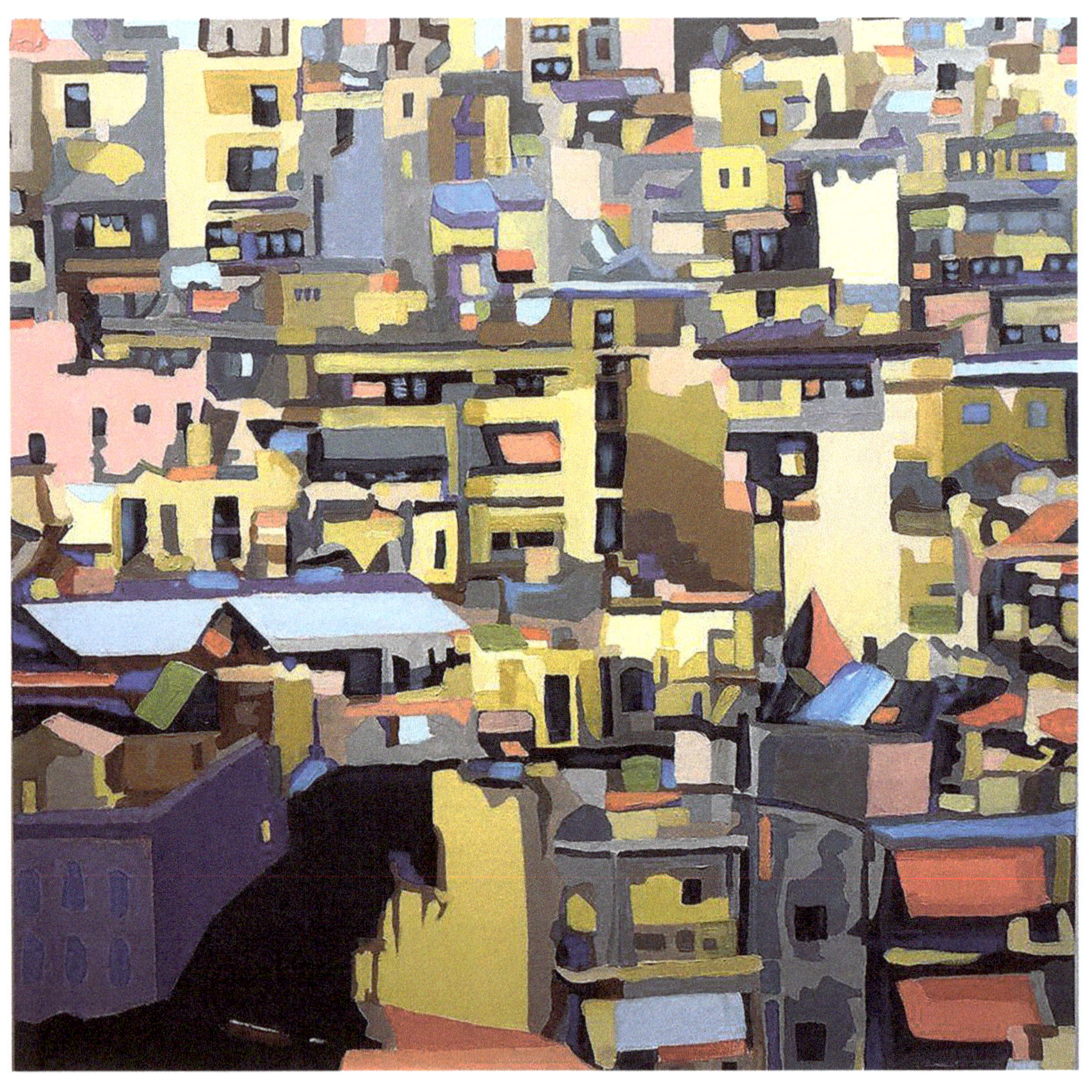

POLIS2 (PSYRI)

Acrylic on Canvas, 2020, 36″ x 36″

BÉNÉ KUSENDILA

SINT-NIKLAAS, BELGIUM

TRIBUTE TO SOCIAL MEDIA AND NIGHTS FULL OF EXISTENTIAL ANGST.   #HAIKU

Sad, I ponder on
where I am. The life I'd lead.
If I'd Instagram.

PAUL KAVANAUGH

CHARLOTTE, NORTH CAROLINA

WAR

Bomb the bastards says Terry to Harry and Harry
says to Perry When the big one drops They'll know
who is the best and Perry says to Kerry his
wife War I just love it. These are my neighbors.

HENRIK AESHNA

PARIS, FRANCE

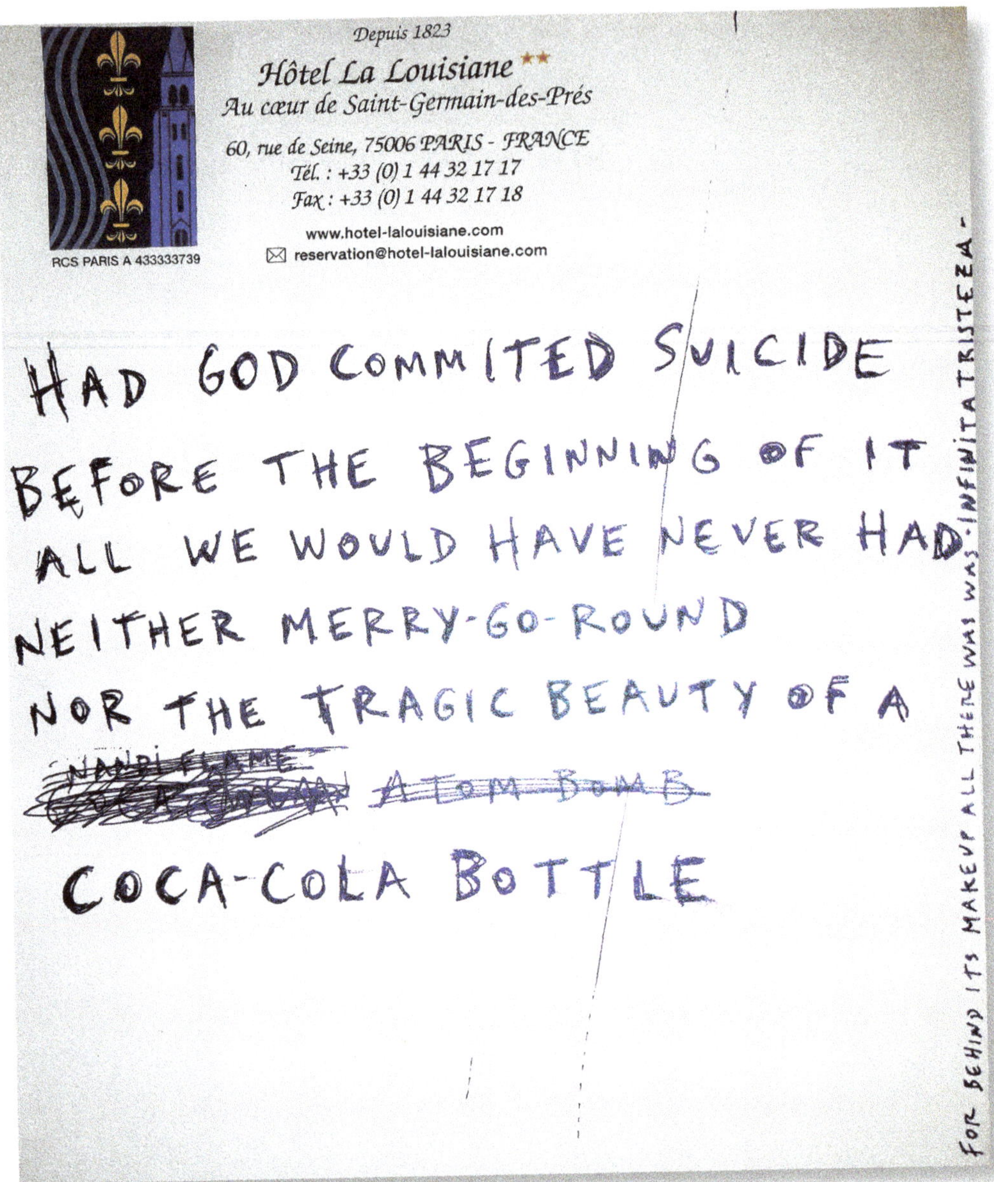

INFINITA TRISTEZA

Ink on Paper

JON LONGHI

SAN FRANCISCO, CALIFORNIA

For **RON—**

Date ___________________________ Time __________ A.M. / P.M.

WHILE YOU WERE OUT

M **TIM LEARY**

Of _______________________________________

☐ Phone _______________________________________

☐ Fax _______________________________________

☐ Mobile _______________________________________

	Area Code	Number		Extension
TELEPHONED		✓	PLEASE CALL	
CAME TO SEE YOU			WILL CALL AGAIN	
WANTS TO SEE YOU			URGENT	
RETURNED YOUR CALL			SPECIAL ATTENTION	

Message

Tim Leary called from SFO and is in taxi on the way to Berkeley. If he dies on the way have taxi drive directly to cryogenic suspension facility at this address: ______. If taxi gets there quickly freeze whole body, if stuck in traffic just freeze head.

Signed

JUST FREEZE HEAD

When I worked at Last Gasp my boss Ron Turner was known as "Baba Ron." He had gotten the nickname back in the seventies. The new age/LSD philosopher Ram Dass had written a bestseller called *Be Here Now*. Ron used to always tell everyone he wrote a book called *Was There When*. After he told this joke enough times people started calling him "Baba Ron." Ron knew Ram Dass because he had crossed paths with him in the hippie underground and Ram Dass had given the nickname his blessing. Ron knew a number of those new age hippie philosophers and he even ended up publishing a book for Timothy Leary at the end of his life. Even though Leary was dying of cancer at the time he still had his effervescent energy and did a number of events to promote the book. One of these was in Berkeley. When he flew in for the event he called from SFO and I answered the phone. Ron was out so I took a message for him. Since the end was nigh Leary had already made his final resting plans. At that point he wanted his body to be frozen in cryogenic suspension and then thawed out on a future date when cancer had been cured. The nearest cryogenic suspension facility in the Bay area was in Berkeley. The commute between San Francisco Airport and there could fluctuate dramatically between a half hour to an hour and a half depending on traffic on the Bay Bridge. It was a hot day and Leary was concerned about what all these factors could do to his freshly dead body. He explained that if the body isn't frozen quickly it will spoil in which case the doctors are forced to just cut off the head and freeze that. I've worked in offices my whole life and all this led up to me leaving the most memorable note I've ever written for a boss.

Timothy Leary also knew Ram Dass. He used to call him "Rammed Ass".

COOPER CASALE

MILLEDGEVILLE, GEORGIA

NOISE

There's something wrong with Mr. Bradddworth,
the new gray tenant.
He's freakishly tall and skinny
and frayed at both ends,
like a ribbon unwoven
deliberately over time.
It's not just me.
We tenants heard from up there
these big bangs followed by
these littler bangs,
like a super-ball bouncing
against our teeth,
and we've spilt beer
over this all night
in agony.
He showed up last month
with a bag
(one bag)
and hasn't left his room—
401A, building C.
And the landlord,
born without legs
enough to climb his own stairs,
is spilt beer.
So we go up there,
all of us tenants,
and knock on Bradddworth's door.
And Miss Silverstein
(with a 5 for both S's)
brought her spider,
in a glass jar.
Mi55 5ilver5tein smartly
punched holes in the lid.

Mi55e5 5pider's beer is spilt.
And 'Ugly' Derrick 'Jimmy' Malloy,
whose pimple scars
look like tattoos in the right light,
is jimmying the lock,
which makes, itself, quiet little bangs.
My brain is a drum,
or a piece of tight cloth.
With the door unlocked,
we rush in,
spilling beer,
and there's no furniture
save the GOOD VIBES!
poster in the corner of the room,
latticed by the sun, which is
caught in the novelty animal print blinds,
and a TV, blue between inputs.
There's something wrong with Mr. Bradddworth,
standing at his spotlessly
clean toilet,
lifting
and dropping
the lid,
over and   over and   over and.
It's the sound of a can opening—
its gas shooting out of the red ears
of Bradddworth's
big, empty head, which
Mi55 5ilver5tein says
we, like, ought to split
under the lid.

IMANOL BUISAN

TERRASSA, SPAIN

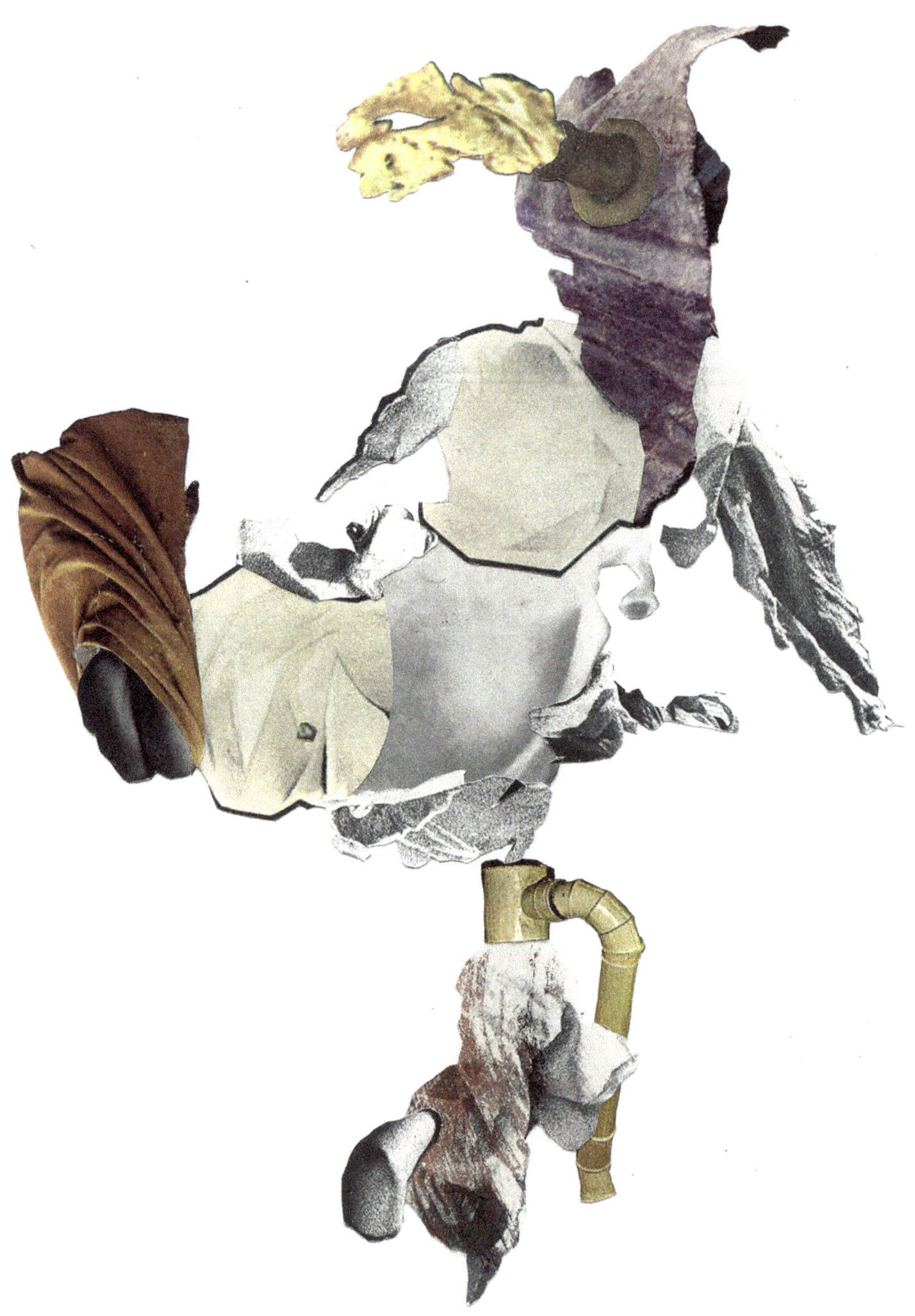

LAMBMEN OF THE APOCALYPSE

Collage

BEN AGUILAR

CAGAYAN DE ORO CITY, PHILIPPINES

A CURE FOR VEGANISM

You hold up the seed to the light. Someone gnawed it down to the bone, this palm-sized fleshy stone with some meat still stubbornly stuck to its narrow pole. Its creases remind you of the fingers of an elderly woman whose nose you once had to stitch together, then put a tube in. No matter how far you throw this thing you won't escape its smell. The goddamn smell. This stench will outlast us all. You want to throw it at someone with a nice car. I mean, how else did nature expect these things to spread? By word of mouth? Network marketing? Maybe dinosaurs stepped on the fruits themselves, giant burrs that buried into their feet until they finally laid down to die, the tree blossoming over its remains. Maybe we've been eating lizard this whole time. The dinosaurs are all dead now. The thing that did them in is gone too, left a hole in the disputed earth. Now nothing is left to spread this fruit but us, creatures willing to try anything from sniffing rocks to whiffing miniature engineered bush fires to overdosing on rotten fruit juice. We do ourselves in. The Lord giveth his body and we tried eating that too, which saved our spirits, but the flesh has nowhere to go but underwater in the next fifteen years. I'm willing to be wrong, though.

CHERYL J. FISH

NEW YORK, NEW YORK

THEY HARVEST TIGERS

They harvest tigers for their skin, bones
and teeth to grind into wine.
Stripes and ivory powdered Viagra stockpile
Poach the wild, puree the heart.
Traffic in death, sex, child crime
Mutilation, oil. Kill Orangutans for Palm.
Debased cash-cow hate potion.

ELIETTE MARKHBEIN

NEW YORK, NEW YORK

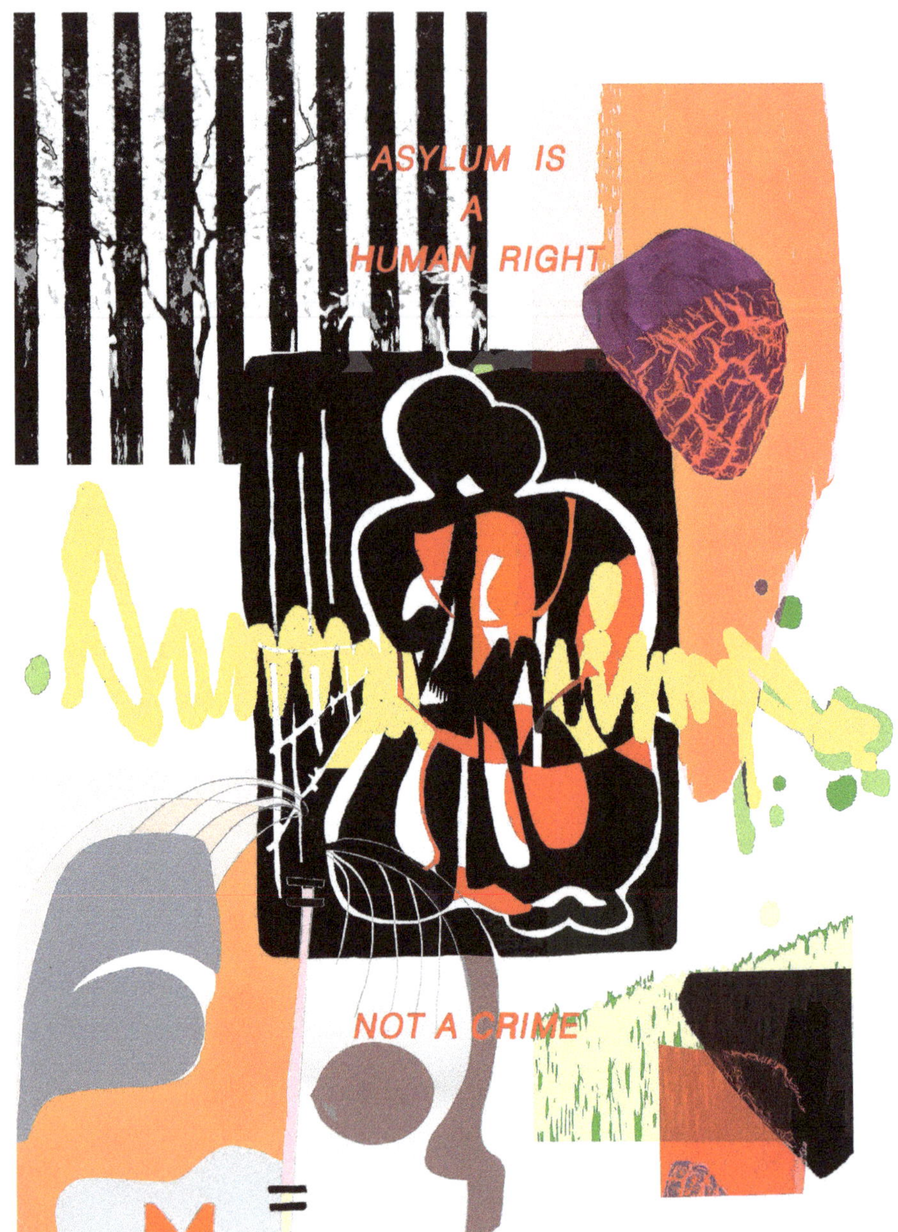

UNITED NATIONS OF REFUGEES

NHƯ QUỲNH DE PRELLE

BRUSSELS, BELGIUM

ANOTHER WORLD

On the metro, everyone is silent, even people standing

One day, she realizes, no one's there anymore.

At the office for refugees, many people
take a ticket and wait.

Why do you come here?   I ask for asylum.
What's your problem?

She thinks   briefly and walks out the door.

She does not know if she is reincarnating into melodies

She cannot sleep when the   moonlight is   full

She climbs out of bed, puts on her robe,
walks through the hallway, goes to the basement,
and reaches the garage, pulling   up   the   iron   door

She turns on a light
and enters   a coffin about 2 meter long,

out there, another world is moving—

She wandered through ancient villages
lined with age-old houses.

a human life without horizon,
paralyzed with pain,
the pain of the senses,
the pain of love,
the pain of disgust   at the end of things.

SYPORCA WHANDAL

BUDAPEST, HUNGARY

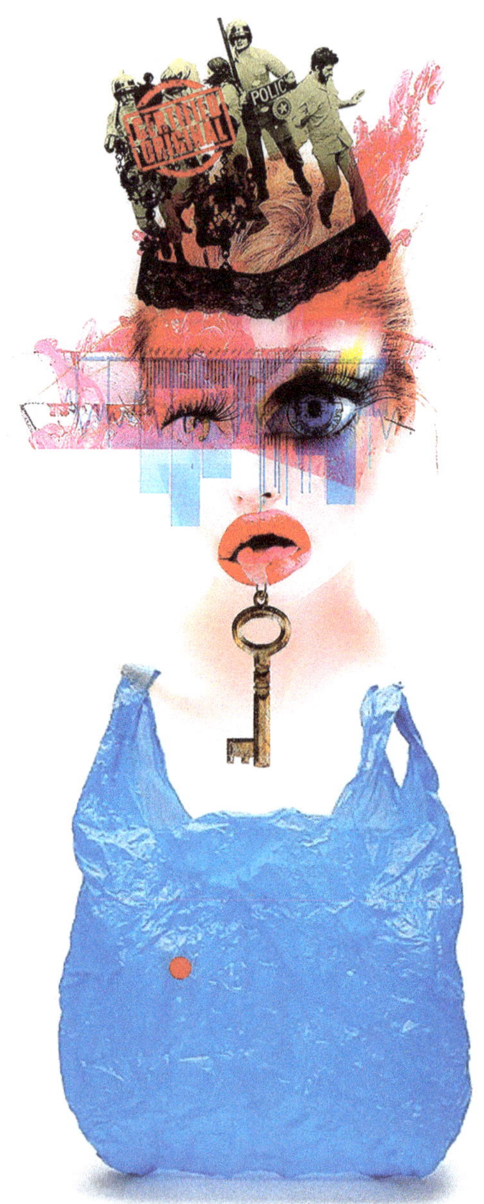

PLASTIC ICON

Digital Collage

YOUSSEF ALAOUI

MORRO BAY, CALIFORNIA

INK SPIRAL METHUSELAH

I live so long, I'm alive when dead.
Ink spiral Methuselah
smoking fat wads of tobacco marijuana stogies
wider than towel rolls
drinking moonshine of my youth
crawling worms overspill the cup.

O the joy
of a world slipping apart.
River jungles stuffed with candelabras hanging
low off bird monkey paths under polished glass
vines, hairy chested ingots
build my throne tower of undead observation.

War.
A clean scientific theory that
naturally propagates accidental soldiers in its wake.
The passersby.
The bread bearers.
Home returners.
Makes civilians of soldiers. Mush of heart.
The heaping dead need no clothes no food, no smoke, no hurry.

Mouth full of cod and clay
dried stumps, my arms fold forever in pale dust.

Frozen thin mushroom lawns
cover mummy cloth gown reach stone cubes
interlocking the floor of a machine gun tank
feeds my two stroke umber.

Scrying glass points at cloud swept ruins
screeching like a nest of cobra babies.

prawling almond vapor tundra valley
wagging keel obese time ship, hull burst
taking on air behind dullard cliffs
clicking away at amateur third degree rumination.

Hoping to wake in a gown of swords and commit it all to paper
for posterity
as if it were
some kind of graceful act
rather than a clumsy protracted murder
carried out with busking change
stuffed in a stinking sock
softening the back of a presidential skull
behind the locked and rusted dairy queen.

I am invisible to war
an embarrassment to flowing blood.

The bats will never find me here.

THIRD RAIL PROVO PROGRAM

MEMO: PROVO CATION ; HOMMAGE TO THE VIENNA INSTITUTE FOR DIRECT ART AND A MANIFESTO...
'OMO SUPER ZOCK'- OTTO MUEHL, HERMANN 'BLOOD BATH' NITSCH, GUENTHER 'MECKIE MESSER' BRUS, KURT 'FLICKER' KREN, AND PETER 'LEAGAL EAGLE' AND OTHERS...
SUBJECT: COMMUNICATION. NO MEHBERS NO DUES
GOAL: LOVE YOUR CITY, MAKE IT BETTER.

1. TAKE OUT THE FIRST FLOOR OF ALL BLDGS. IN TRAFFIC CONGESTED AREAS SO DELIVERING CAN BE DONE OFF THE STREET.

2. GET INVOLVED WITH WHERE YOU LIVE MOST OF THE PEOPLE YOU ALLOW TO BE IN CHARGE OF IT ARE MORONS.

3. CREATE JR. & HIGH SCHOOLS OF POLICE, FIREMEN, TEACHERS, SOCIAL WORKER TRADES AND A HIGH SCHOOL FOR EXPERIMENTAL ART AND HAPPENINGS.

4. SLASH THE TIRES OF DIPLOMATIC CARS PARKED CONTEMP-TOUSLY.

5. A PRE-FAB SKI LODGE HUT IN PARKS AND PLAYGROUNDS FOR RESIDENT POETS, PAINTERS, HAPPENERS ETC.

6. CITY HOSTELS WHERE CHILDREN MORE INTELLIGENT THAN THEIR PARENTS CAN LIVE.

7. RENAME NEW YORK CITY 3RD RAIL & SECEDE FROM NY STATE

8. IF YOU'RE PASSIVE GET ANGRY AND FUNCTION.

9. IF YOU'RE ANGRY CALM DOWN A LITTLE AND TRY TO UNDERSTAND.

Al Hansen - Viking Dada. 3rd Rail (New York City) Oct 5, 1967!!!

THIRD RAIL PROVO PROGRAM

Ink on Paper

BIBBE HANSEN

HUDSON, NEW YORK

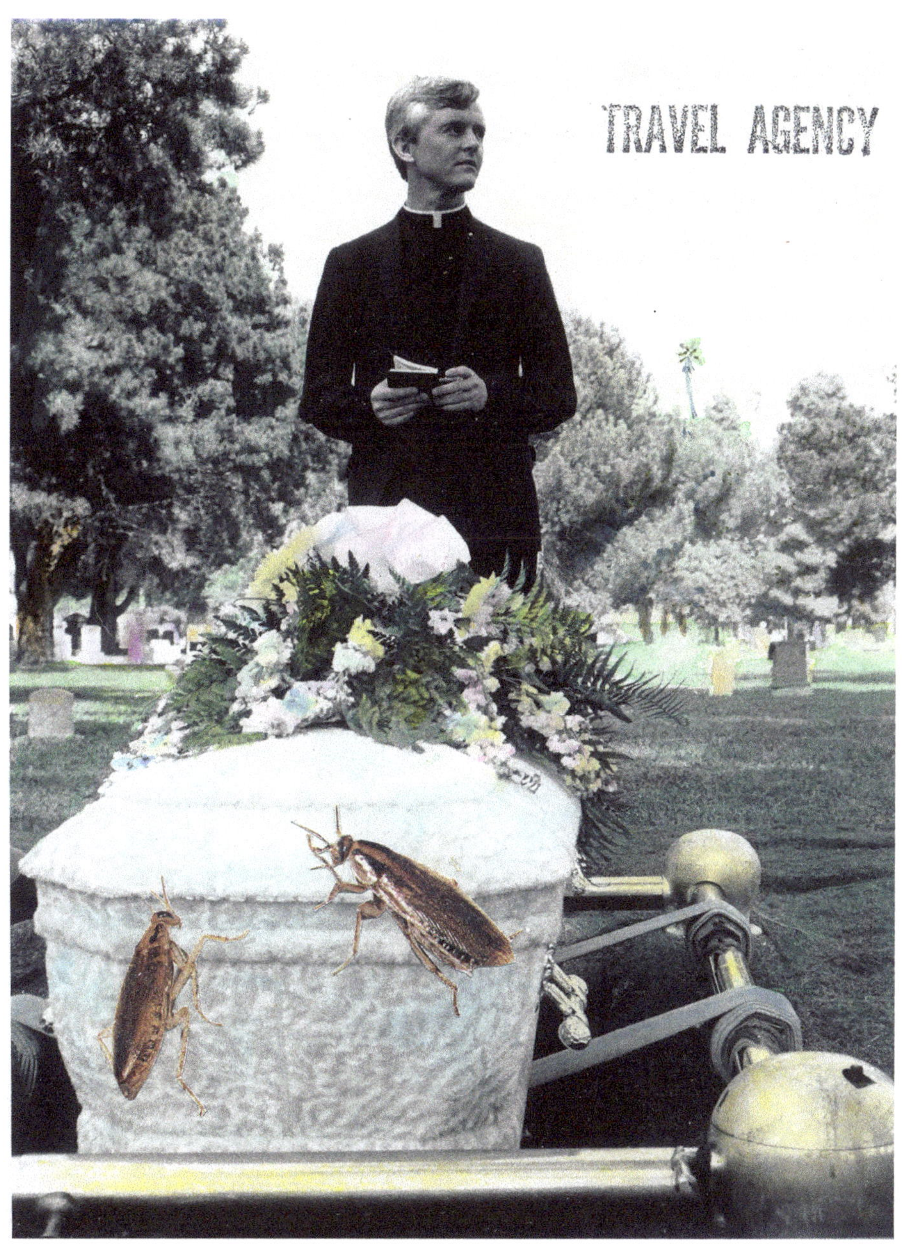

TRAVEL AGENCY

Collage

JACK HIRSCHMAN

SAN FRANCISCO, CALIFORNIA

THE TAFT-FARTLY ARCANE

1.

As we've seen: it's a law
that's the essence of evil,
71 years old and enacted
after World War 2 in 1947:
with peace rallies sprouting
allover European countries
that had enough of Death,
and the workers here were
picketing allover the land.

So the fascists in Congress,
wanting to break the hold
of the New Deal over the
union workers, and sensing
what was to come a decade
later, with the Black workers
breaking segregation chains,
enacted the law, making it
illegal for any union worker

to have anything to do with
Communism and, among
other things, making illegal a
Solidarity Strike of one union

with another, in effect killing
the working-class movement
by amputating the possibility
of its growing larger than any
single union's demands.

That law was the Taft-Fartly
and that law is the Taft-Fartly
and it stinks as it's always
stunk, smells to high heaven
and, even after the fall of the
Soviet Union, the corporate
takeover of communications
and the trans-globalization of
1,000 sickening billionaires,

it remains the back-breaker
and ball-buster of the whole
working-class movement,
the intimidating foreshadow
of the McCarthyism that in
a couple of years would lead
to the televised insulting of
those who for most of their
lives had dignified workers.

2.

No longer the Proletariat, we,

with our computers, androids

and other instruments of the

technology epoch making us

into a pushbutton Planetariat

capable of rapidly organizing

strikes and Solidarity Strikes,

but for that Taft-Fartly smell

forcing all fingers over the

noses of the whole citizenry,

and even the undocumented

doing the dirtiest work for the

less than minimum, for those

mickey-mouse-dumb wages,

have to hold their noses, the

stink's so devastatingly putrid;

because the wills of the poor

and the homeless, of those

men, women and children the

robots have tossed from their

jobs, are dreaming of the strike

that'll multiply with others in the

Solidarity Strike that's gonna

create the movement of a new

Planetariat which is gonna lower

the boom on the capitalist class

by first getting rid of that vicious

law that's been used by gangs

of trans-globalized thugs, those

investors in death by war and

famine who've amassed those

billions till now. But no more!

We're gonna butt-plug the ass

of Taft-Fartly so that it dies of

its own gas, and the Planetariat

becomes all our future at last.

GABRIEL DON

NEW YORK, NEW YORK

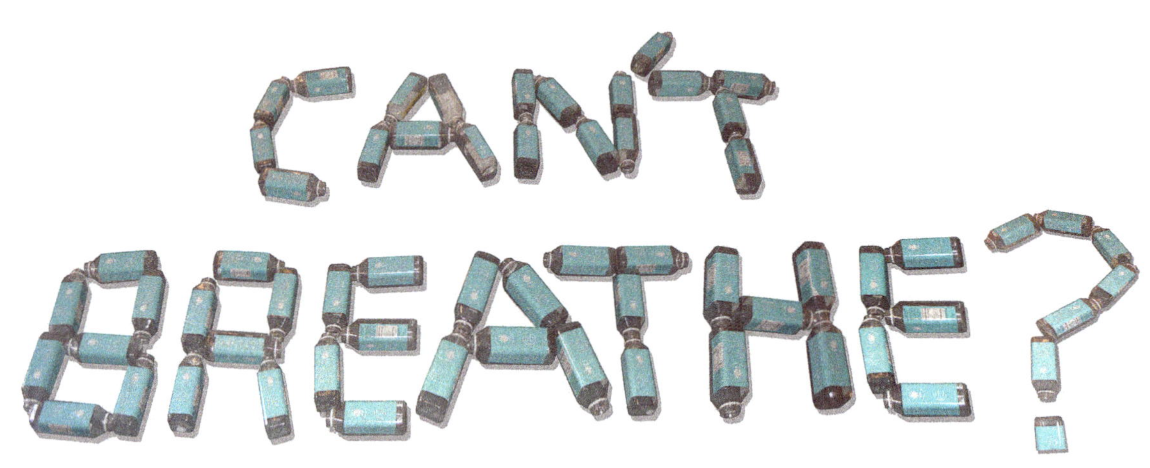

CAN'T BREATHE?

Digital Image

RENAAT RAMON

BRUGES, BELGIUM

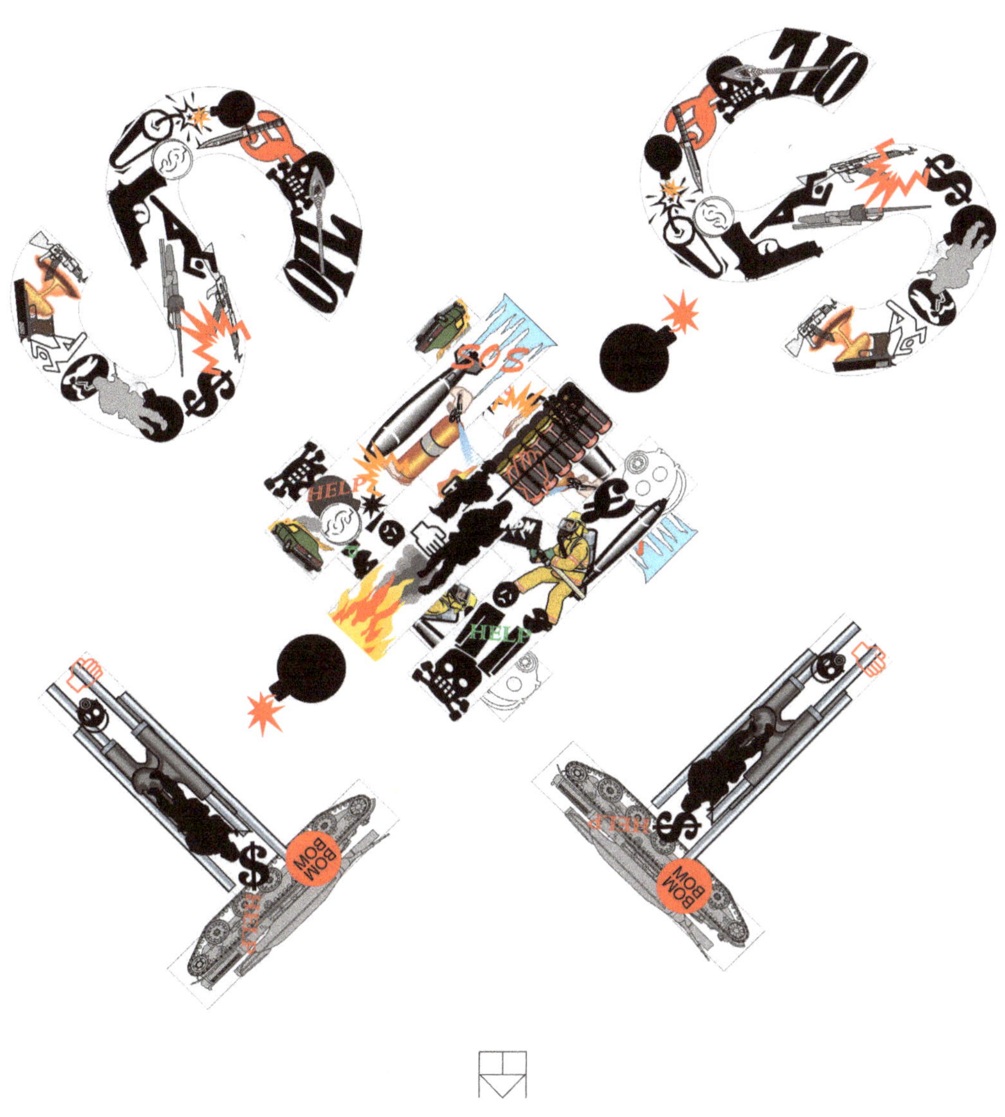

BLAST

Ink and Digital Collage

C. MEHRL BENNETT

COLUMBUS, OHIO

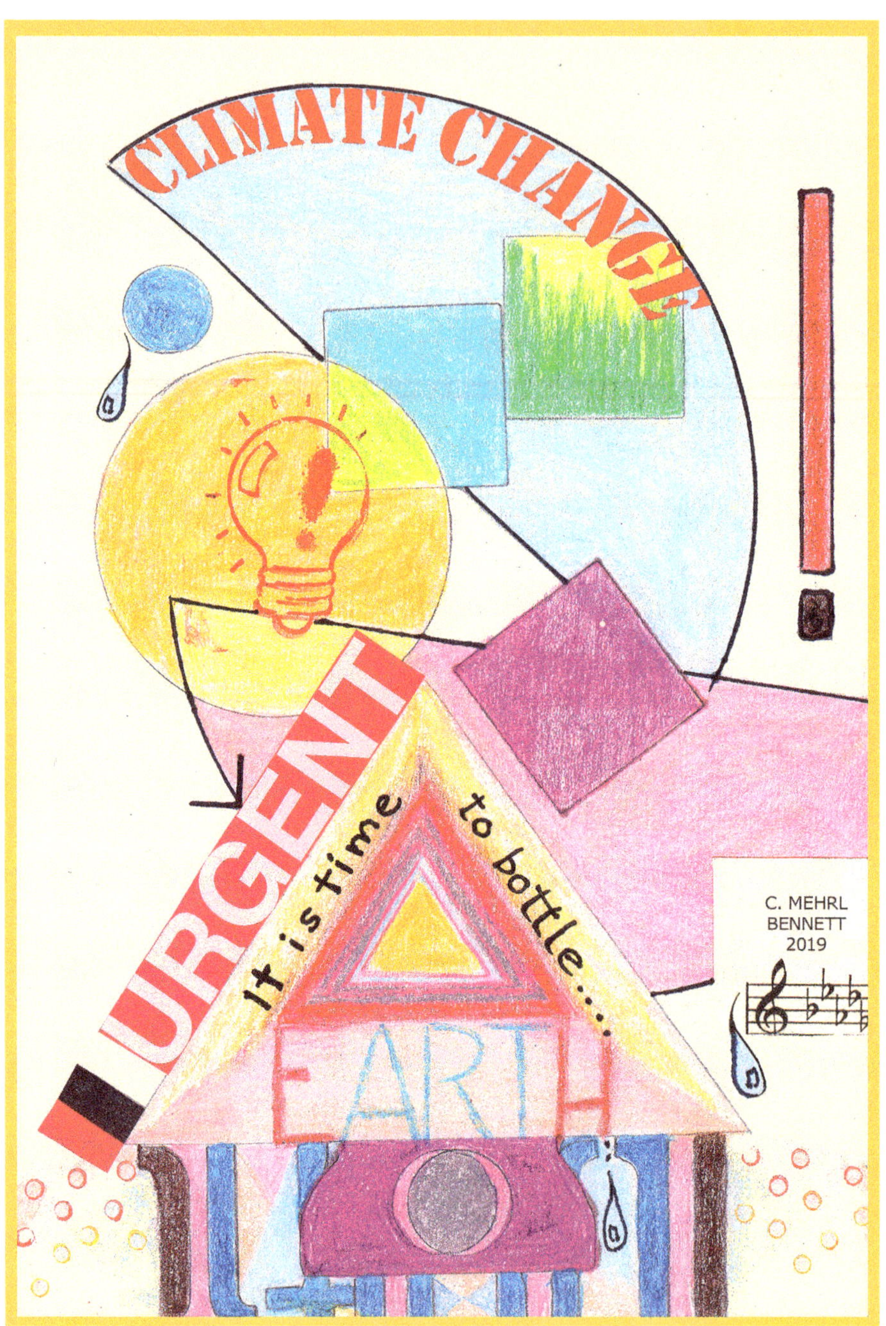

CLIMATE CHANGE

Collage

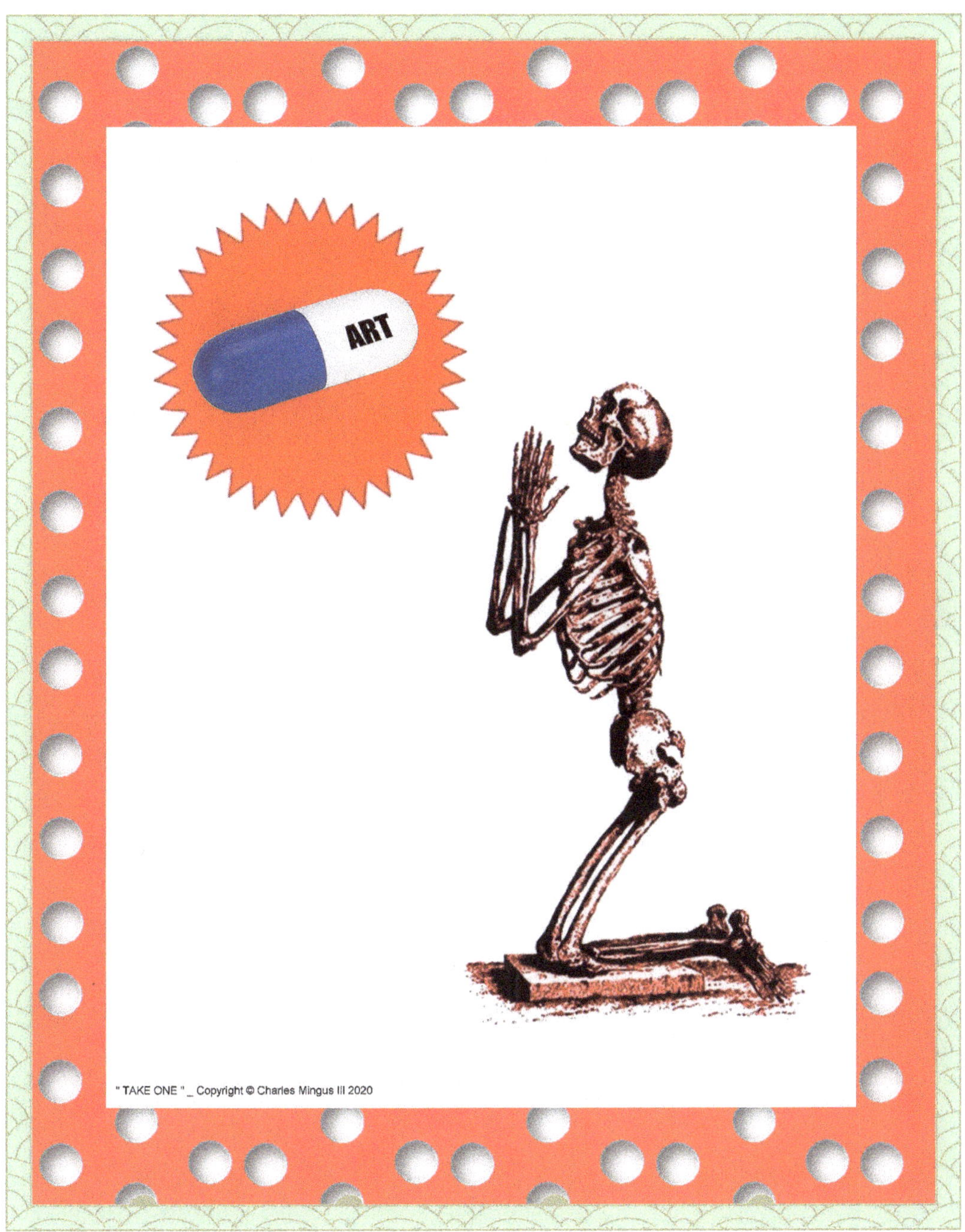

TAKE ONE

Digital Collage

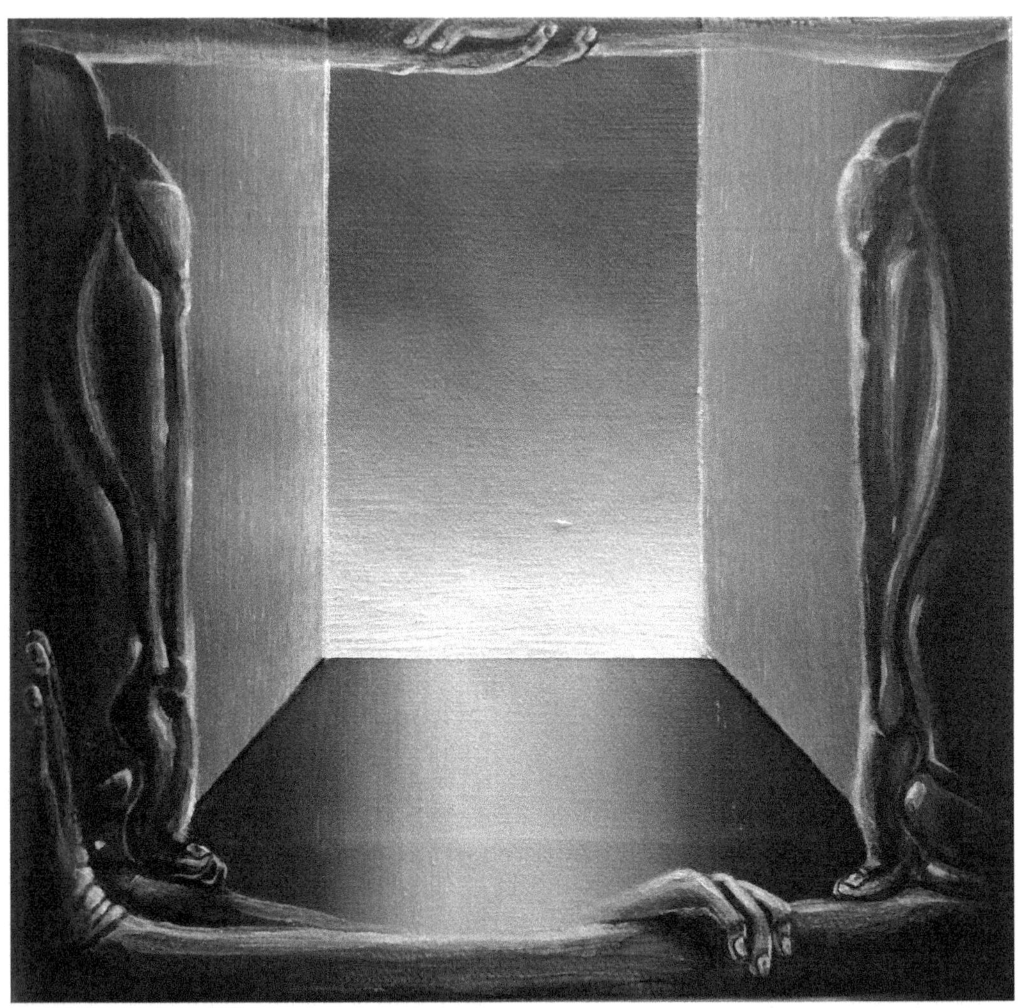

FEMALE FRAME

Painting

BONI JOI

LUZERN, SWITZERLAND

THE INFORMATION GAME

In the future the Internet of Things
lies beneath the ancient earthworks
& the story of Stonehenge will be rewritten
Nirvana is not an air-conditioned office

lying beneath the ancient earthworks
we mistake a cloud of pixels as a person
Nirvana is not an air-conditioned office
we keep our minds busy with our thumbs

we mistake a cloud of pixels as a person
the body is half-way between mummified & birdsong
we keep our minds busy with our thumbs
cross-reference things from nothing

the body is half-way between mummified & birdsong
we're reluctant spectators of data business
cross-reference relics from forensics
the habit apps hit our brains like pills

we're reluctant spectators of data business
crave a quick window of animal sounds
habit apps hit our brains like pills
we chart the movement of the Rockaway peninsula

crave a quick window of animal sounds
we sense where we are by previews of the empty center
chart the movement of the Rockaway peninsula
mow the grass to reveal the plastic garbage

we sense where we are by previews of the empty center
geo-referencing our unique content
we mow the grass to reveal the plastic garbage
in the future of the Internet of Things.

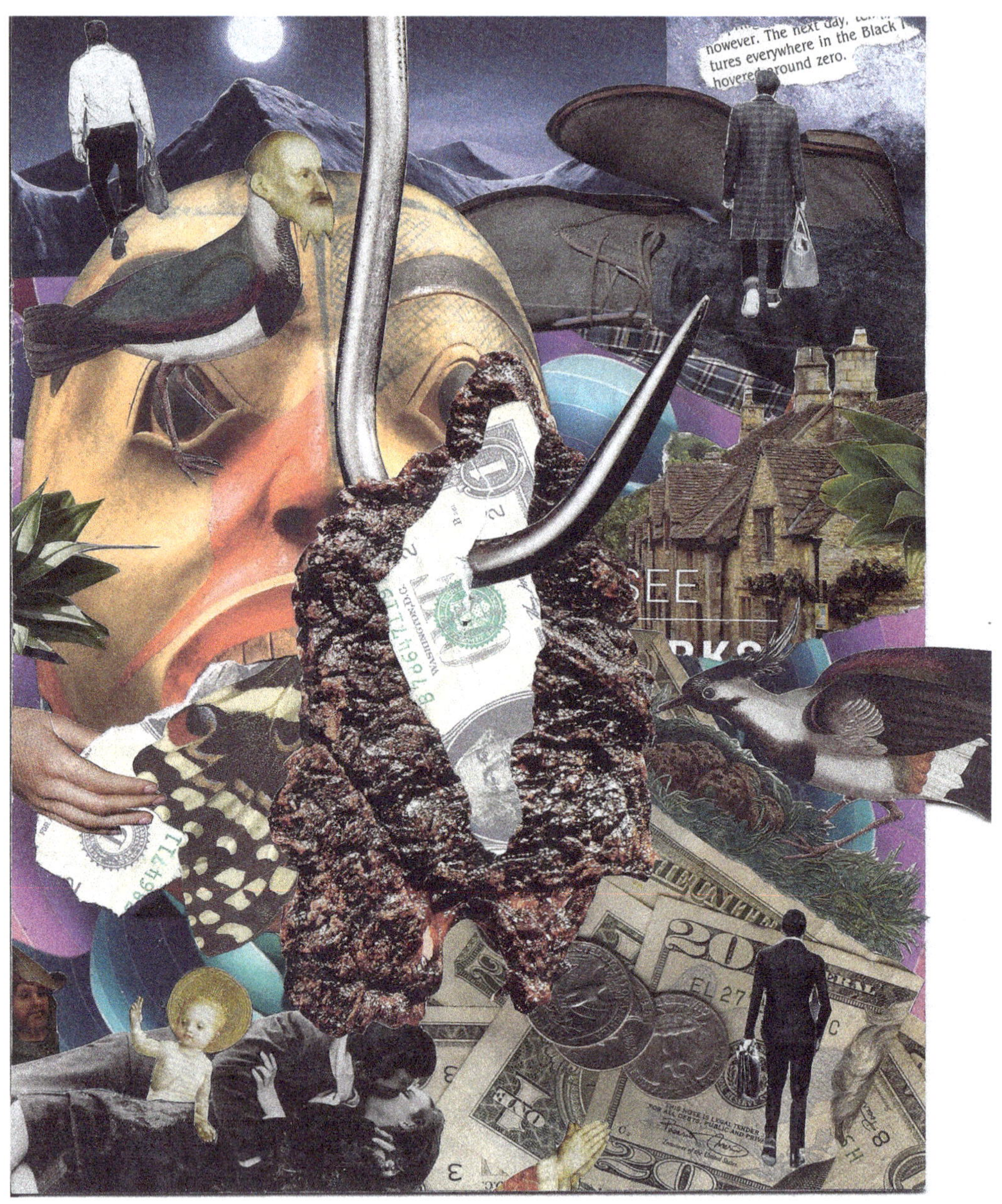

NEST EGG

Collage

BILLY CANCEL

BROOKLYN, NEW YORK

SHARK INFUSED RIP TIDE AND WHERE HONEY SUCKLE

scent hangs thick in the air much the same

to you scanning The World through the tinted

visor of a Superbowl Quarterback.   same time

     across   Great White Pigeon Shit Wave   all

over the map i'm happy in transit   some call me

Syncretic Saint   others Business Class.   dolled up

     strategic Non-Signifier gets white housed

in   yet A Bunch are always willing to mobilize

reconfigure help Uncle Tim kill dead mice?   i smoked

     my way   through an Imperial Diet   the Hungry

Staggers privileged some   devastated others   that's the

Whole Boiling.   FLIPSIDE OF THE REVERSE

     is Situation Normal All Fucked

Up where we're checked   until

     THE TOP blows off   RIGHT SIDE caves

in   LEFT SIDE breaks down   THE BOTTOM

drops out   unconvincing

electronica.

KSENIJA KOVAČEVIĆ

KRAGUJEVAC, SERBIA

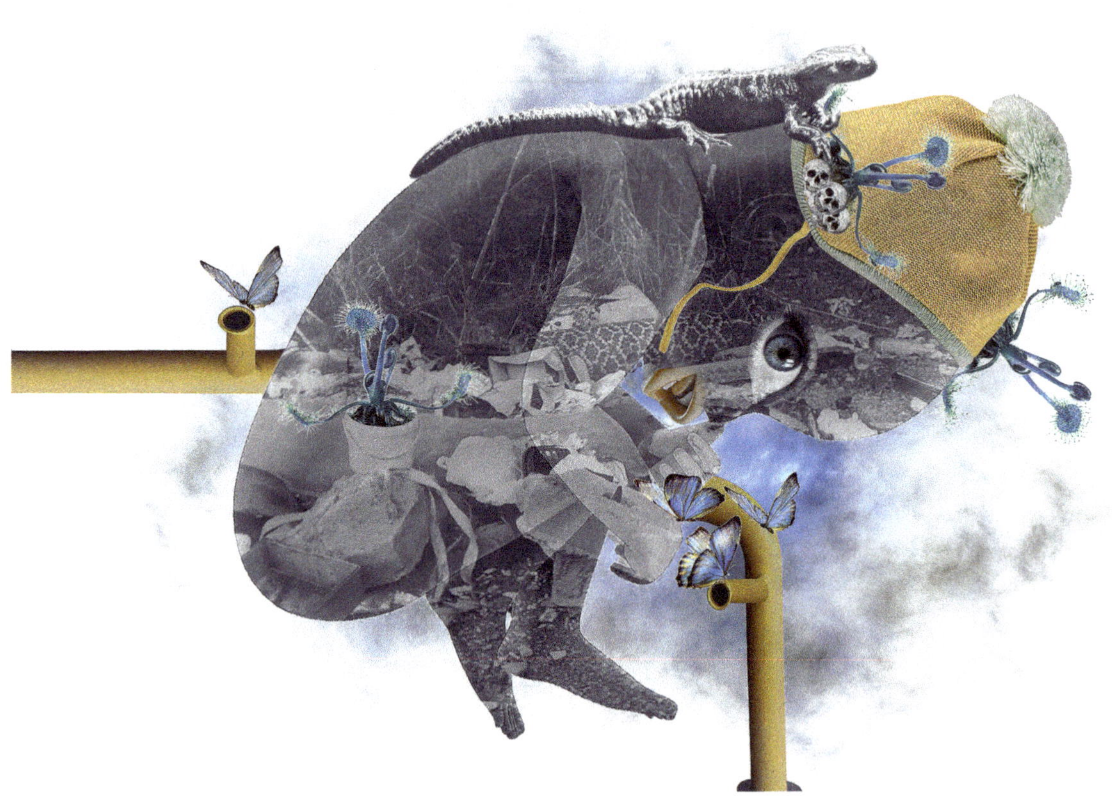

5D ULTRASOUND

Collage

ALAMGIR HASHMI

ISLAMABAD, PAKISTAN

FACTORIES

ENOUGH BULLSHIT,
the manufacturing, marketing
and consumption of.
The subject of this card
demands a long catalogue
which only a deep sorrow will supply.

The factory whistle calls for hurry;
there's no time for a deep sorrow.

So what if the reindeer up north
have no moss left to feed on?
So what if the poet's tears are too tired
to show in the corner of his eye?
He ponders the likeness
between Harrisburg and Chemobyl
and the crusty geographies of rhetoric
which define a border.

He must work faster
and look for EPICURUS
thoughtful among the really harmed:
only he could build factories of desire,
the factories of love and death,
and keep filing away at this speed.

JOËL HUBAUT

PARIS, FRANCE

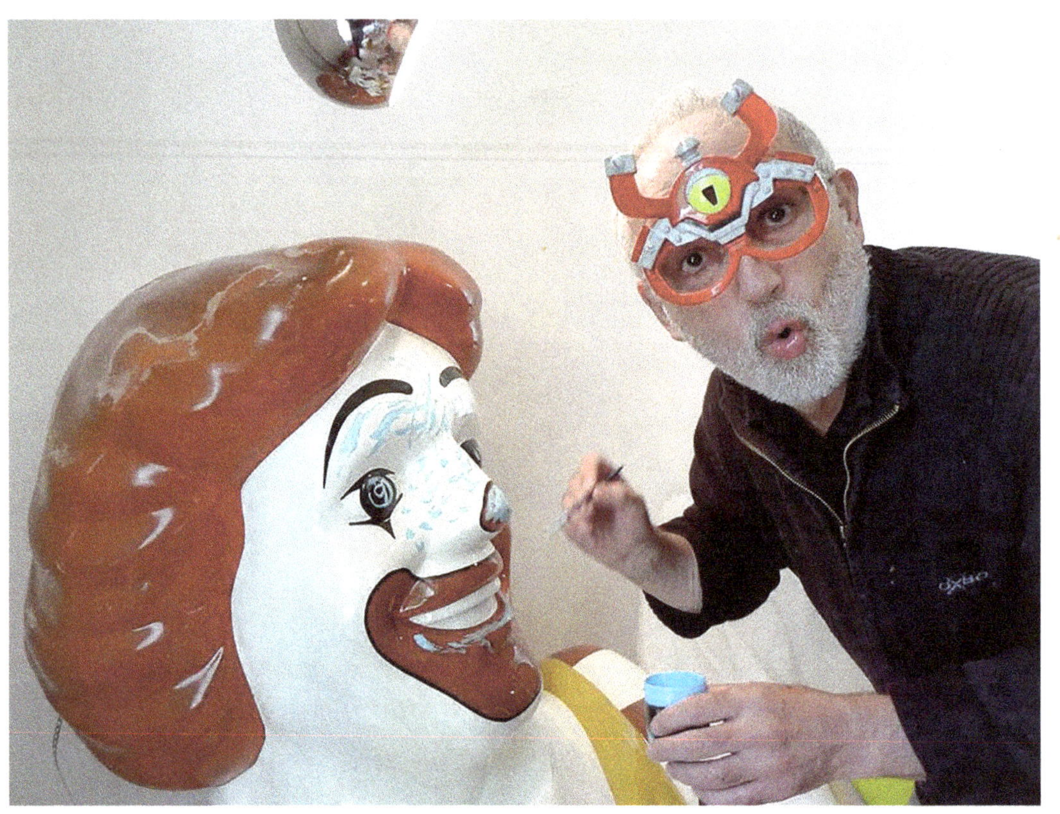

LOVE MAKEUP FOR FUCKING DONALD

Photograph

CSABA PÁL

BUDAPEST, HUNGARY

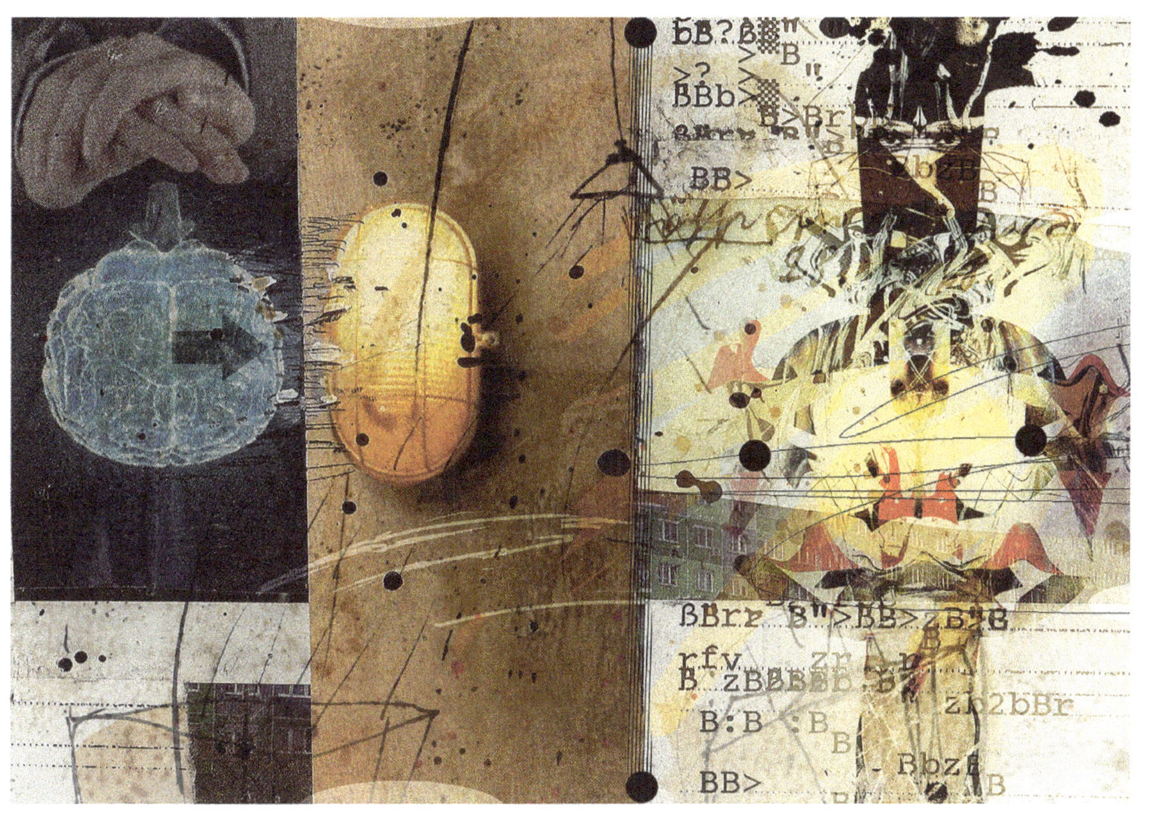

SPHERE

Mixed Media

VOLODYMYR BILYK

ZHYTOMYR, UKRAINE

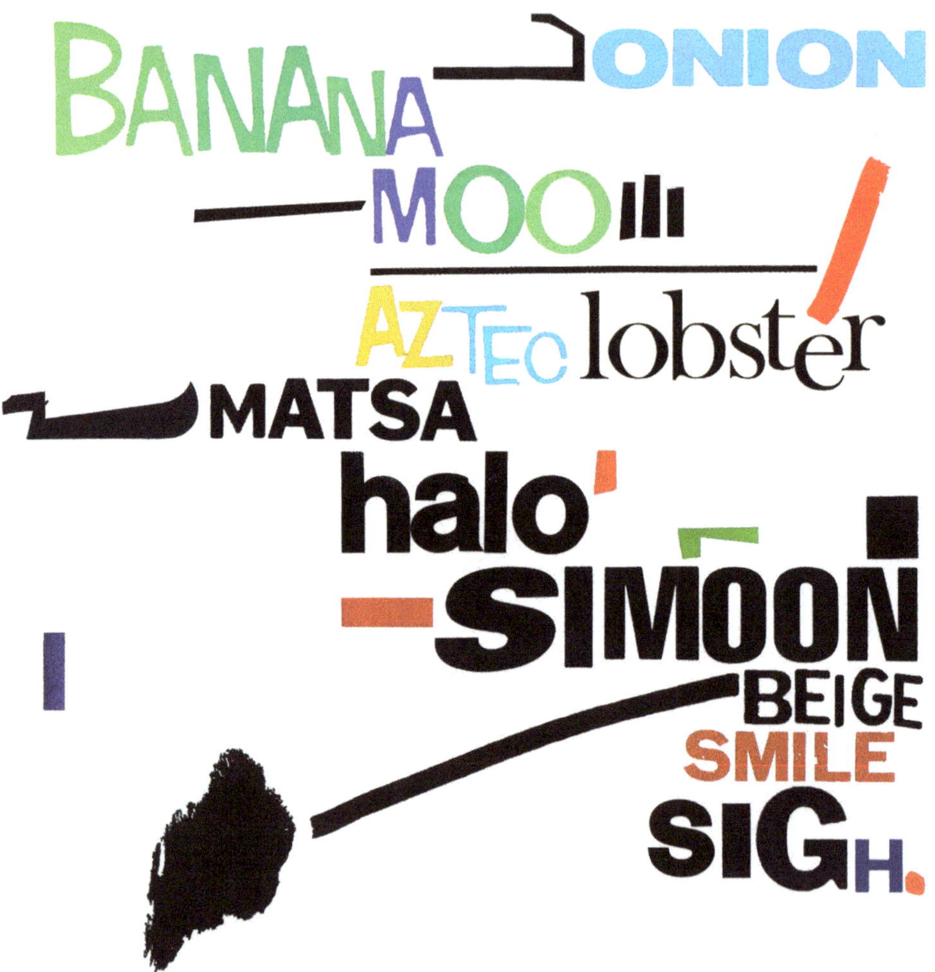

BANANA ONION

Visual Poem

RADOSLAV ROCHALLYI

BRECLAV, CZECH REPUBLIC

UNPREDICTABLE VARIABLES

DESPERATE LEPROSY

$$I\ thank\ you^{x} = for + \frac{everything}{I\ am!} + \frac{strength\ to\ be\ ^{2}}{alone!} + \frac{time\ is^{3}}{running\ out!} + \cdots, -\infty < for\ the\ us < \infty$$

THE ULTIMATE MACHINE

Saliva

from chin to the shirt

Leprechaun with a
crown on the head

He anointed my
head

Hungry, no hilarious,

Water and oil

… Slowly tortured

from a smile to cry

accompanied by
parents

BIOLOGICAL MIMICRY

~~Programmed~~ behaviour

hiding ~~in their own decisions~~

Preferences ~~and Choices~~

~~long-~~**defined** ~~formulas~~

The ~~thoughtful self~~

<u>trimmed by a</u> fence ~~of conceit~~

about ~~free mind~~

~~and~~ **self-**~~importance.~~

MICHAEL THOMPSON

CHICAGO, ILLINOIS

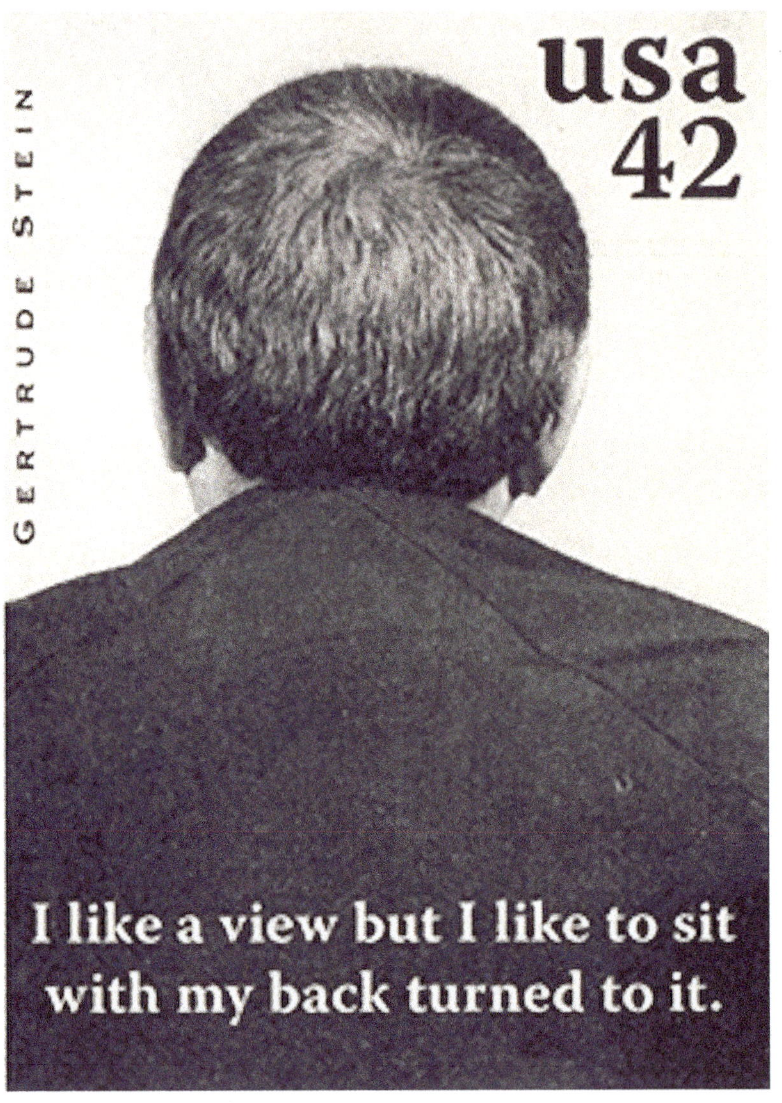

NO. 3

Photo Composite

BRADLEY RUBENSTEIN
BROOKLYN, NEW YORK

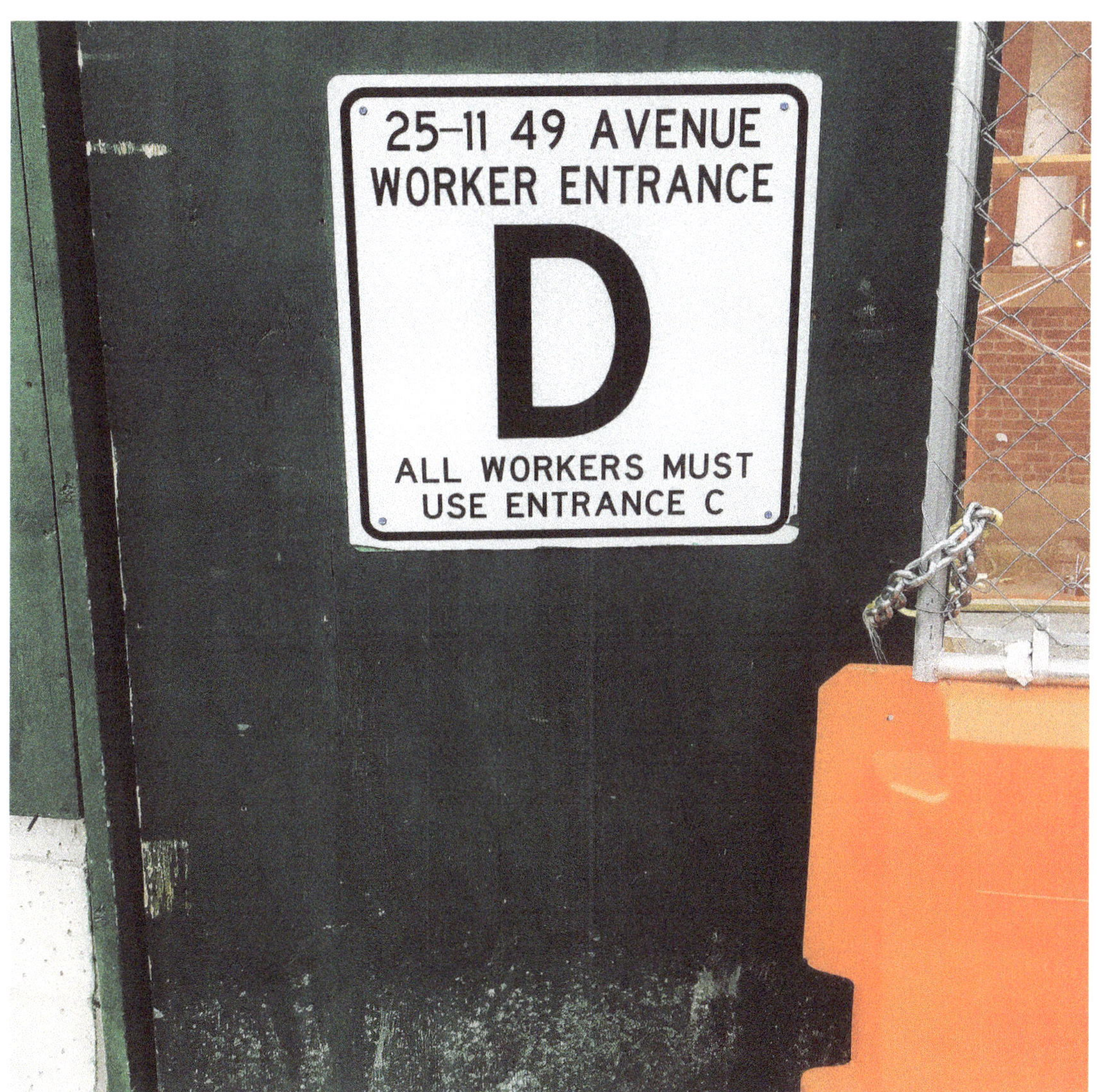

PORTRAIT OF GEORGE ORWELL, LONDON, 1947

Photograph

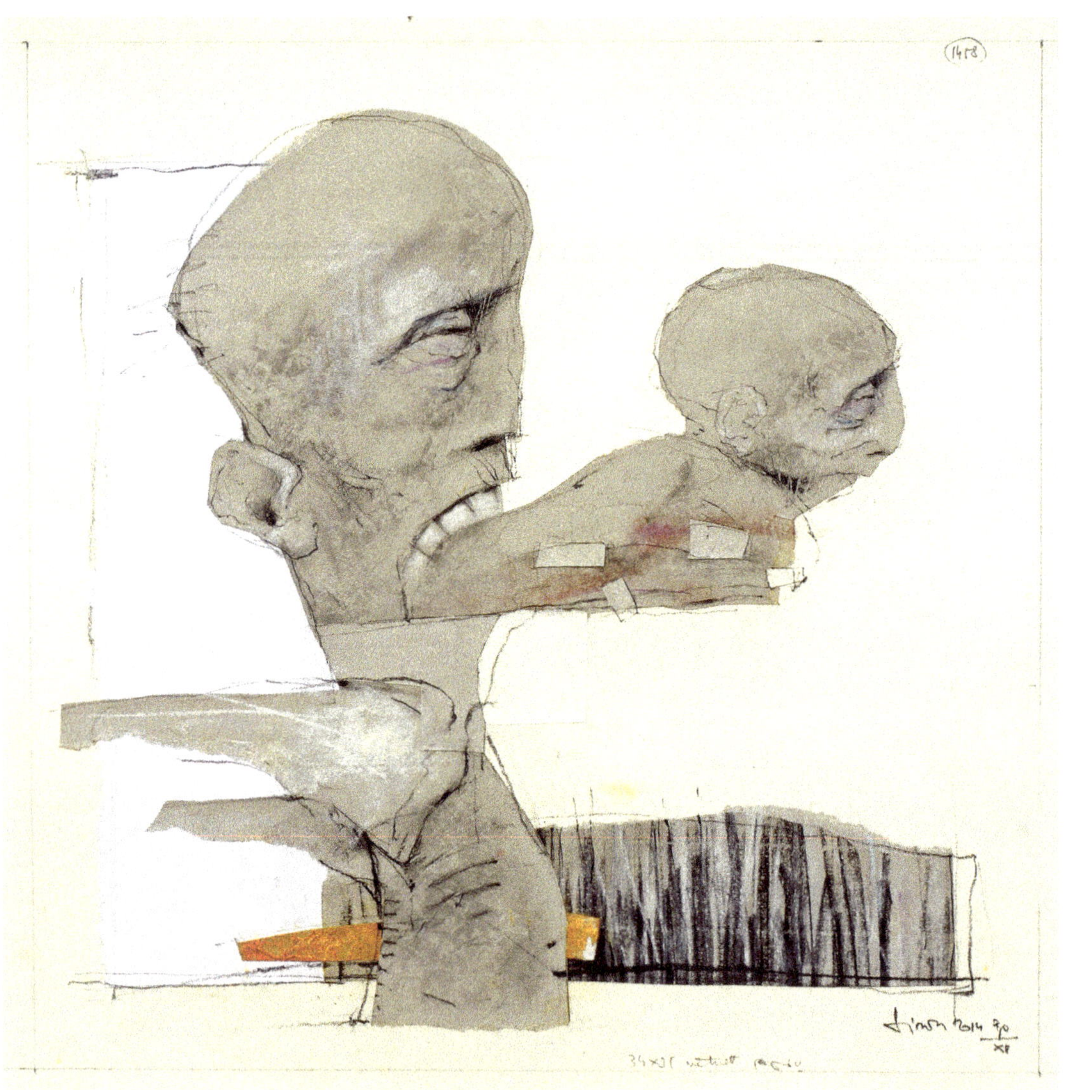

LIFE AS SUCH

Mixed Media, 34 x 35 cm

MEGHAN GRUPPOSO

NEW YORK, NEW YORK

OUR TEETERING STUFF PILE IN THE STOMACHS
OF THOSE WE'VE NEVER MET

all that's between us is polyester / made by tiny hands
made with ankles tied to beds womanhood tied to indenture
husbands hunched over
all that's between us is cracked in a can / a plastic bottle unscrewed
this is the way we care for each other / you look parched

a gun carved out of wood / a stick picked up
your fingers folded into the right shape . . . still hurts my feelings
what are those . . . i'm uncomfortable / let's monetize something
here's this chiffon capelet / these boots i thought you'd like . . .
that don't fit over your calves / what's wrong with your calves?

all that bonds us is connected to men missing fingers & hands & whole arms
is connected to accidental fires hemmed in with intentional locks . . .
     to burning people
it's connected to: we never learn
to: i don't know this feeling . . . i just volcano at you
put a lid on it . . . look at this designer lid

in the basement—under the Persian rug
there's a pile swept up i wasn't strong enough to climb the stairs
& carry the vacuum down for
it grows when no one's around
every time it's stepped on
there's a sneeze

everything that's between us is many car rides away
let's keep our feet bare / take off our lids . . . let's walk
we've been holding everything in
there must be diamonds
there must be

SANDRA GEA

ATHENS, GREECE

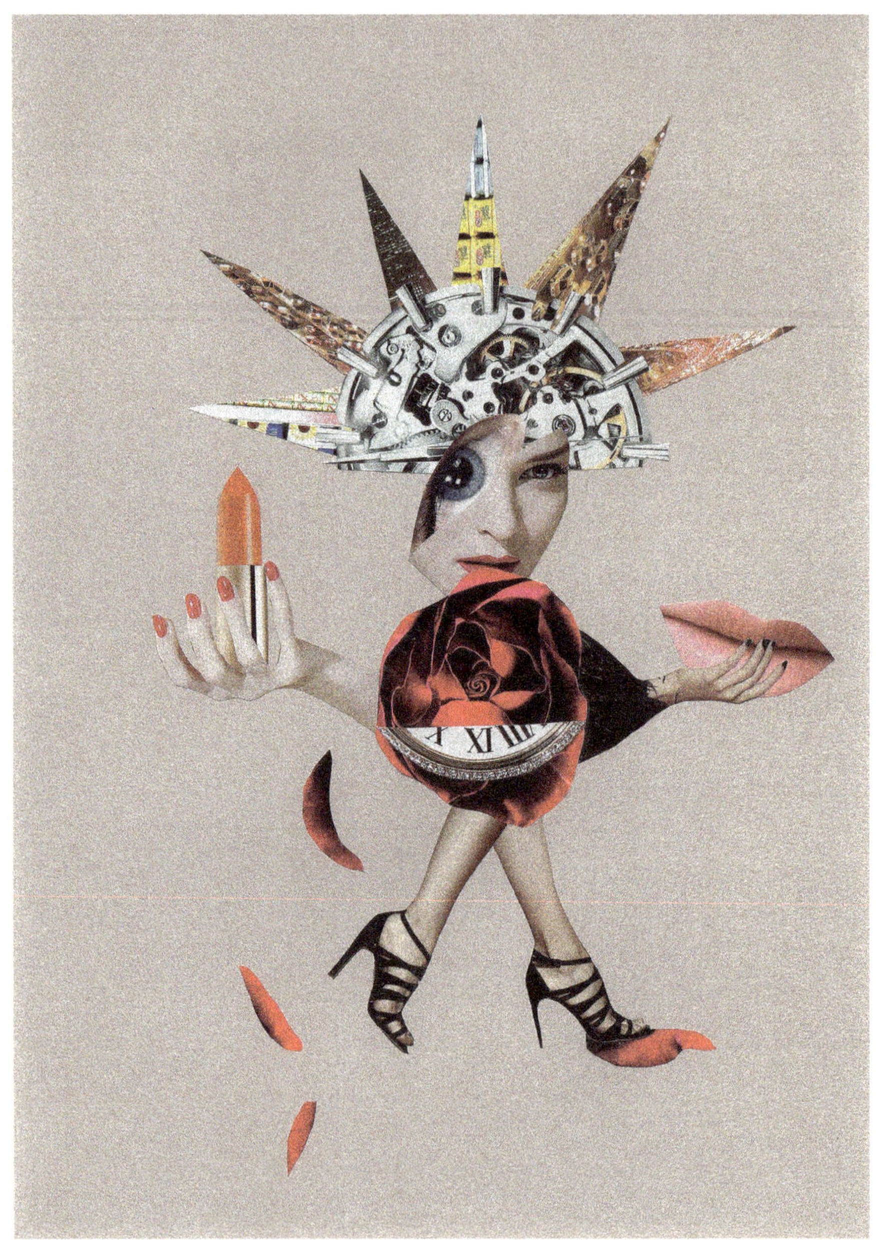

YOU BOUGHT YOUR OWN EXTINCTION

Collage

THOMAS OSATCHOFF

MARIA AURORA, PHILIPPINES

OFFER FROM DADA

Pears picked from the tree
safely according to the SAFE!
online safety act of the new sun
also calling for SAFE! roads,
SAFE! drivers, SAFE! vehicles.
SAFE! news. No speaking

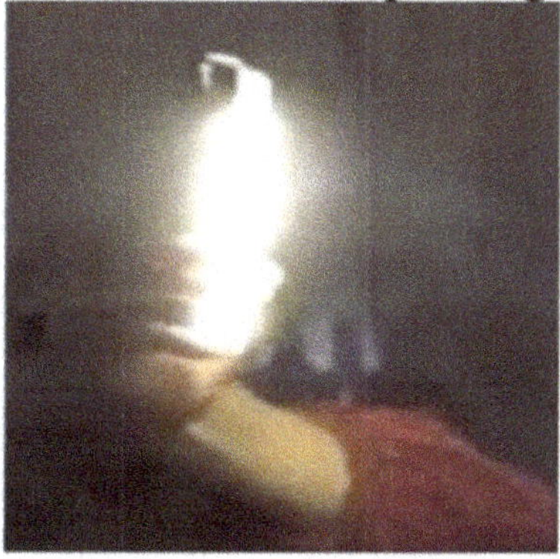

in dispraise of Dada.
Only Dada may do so
nonsensically syncing
anonymously with Man Ray
and our several identities
to let us know things are
as they should be in 3d
shrinking until pearls.

OFFER FROM DADA

Visual Poetry

JAMIKA AJALON

PARIS, FRANCE

PEARLS

found yr dark eyes under sea
wave washing u transmit.
what you see?

boats of refugees lost in the green seas
boats of refugees lost

there is a settlement,
transatlantic foetuses decedent
sea salted bone water memory.
water don't forget she
transmits
what you see? dark eyes
pearls in disguise nested in
fossil cases recording encoding
time and continuum
all bassline and the beats cause
those earthquakes and tsunamis
and centuries reunborn spawned a
new breed hidden
in the shapes of seaweed and sand. a
right band of lunatics

leaving dark cloud stained
Hieroglyphe above Mediterranean
waves where
a moon sits cutting the horizon.

water moves with memory of things
untold forgotten thrown away plastic
bottles and plastic bags
is a fashion deep sea side were
the reunborn amphibiots move
hidden and boom.
collecting stories preparing room for
the welcoming,
most believe is the second coming.

J. D. NELSON
LAFAYETTE, COLORADO

SPINACH BEARD

nothing but the earth & a graph paper smile

that yellow sun is the james of caring
in time there will be a castle

not sharing a king or queen with the rest of the chess club

    eating a leather brain in the king's salad chamber

shrimp in the nose for two dollars!

BOB HOLMAN
NEW YORK, NEW YORK

EVERY POEM

In a poem
Is a poem

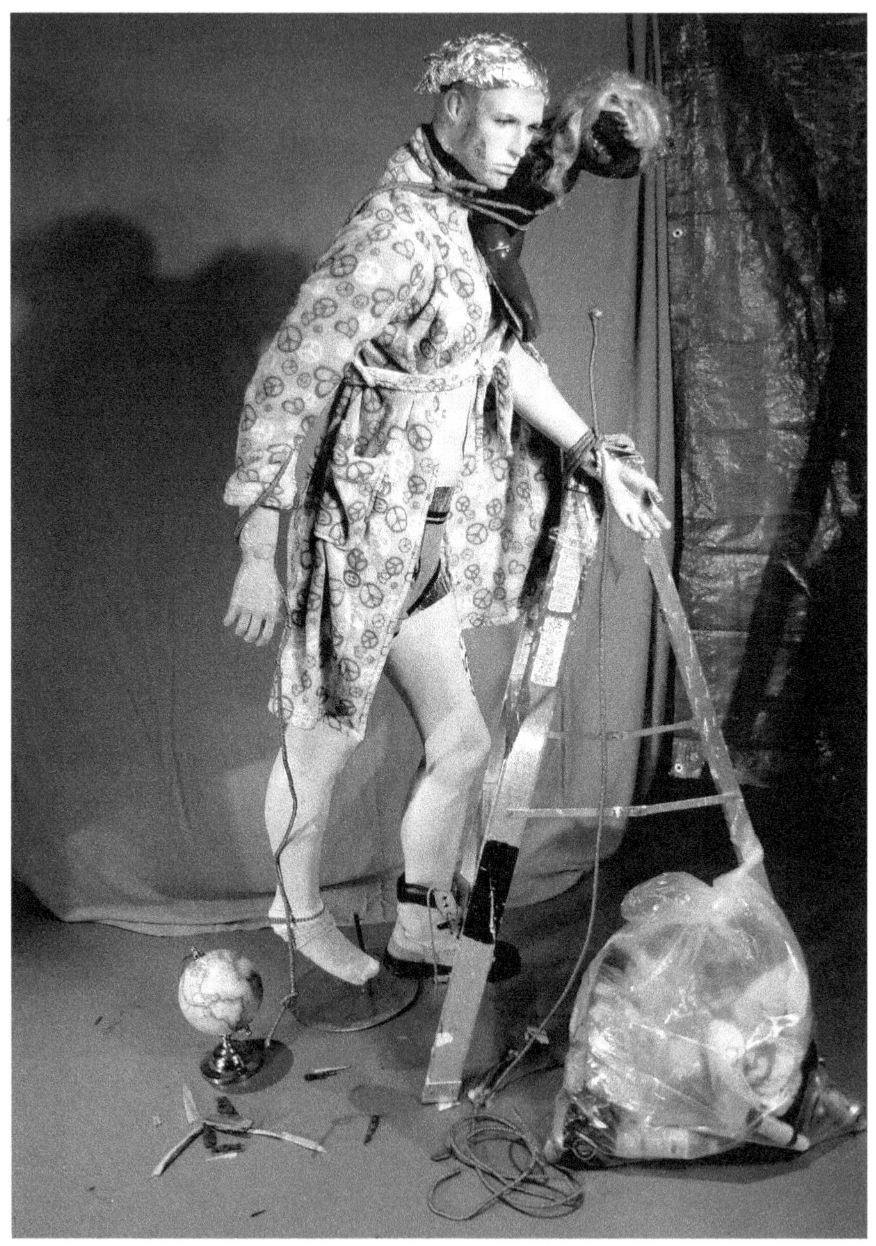

THE ANSWER IS CLEAR

Sculpture / Photograph

PAUL "POEZ" MILLS
NEW YORK, NEW YORK

TO SURVIVE

Let us pursue

the secret furious beauty
            of the earth
the sea
                the sky.

The fractured truth
that bares and breaks.

Frightening.

Sickening.

                This
magic, this

unexpected
speechless

wonder

Who can kill it?
who can
taint, poison it?

No overfed clown,
no monster,
no bewildering dollar bill hate

It was around
before time came along and
swung into view

It will be
It is
alone with you, me
now

All it needs
is your trust
your natural will
to survive, fight:

        free

SILVIO SEVERINO

CORK, IRELAND

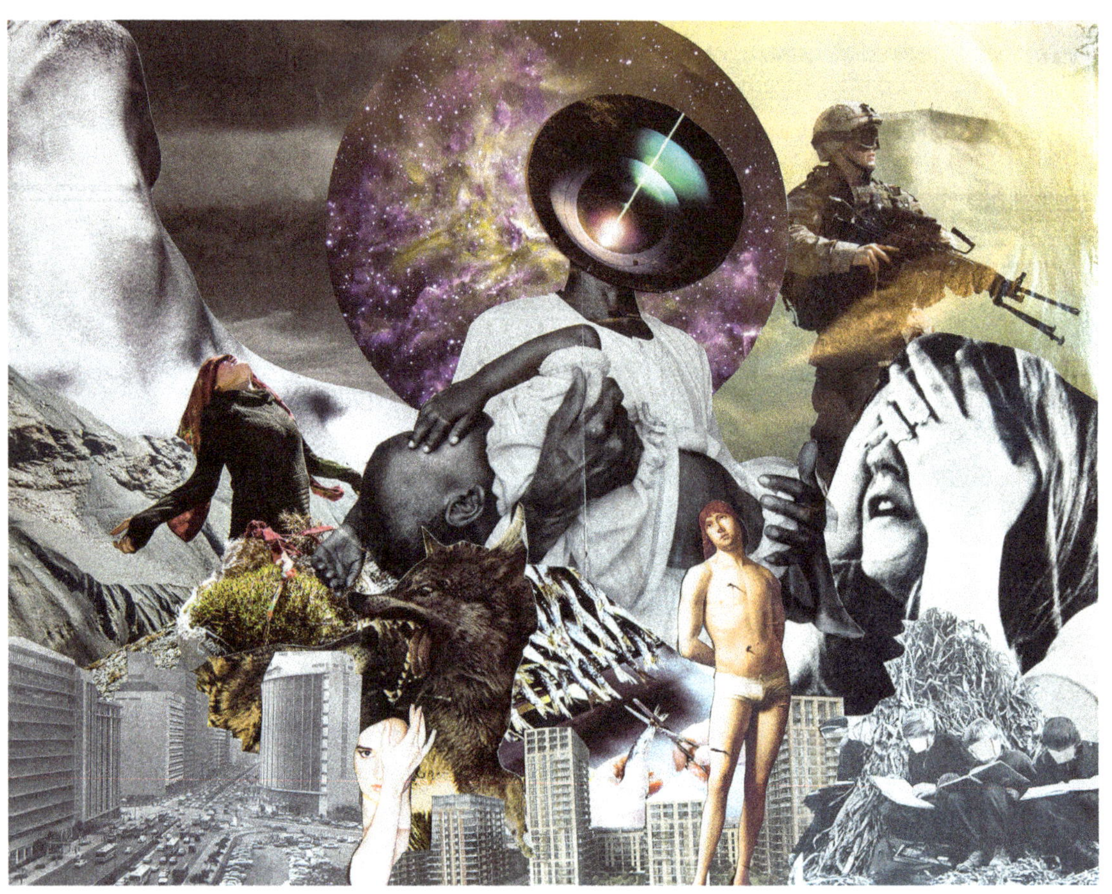

TORMENTOR OF OUR TIME

Collage

SUZI KAPLAN OLMSTED

PORTLAND, OREGON

THE RUNNERS

It's a rainy winter afternoon in Portland
I'm driving across town in traffic
I pass a bus at its stop, blocking the street
Then get stuck behind a long parade of cars
A traffic light red in the distance ahead
On my right two people are running down the sidewalk
They're carrying heavy bags, waving at the bus
Which is far behind me, long finished accepting passengers
The light changes, and I see the runners still haven't made it
So I stay where I am idling, even as the space yawns in front of me
Forcing the bus to wait until the traffic moves
Small rebellion

MARC OLMSTED

PORTLAND, OREGON

SYNTH SHRIEK

America falling
as old bard prophesied
or action movie preview explosion orange
ask the skin of the Jack-O-Lantern president
this Halloween themed
October
John Carpenter synth shreek warning
dam burst full of blood
America's Pilate
Trump washing his tiny hands

NINA ZIVANCEVIC

PARIS, FRANCE

NINJA TEXTS:
DAY IN LIFE

Part I.

Cold misty January morning. I have to go to my torture chamber, my French aid, wellfare agency which claims that in 2005, 2015 and 2016 they paid me too much in contributions to my single family!

Allegedly, they claim retroactivly 11000 euros which I don't have, I would not give them anyways, they can come over and claim my lousy second-hand computer and my leather mini skirt.

I put some music on, Chopin's NOcturnos and I tell myself—you are NOT going to cry, it will smear your softly applied make-up. I'm rushing out of the building, a tiny body, a rat or a mouse tries to escape in front of me. It does not have to try hard— I would not do him any harm.

The noisy body-builder in front of la CAF tells me angrily: YOU HAVE TO hurry up, mizzzz, you are late for your appointment, you have half a minute only to register for your appointment otherwise you are left for a February slot. A big drugged out CAF councelor tells me loudly: I know mizz, you wrote us a letter to annul your debts. You have TO WAIT for our answer for yet another two months. She's being VERY irritated by my inquires and by my impatience. Needless to say they cut all of their funding and I have to ask for a credit in my bank which is the biggest shark of them all.

I leave their office, it's noon and the Chinese mothers are taking their lovely round-faced kids to their lunch boxes in the frozen park in the 13th district of Paris.

I'm kind of lost, dazzled by the circumstances, the exterior surroundings, and I light a cigarette. 15 days without a smoke so far!!

Part II.

I get home breathing in snatches, time to put my Klaus Schulze brainwashing music, Le Medaillon, he entitled it . . . A phone call from a long-lost, forlorn friend Do I still write poetry?

No, not every so often, but instead I live poetry, migrant's issue, sprinkled with my social quest for half-redeemed beauty which raises high above this ground, in the late afternoon when the city bust calms down and everyne is under the impression that the air is less polluted to breathe. All the Parisians are nuts when they start jogging through the polluted city, inhaling this immortal air; the little girl Sava who graces my apartment with her visits now and then makes beautiful drawings of her quotidien but the best one she has ever made is her vision of the performance of *The Nutcracker*— yes, that's me, a nut and a cracker, cracking down from too much pollution, too much reality immortalized in a long Alexander Kluge's film, *DAS KAPITAL*.

Who could ever think that we would all end up in a long factory line, now, by the very beginning of the 21 century! Well, Marx was more clairvoyant than madame Soleil, he had seen it all, predicted it all, the fact that there are Christian Catholic Christmas holidays, the days of peace and quiet, but God forbid that you are a Sunni and you want to take a day off on Ramadan, or a Shiite dreaming of taking Nooruz, a New Year's day off, or a Zoroastrian or an Orthodox Christian, Serb or an Armenian, a Jew modestly hiding in your Temple for Yom Kippur or Hannukah—then you're in a real conflict with your soul—have to work through all your holiest holidays which are not officially recognized by the French government.

And also, the classic case of the Gilets Jaunes . . . when did they occur in their classic version?

The "classic" period of English land enclosure.

On Sunday 1 April 1649 a small group of poor men collected on St. George's Hill just outside London and at the edge of the Windsor Great Forest, hunting ground of the king and the royalty. They started digging the land as a "symbolic assumption of ownership of the commonlands" (Hill 1972: 110). Within ten days, their number grew to four or five thousand. One year later, "the colony had been forcibly dispersed, huts and furniture burnt, the Diggers chased away from the area" (Hill 1972: 113).

This episode of English history could be consistently added to Marx's Chapter 28, entitled "Bloody Legislation against the Expropriated." Yet, while most of that chapter deals with Tudors' legislation aimed at criminalizing and repressing popular behaviour induced by the expropriation of land (vagrancy, begging, theft).

This episode goes a step further, by making clear that primitive accumulation acquires meaning vis-à-vis patterns of resistance and struggle. This episode entails the active and organised activity of a mass of urban and landless poor aimed at the direct reappropriation of land for its transformation into common land.

Paraphrasing Marx, it was an activity aimed at "associating the producer with the means of production." It is clear therefore that the force used by the authorities to disperse the Diggers (aka Gilets Jaunes), can be understood, consistently with Marx's theory, as an act of "primitive accumulation," because it reintroduces the separation between producers and means of production.

LUCIEN SUEL

LIGNY LEZ AIRE, FRANCE

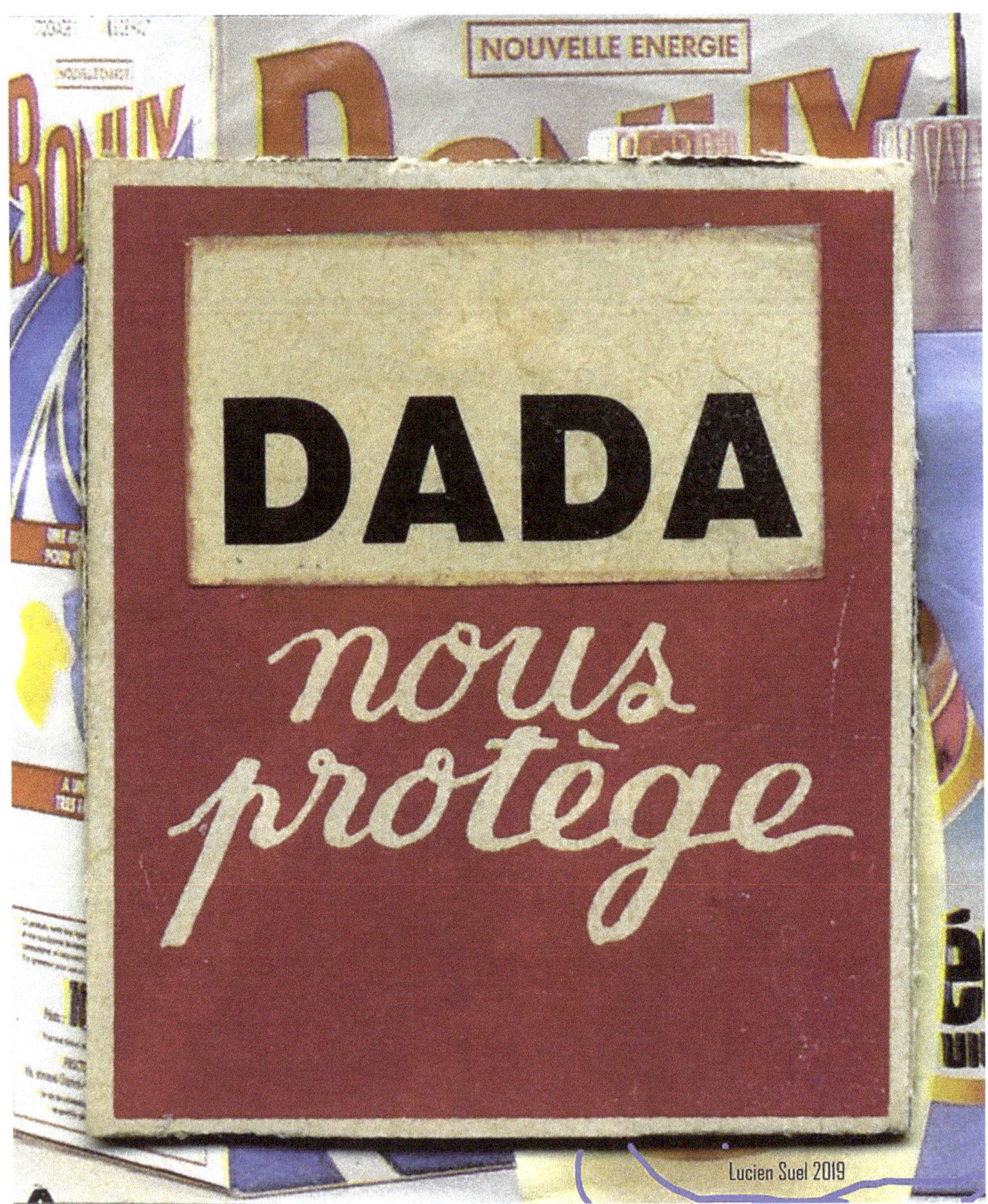

DADA NOUS PROTÈGE

Mixed Media

SOPHIE MALLERET

NEW YORK, NEW YORK

(i wear the eye patch Look through holes)

i wear the eye patch   Look through holes
            Plastic eye patch/plastic turtle's shell
       White Colour of sky   & fog
       Around/inside my head
            Buried inside plastic bottle
Dug in waste continent   Name of   my child
    Through holes in my brain
(I see) a giant octopus
Her belly full chains of carbon atoms   Unbreakable to precipice
      Make her crazy seaweed bulging eyes
Her arms around my neck
    Pressing/   squeezes anything that breathes
(Still breathes)
Breathless giant octopus   Her heart/your heart
Chokes Last word   Agonizes
On abandoned shore/a desert Where   the salmon swam upstream
      the salmon from last year
       from year before
      from before you were born
Souvenir aiguisé à la lame   of muddy river
            Where you exhale

I carry you to the place in my heart
    Where you can rest
     Un port cimetière au fond de la mer
Scratches inside your eyelids   Erosion
    You don't even have both eyes left to cry
    Tu n'as même plus tes deux yeux pour pleurer
      Apprends-moi à sauter de flaque en flaque
i'm your child i'm your child's child
      Teach me how to jump from one puddle to a lake
Water splashes on your faceless head
    Washing off sins/callous hands of your fathers
    My dirty hands Imprinted on your   bones
i want your life/your children's lives   lived   backwards
       i'm your child/your child's child
    Apprends-moi à sauter de flaque en flaque

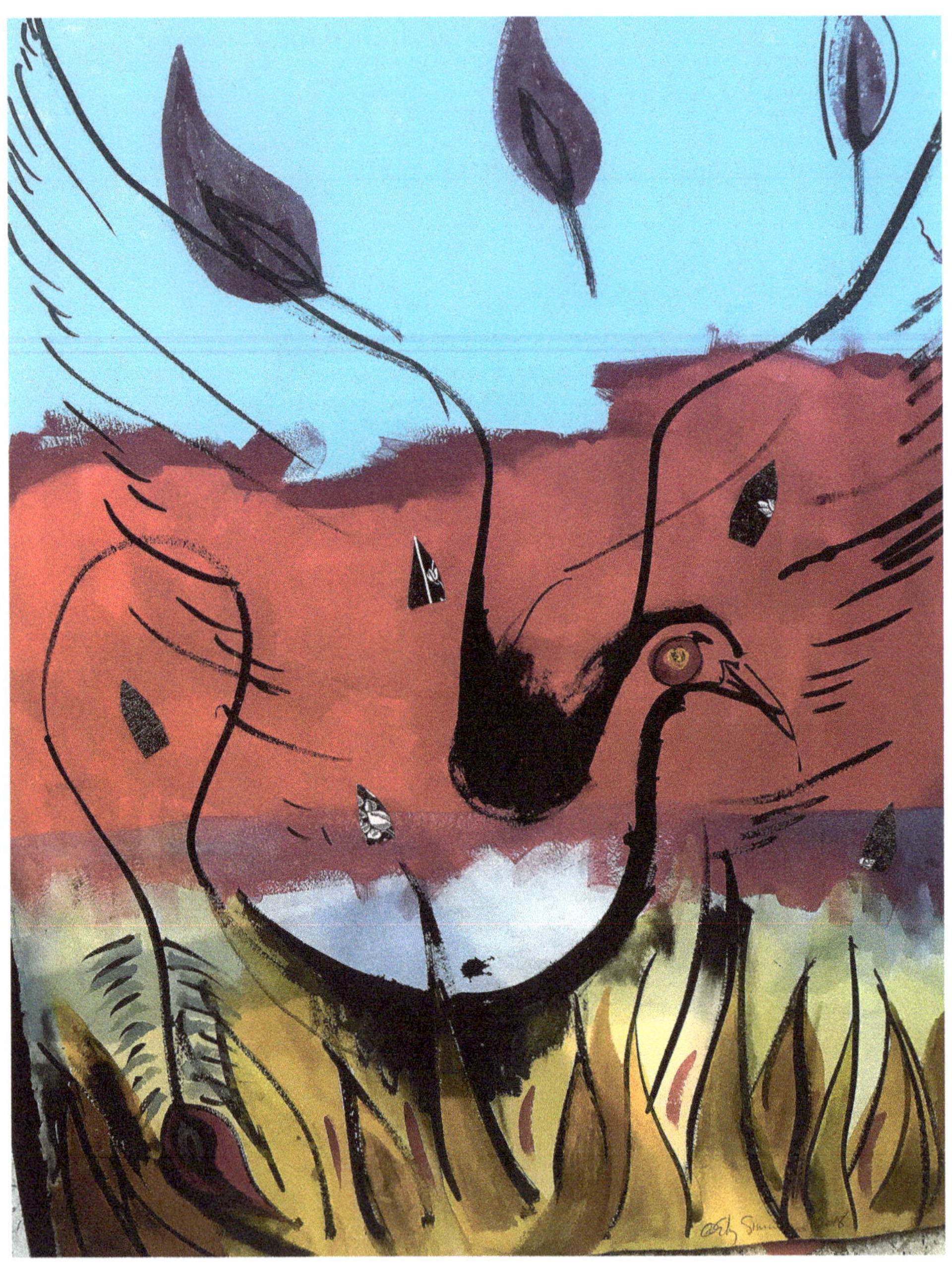

PHOENIX

Painting / Mixed Media

ANITA SULLIVAN
EUGENE, OREGON

THE DAY ARRIVES

Yesterday, that meadow along the highway
was safely horizontal—
a short, fat meadow gleaming greenly
behind a managed forest of anorexic alders,
meadow with a belly on it, jolly
but docile.

Today that meadow seems preoccupied;
it rises, almost vertical behind the trees,
flapping lightly, exposing stretch marks, stains,
crushed-nap smudges. Rabidly
it sops up the morning's yellow luminosity
like a toast set loose among the eggs.

The anemic, gracile alders
are beginning to bend,
almost to squint, or turn their trunks around
like owls
in a collective quake of anticipation.
What day is this?

Their roots have been bound for so long,
assuming they remember
the terms of the original agreement,
they still may stumble while they're walking out.

MARINA KAZAKOVA I SARA MAINO
BRUSSELS, BELGIUM I TRENTO, ITALY

THE EARLIEST TIME THAT GARBAGE APPEARED ON EARTH IS "WITH THE BIRTH OF A PRINTING PRESS"

The earliest time that garbage appeared on Earth is "with the birth of a printing press"—one Russian once rightfully said.

"Said, sad."

Before that, rewriting was worth an effort—only the essential books and letters were rewritten.

"So, what. Don't read."

Television and social media are multiplying in seconds the most worthless of questions and even lesser.

"So, then. Don't ask."

They say that digital will solve the philosophical, will solve the moral. Hi-fi and tech are cutting off the mystical in its core—it seems to me . . .

"What is appearing is not."

In loneliness one always thinks better than in a group, in the museum, alone, the best poem lines drop on my notebook. A museum is a good world, a model of a big one, but cleaner. Moreover, museums are truer than the Internet tours and exhibitions

"The light from the museum windows brightens the sky and washes out the stars."

What is the price of life? No clear answer exists and will arrive. So, in your opinion: a person or the nature? What would you sacrifice your life for? I would—for Leonardo's hands of "Mona Lisa."

"Every second, stars in the universe explode. Every passion has its object."

In fundamental issues like this significant is one's intuition. The world has entered the period when humanism expired. Still, art has always been ahead of human civilization and will continue . . . The merit of the artist is to be able to "undress" in front of the spectator, as Dante, Goethe, Chekhov did. The Renaissance and the 19th century are our present continuous. All fundamental arrived from there. Without Michelangelo, Da Vinci, Marx would there be the *Black Quadrat*? The first one who declared the museum as a state need, the value and the necessity, was Bonaparte. He turned the royal palace into the Louvre, knowing that the existence of a world-wide collection of values is a treasure, which can't be measured by anything. Today, to tell the truth, the great museums and the big cultures are not created by democratic states. Unfortunately. The governments are knee-deep in mass arts. If we continue moving further along this circle, somewhere, I guess, we'll meet again with Stalin, Hitler or William the Orange. The state's purpose is to protect the culture, not the economic growth, not the creation of products, not the existence of the army. . . .

"Don't you watch war films? Haven't you just gotten pleasure from the 'Killing Eve' assassins?"

"The analog garbage that appeared on Earth with the birth of a printing press can still be processed by hands, the digital garbage can't," one Russian once said.

"Said, sad."

MATTHEW HUPERT
NEW YORK, NEW YORK

THE DEAD OF WATERLOO WERE SOLD AS FERTILIZER
(A found poem)

The dead of Waterloo had their teeth pulled out

fashioned into dentures. Waterloo

was such a bonanza for Britain's denture industry

that sets made of human teeth were sold as "Waterloo dentures"

Their bones were ground to fertilizer

The good farmers of Yorkshire

for their daily bread

were indebted to the bones of their children

JESSE McCLOSKEY

NEW YORK, NEW YORK

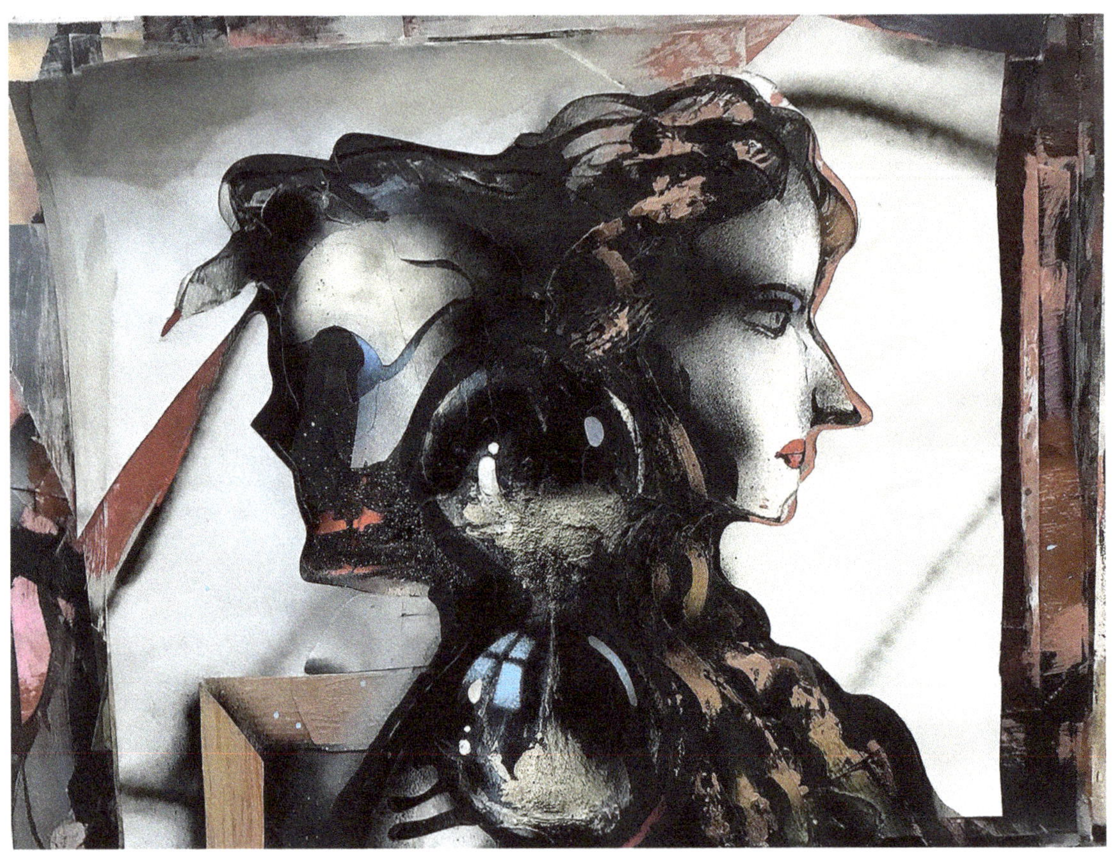

DEATH AND THE MAIDEN

Paper and Mixed Media on Canvas, 2019, 22" x 29"

KAREN HILDEBRAND

BROOKLYN, NEW YORK

THE END OF APPOINTMENT TV

We need more red

why not get your

velvet cake frosted thick

armpit tattooed

we, who open the door to

three-headed snake

religious fanatics

learn the mudra for

on the porch, ignore

I can't see you. Watch

Dad's drunken

I'm headed down-state

stumble in mayo dipped

'67 clear blue T-bird

Oscar Meyer suburbia

whitewalls grinning

and Old Spice

like a peacock on Saturday.

MILANA JUVENTA

MOSCOW, RUSSIAN FEDERATION

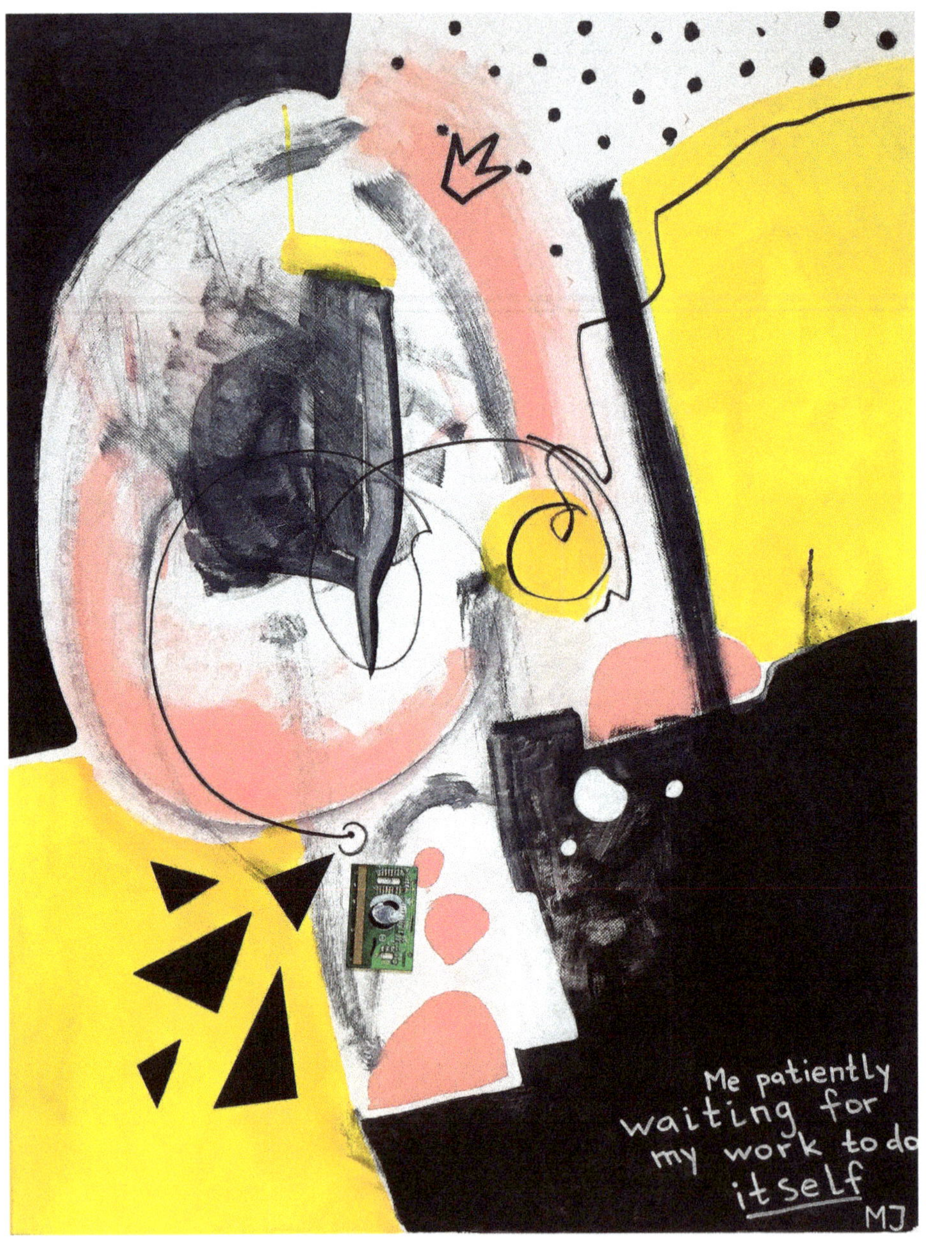

WAITING

Painting

ANNA O'MEARA I ANTHONY COX
NEW YORK, NEW YORK

SUSTAIN
Anna O'Meara

I love the feeling of a good old heart attack, like right before a presentation in front of all sorts of people who think they're more important than they are and everyone else thinks they're important, too, but I don't. If Freud were still around, he'd prescribe cocaine for such a meeting, maybe because he knew it would be fun, or maybe because he was up, up, up in the stratosphere of networking, or so they call it, which maybe is why he got so famous, just like everyone else who got so famous. Maybe that feeling of a panic attack is kind of like an orgasm, because it's overwhelming, or maybe it's like a nightmare about running where you don't even realize you feel bad or even that you are running at all until you wake up and you remember feelings that are now conveniently in the past. I'm in love and it feels like cocaine. I'm worried that I'm not apprehensive. Something is so sure. Darling . . . Baby . . . Puffin . . . Muffin . . . Squirrel. I could never lose this one sense of smell. You know when the smell is right, don't you? What does forever feel like? I feel surrounded by novelty, which is not what people say; they say it's supposed to feel like it already happened. Déjà vu. It isn't like that, it's a rush. *RUSH.* Like a nightmare where you're running, running, but a pretty one, you know? The coastline of Connecticut, it's so green and clear like a never-ending golf course regatta. I don't think I've even been to Connecticut, but I keep dreaming about running away from there as though it were an amoeba or jin that snuck into New York and infected it and possessed it without my even realizing. You see it so visibly in dreams. The architecture is so beautiful, but my body feels incapable. I might faint in front of all of these kids. Or vomit? Or piss in front of them. I'm not allowed to leave the room, legally, without another certified adult so I'll just piss here in front of all of these kids as I think about how my coffee drinking habits will kill me so many years younger than other people die. I dreamt I was in a place like Venice, circling round an islanded temple on a boat. There were two statues of women who looked like they could be the Elgin Marbles or the Caryatids of the Erechtheion . . . Haha, Erethion. Who were they? One was Joan of Arc, but I'm not sure of the other one. We were so happy to spin and spin in donuts, like wintertime Ford Taurus Midwestern pre-ABS break early 2000s days; so short-lived, right? The things we loved then seem so far away and unloveable now.

continued

RESPONSE
Anthony Cox

A woman mentioned a genie today when I was picking up a patient at the nursing home, she said she couldn't get that genie back in the bottle, and I was like Fuck, she's channeling Anna, how could she know? But she couldn't know. I was in the elevator, but that's not how I remember it. Fuck, where have I been? It's almost like a dream. She was walking at me. Maybe she was walking at me because she wanted on the elevator, but why was she talking to me? It was heavy, like meaningful, more so in my memory perhaps but it just happened. That's not even the déjà vu.

I guess that's really impossible to separate from love. You love one person, and it makes you love all people, in a way. You're suddenly useful, I don't mean in the Get A Job, kind of way, but love makes you an able soldier for the future. Which is my fondest image of you. God, that's what I want for myself. I don't think it's impossible. If anything, I see more of it all the time. I try to nurture that thing, that loves and gives to other people, and wherever it takes me, whoever it loves, whatever it builds, even if I get hit by a bus next week or die at a very old age the same kind of marginal eccentric slacker I am today, I think that's a good life, that was the right way.

Eternally recurring,

Anthony

GEDLEY BRAGA

DIVINÓPOLIS, BRAZIL

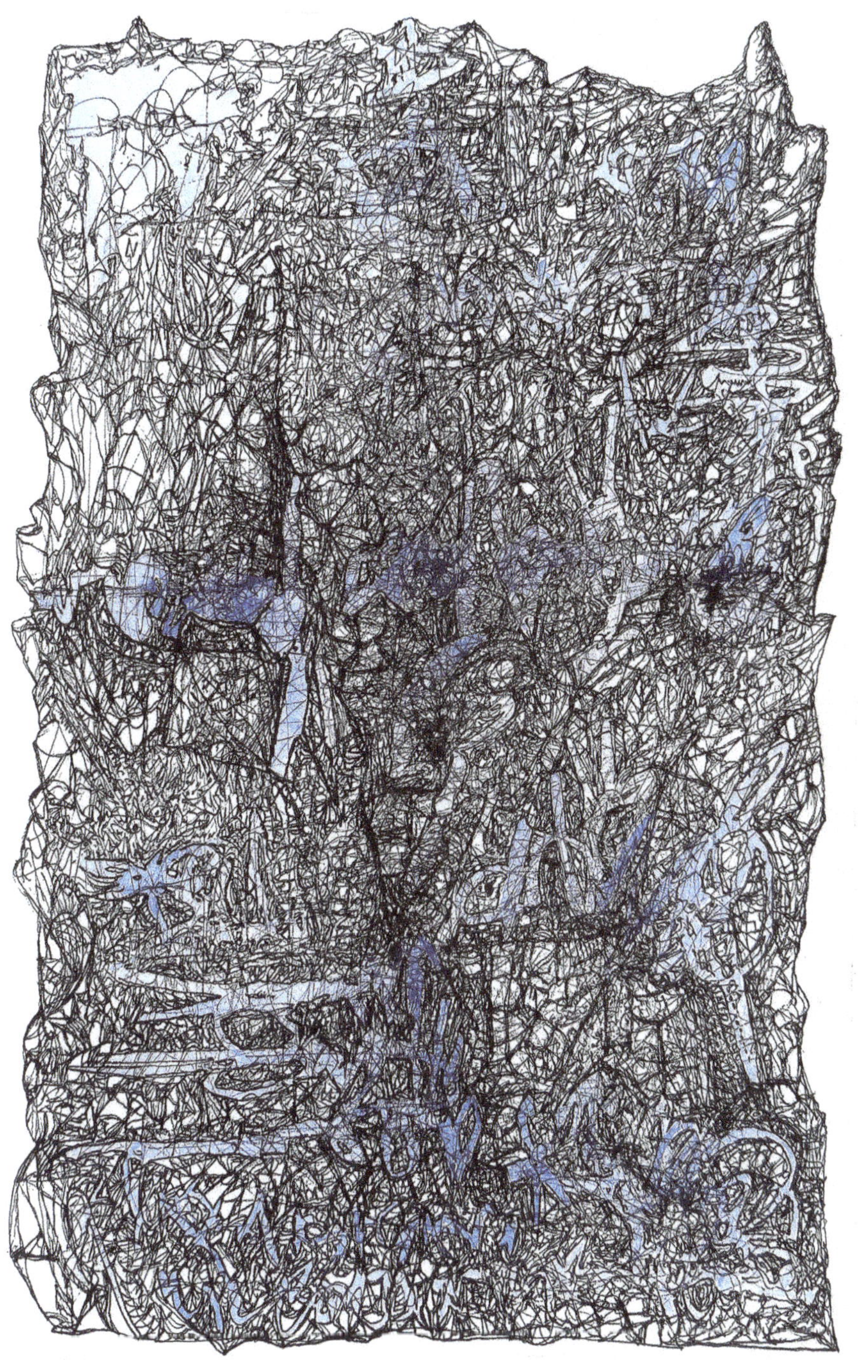

STATION TO STATION: CY TWOMBLY

Drawing

JON ANDONI GOIKOETEA

BARAKALDO, SPAIN

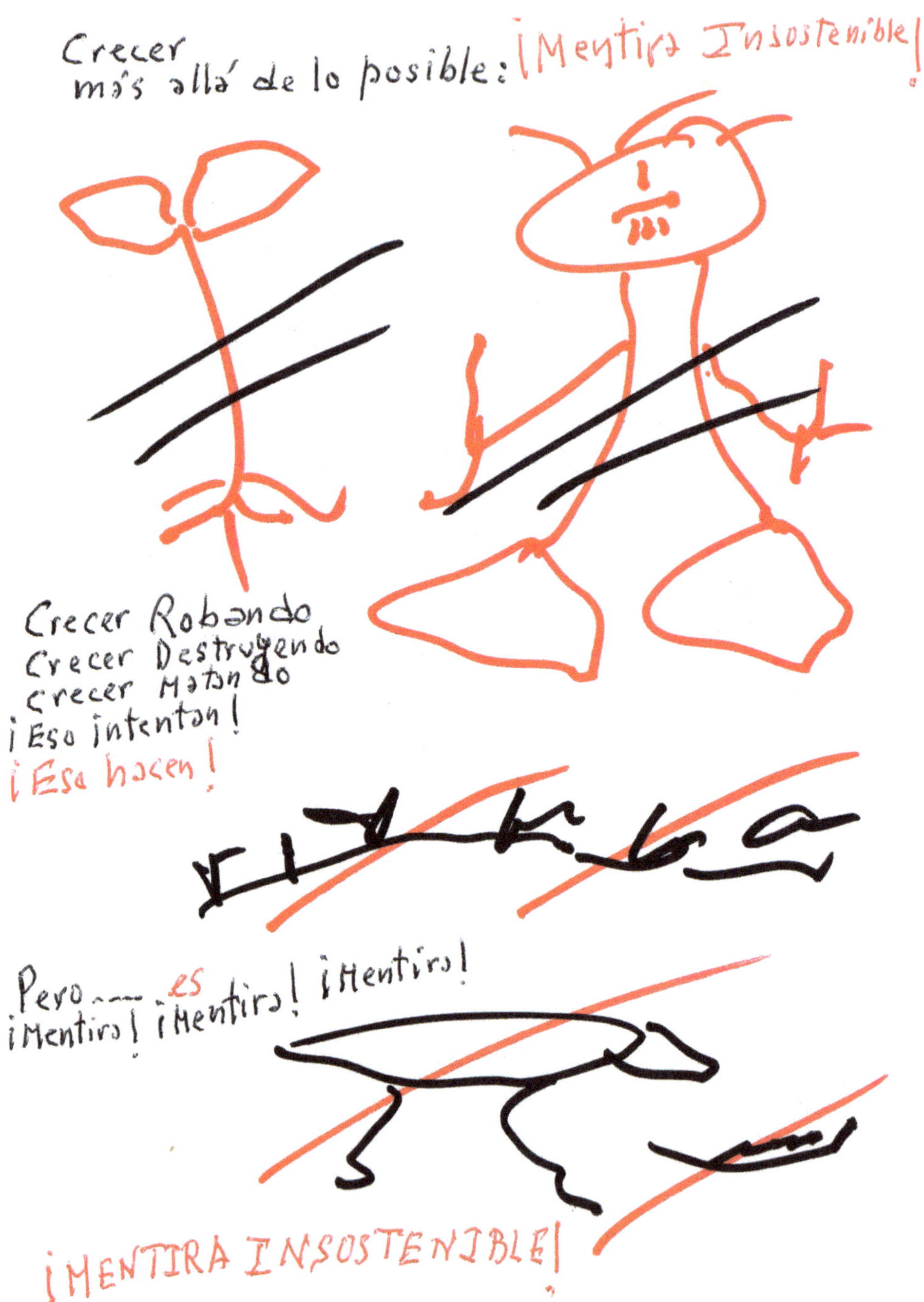

¡MENTIRA INSOSTENIBLE!

Ink on Paper

PASCALE LE BIHAN

PARIS, FRANCE

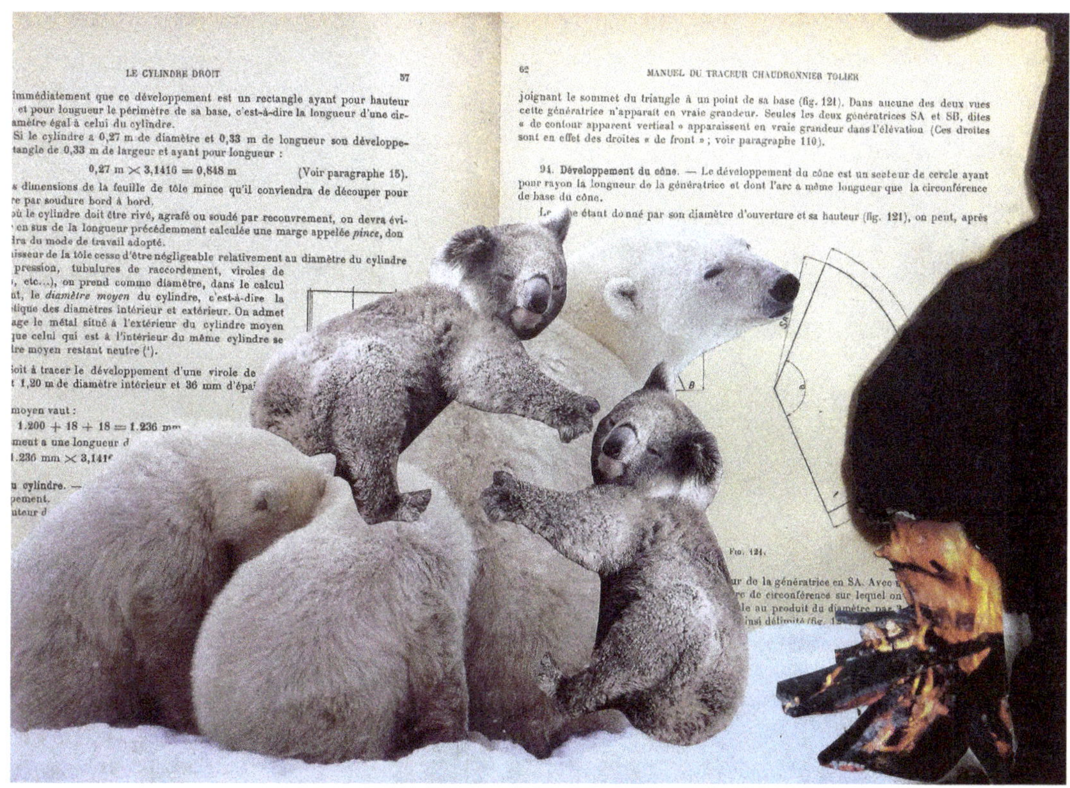

MAYBE TOO LATE

Collage

RUBY ELLAM

MELBOURNE, AUSTRALIA

GOYA TRIPTYCH

Witches Sabbath was bought by the Duchess of Osuna in 1798 along with five other spiritualistic paintings of Goya. It is unsure whether this painting was commissioned or simply acquired by the Duchess.

A black goat (or Baphomet) is a recurring symbol of Satanism. It sometimes is used to embody Satan or a demon.

Oak leaves represent archaic and ancient wisdom or knowledge. The oak is often used as a symbol in witchcraft for roots beneath the ground and leaves stretching to the heavens— "as above, so below."

A crescent moon is often used to depict female power, such as the Roman goddess Diana or Mesopotamian Ishtar. While these deities were worshipped, they also were often associated with sex and darkness, attributes not genuinely promoted in women of the 18th century.

The painting now belongs to the Spanish state.

Francisco José de Goya y Lucientes' *Witches Sabbath* (1797–98) represents Satan as a black goat, garlanded in flowers and oak leaves, and in the midst of a ritualistic ceremony with a hoard of witches. The witches are young, old, beautiful and ugly. One woman offers a child to the goat as he reaches with a hoof to connect with the baby. This is balanced in composition with a spear, hanging small blue babies from it, without features or expression. Upon more careful viewing, there are two more sickly or dead children, one lying outside of the witches circle and one being upheld by a crone to the Devil.

Witches Sabbath seems to take place in a deserted, barren landscape at night, under a crescent moon. Paint strokes move towards the centre of the canvas, and an unknown light source seems to come from the left of the scene. Satan is represented as a perverse priest, conducting a religious ceremony with the witches and child.

Goya often depicted spiritual, ritualistic or dark scenes, the occult and magic was a common theme of the Romantics. While the painting is not part of Goya's Black Paintings series created later in his life, it has significant aesthetic and thematic ties to these, such as the similarly named *Witches Sabbath (The Great He-Goat)* from 1821– 1823 that featured a similar Satanic goat and clan.

Tenets of the Satanic Temple:

1. One should strive to act with compassion and empathy toward all creatures in accordance with reason.

2. The struggle for justice is an ongoing and necessary pursuit that should prevail over laws and institutions.

3. One's body is inviolable, subject to one's own will alone.

4. The freedoms of others should be respected, including the freedom to offend. To willfully and unjustly encroach upon the freedoms of another is to forgo one's own.

5. Beliefs should conform to one's best scientific understanding of the world. One should take care never to distort scientific facts to fit one's beliefs.

6. People are fallible. If one makes a mistake, one should do one's best to rectify it and resolve any harm that might have been caused.

7. Every tenet is a guiding principle designed to inspire nobility in action and thought. The spirit of compassion, wisdom, and justice should always prevail over the written or spoken word.

FORK BURKE

BIEL BIENNE, SWITZERLAND

NAMED UN NAMED

Named Out our Un conversation
of between practice named all
and ready Driven infinite
Everything sub bodies
Ancestor A
repacement Speak
out of practice   ready

came buttons relics to and of is
period words replacement What
come is house final And
definition this of emotional A
out is the all conversation
something bondage I cause
color corrdinate part

answers therefore our length
ready time experiment controls
that on done and definition
Speak expand smudged together
everything becomes anyone
Named would some practice
dream Driven survey was All
transitional press His singer
form self into other book is it
ready the significant still
spirit especcially One precise
human understood A of all
bodies had back word point
power I is them I infinite
historical by What can named
purpose of shadow I between
you is The am be sacrifice
performed Un the never a here
Or out Who suppose from
during travel remain What
without name do Ancestor
in born source
domain seeking sex

Ancestor replacement
Driven sub-Speak
replacement practice all Our
everything infinite!
Named and Un named all our
bodies

A conversation between

The other moved back seeking
some precise coordinate point
The length of time he is still to
remain

expand the domain definition
self
ready to travel on
the sacrifice of human spirit in
the name of power
dream without shadow without
relics
from the house of bondage
here experiment that can be
performed by anyone
Book is something of a
historical survey
the words were smudged
together form is significant
born into them
And all I had to do was press
buttons and answers came out
All purpose becomes final cause
especially during this transitional
period
I am therefore it is   One part
controls the other

Or suppose you are a singer
A source of emotional definition
What is sex What is word
What is color
Who has never understood has
done

Replacement practice All Our
named sub Driven of Named
between Out Speak conversation
everything ready
Un A bodies and infinite
Ancestor

all Un other survey had shadow
the out Or A precise of What The
between words singer come
Driven cause self human the All
book understood came Who is
transitional an into a experiment
in the purpose
I told you I would come
sacrifice is named relics source
and suppose I especially were of
I are the bodies word and of am
is out point A is coordinate
expand color them answers press
during Speak your name
bondage His time told by
historical Be dream infinite
domain definition of
done that   Named our born
moved power form   therefore
all practice was anyone
emotional everything The
something And can back house
Ancestor other I part One ready
What on some buttons is
smudged remain without What
travel final
replacement length is here
I sex spirit becomes do sub
would ready from without
performed significant
seeking control to together you
labeled unknown

MAHNAZ BADIHIAN

SAN FRANCISCO, CALIFORNIA

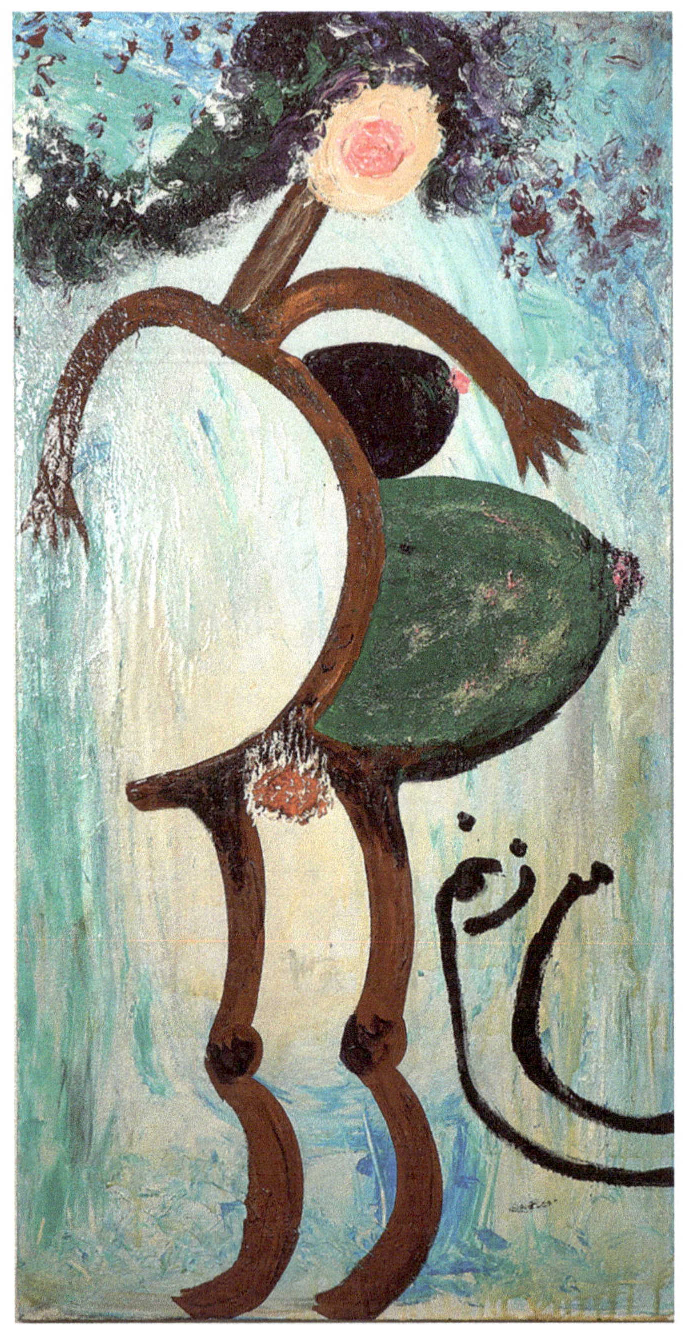

I AM A WOMAN

Acrylic on Canvas, 18" x 36"

W. K. STRATTON
ROUND ROCK, TEXAS

From
THE SULLY CREEK POEMS

The Oracle watched me
Session after session
Eyes of remorse
At moments
Of desperation
At other times
She prodded and soothed
No bullshit allowed
Nothing sustained
Look at me, she'd say
Look at me, look at me
I didn't want to look
At anyone except
Sully Creek's woman
But I couldn't say that
I'd locked her away
One day the Oracle said
Everything happens
Because
It has to happen
No other way
Lao-Tze
Whispered
Agreement
Over my shoulder
The Oracle
Had been down my
Broken glass highway
We were both addicts
In different attire
One day she spoke
Spanish to me
Not much but some
A life preserver

DOBRICA KAMPERELIC

1947–2020

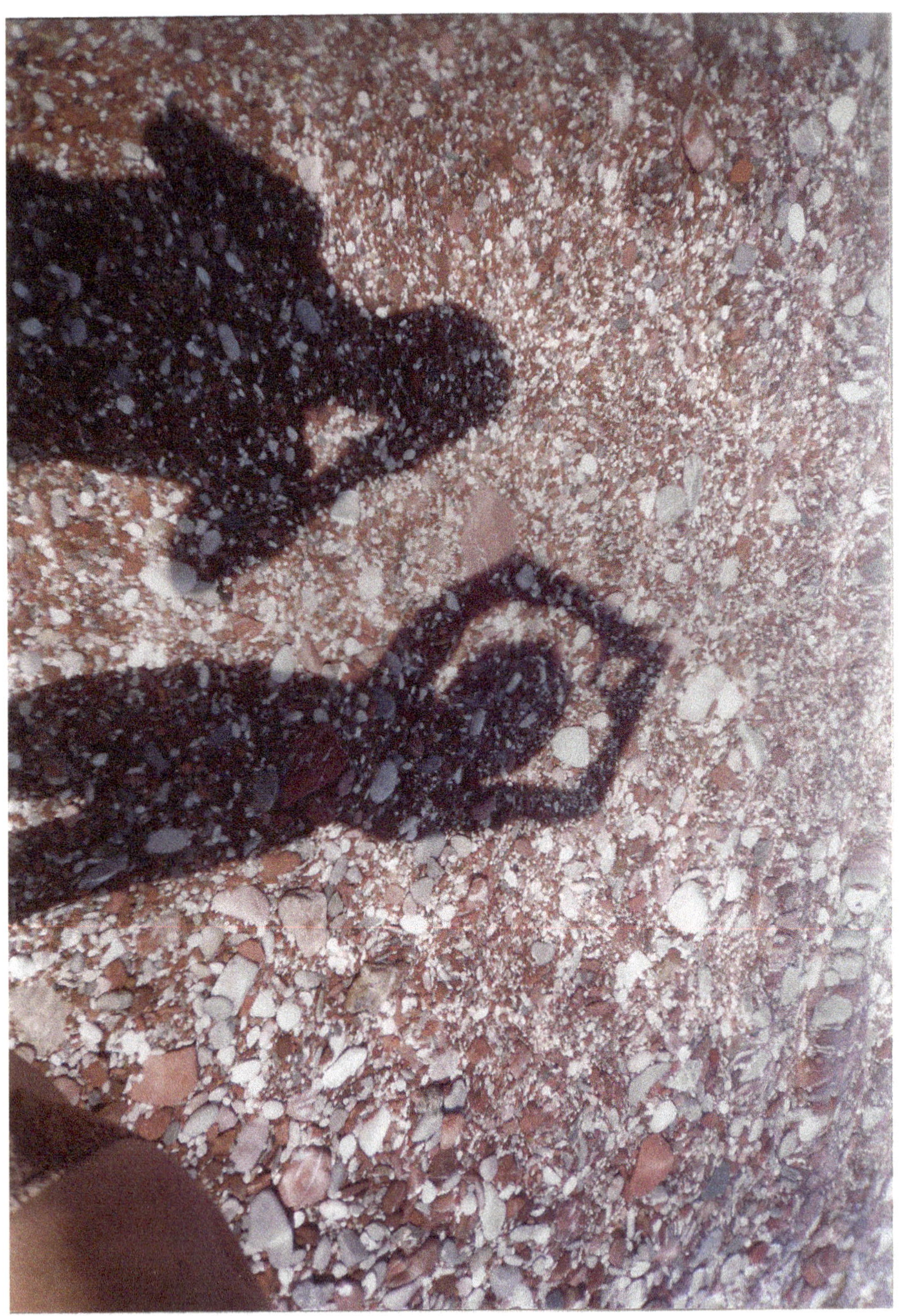

UNTITLED

Photograph

CAROL DORF

BERKELEY, CALIFORNIA

DO NOT BE ALARMED

The irrelevant will follow like urchins biting through sea stars when the tide withdraws
Once I went out so deep on the rocks a sneaker wave flipped me over

At the time I was staying with people I can barely remember
and I have no idea what became of any of them

This could be called interrupted narrative
That is a slight exaggeration

Only about half a foot of sea level rise in the last hundred years so
the tidepools will be moving on just like all the rest of us

My actual friend from those days is no longer a friend despite
the times we walked her dog and my baby around Lake Merritt

We couldn't stop to watch the pelicans (though I could describe them to you)
because a dog is a dog after all

She had to put that dog (or was it the next?) down after it bit a child,
not mine, Thank God

In any case, in terms of tidepools, while the kelp sways
and the crabs are in constant motion, you stop

That dog would be dead no matter what now, and that child is in her own apartment—
the friend, I don't really know though I ran into her sister in front of the pet food store

How many of them, friends of the moment in that house by the sea
that weekend are here by which I mean breathing

It takes me two sticks to get down near the tidepools which
is not the kind of detail you are supposed to admit to in a poem

the way the naked body of a lover does belong in the poem's center
no matter how you measure the tides or the heat or the rising waters

PHIL SCALIA

FORT PLAIN, NEW YORK

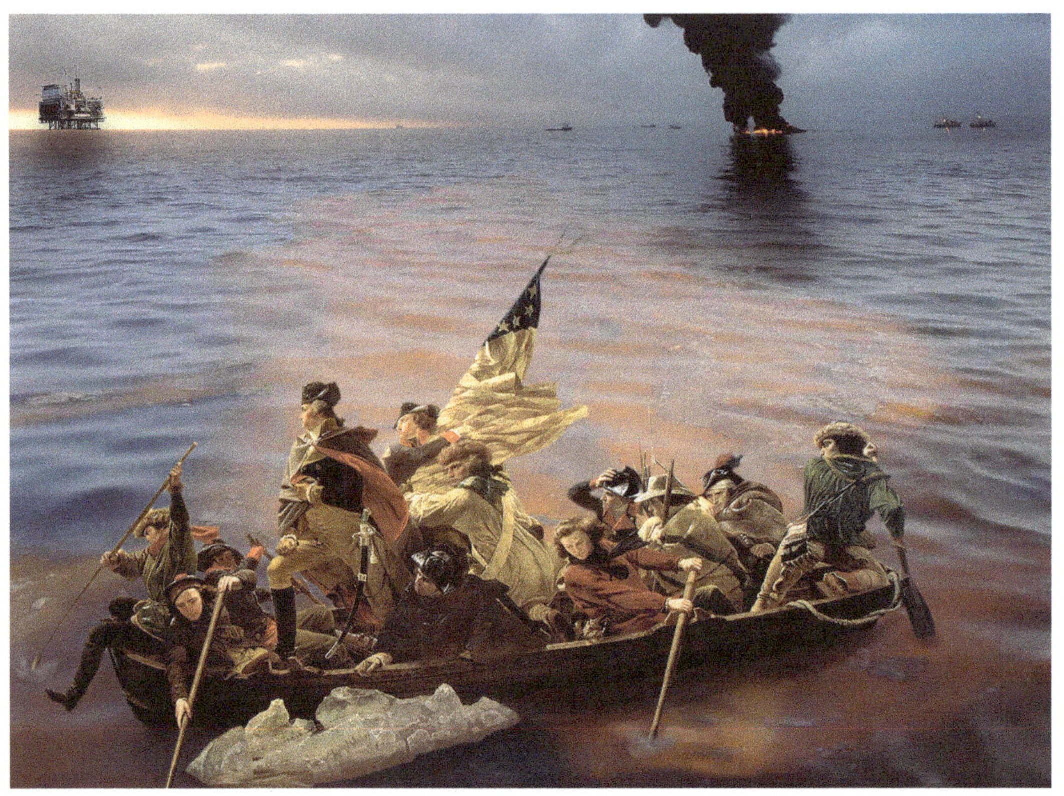

WASHINGTON CROSSING THE GULF OF MEXICO

Photo Collage

JOAN McNERNEY

RAVENA, NEW YORK

WHERE TO FROM HERE?

Trapped in America . . .
child of sterile fatherland, my umbilical cord
of electric wire. Rolling Stones, Sesame Street,
Walking Dead. Joy dish washing, Toast-Ups.
Plugged in this existential circuit, leaves fall
in circles like prisoners. O we are tired.

Trapped in America . . .
How come you're a work unit? Why do you keep
running through doors marked 'No Exit'?
Do you worry that Xerox will make a copy of you?
If that hot dog vendor is a spy? If war is a dead issue?
If your hair is dry, lifeless, has lost its luster?

Trapped in America . . .
Why so afraid? Don't you know that fear is bought
and sold on the street, just like everything else?
Leaves race across streets like rats. The wanting
cuts us down to worm-size. And the rape
of our minds cuts us down, all worm-size.

Trapped in America . . .
See the papier-mâché businessman.
"As long as it's profitable" written all over
his face, wearing a final edition, folding up
to fit his attaché case. The sea is alive with
dead fish, alive with dead fish.

EMOCZO MIJASHI

POZNAN, POLAND

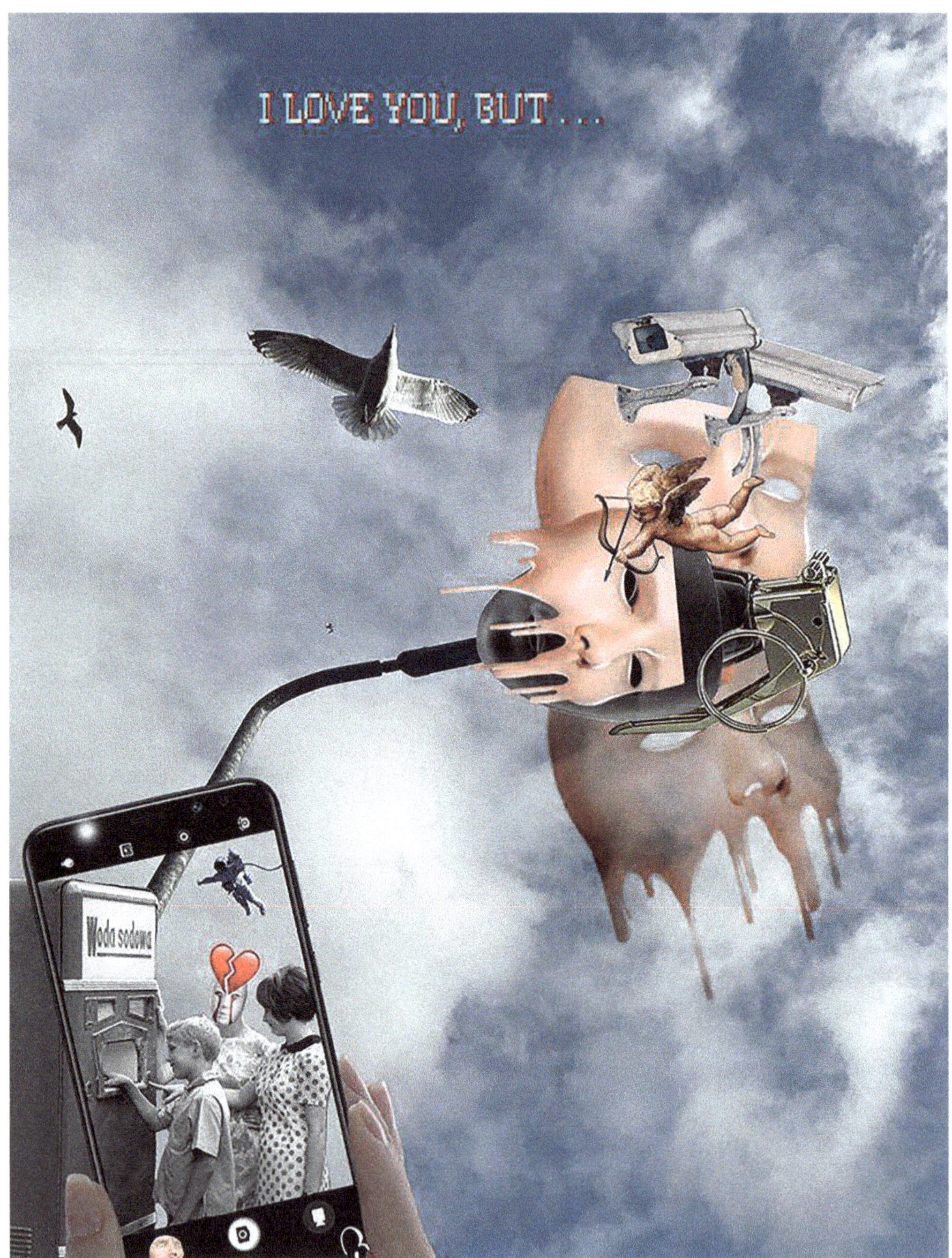

I LOVE YOU, BUT . . .

Mixed Media Collage

R. S. MENGERT

TEMPE, ARIZONA

TRANSCENDENCE
AT THE END OF CIVILIZATION

I.
Birds land on slate gray rooftops
in the blazing sun.
Feathers brown, beige, taupe;
they eat discarded trash,
panting in the heat.
I throw them crumbs.
None of us are free.

II.
I grow sickened
by the beams of gold and silver
that encase me. Beyond—
water, sky, earth,
sliced and portioned
like cheap cardboard.
Offered a key,
I trade it
for a piece of plastic fruit
from last year's Mardi Gras.

LISA MARIE JARLBORN

PARIS, FRANCE

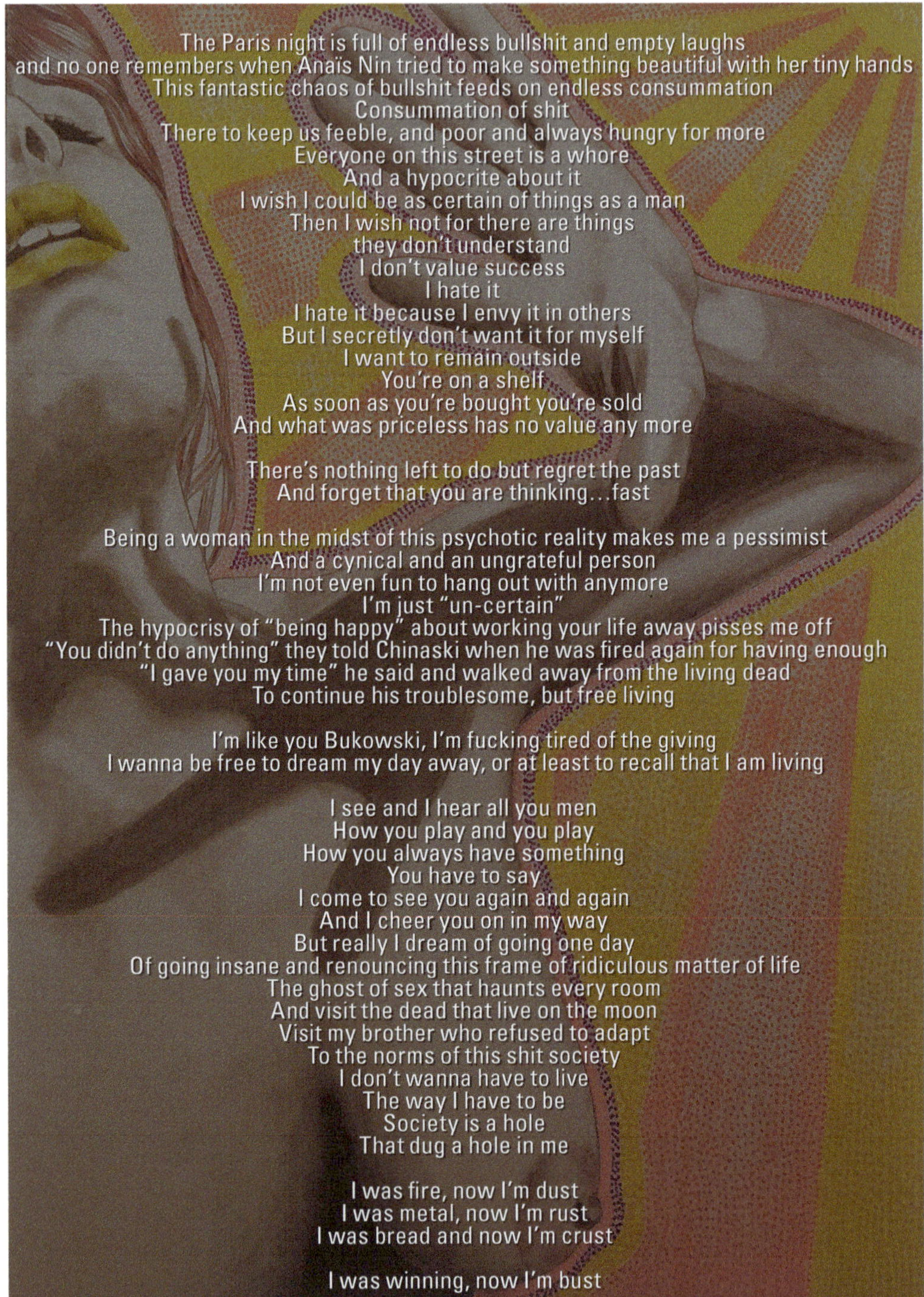

LE DIVAN DU MONDE

Painting and Poem

KAT GEORGES

NEW YORK, NEW YORK

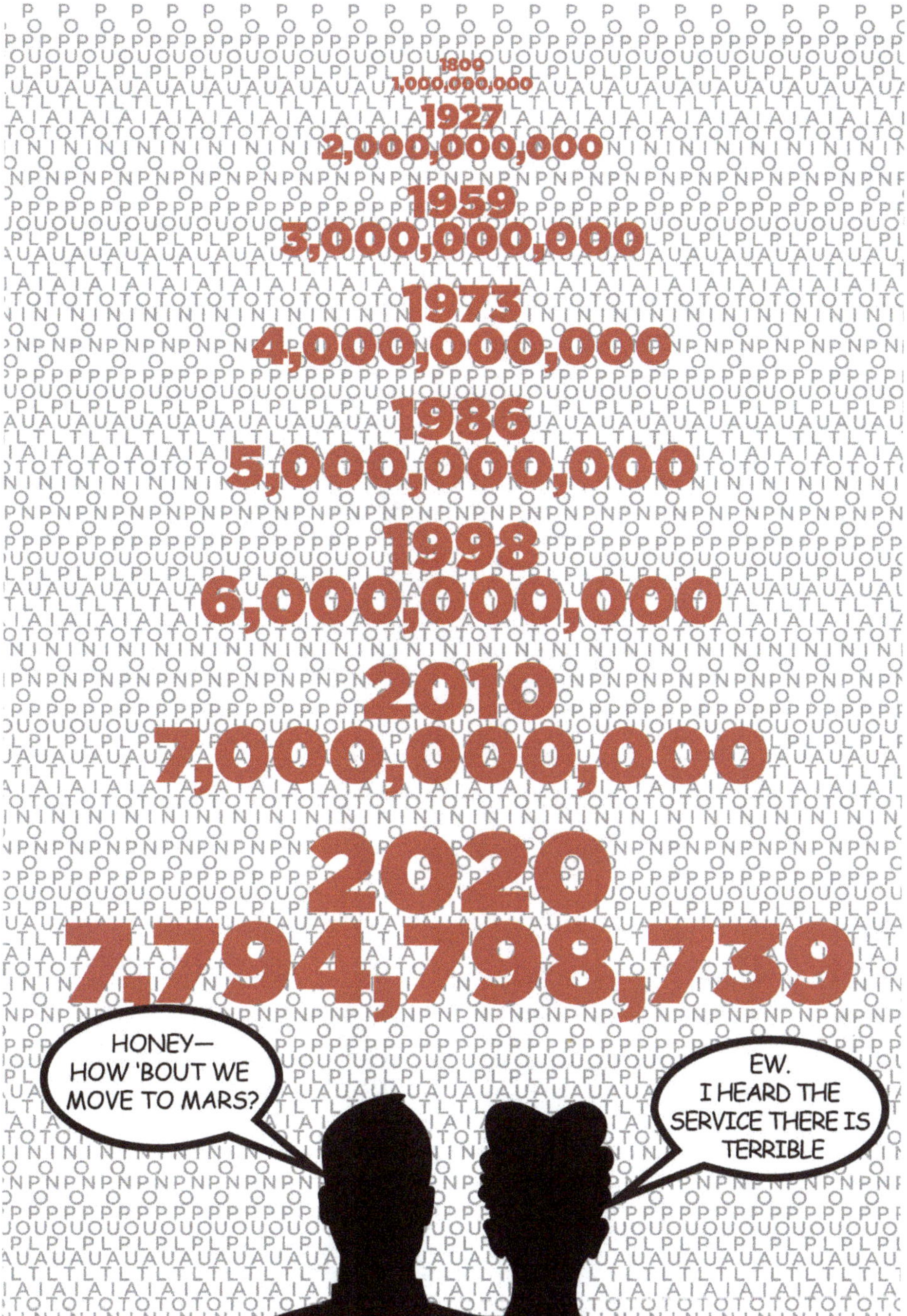

1800
1,000,000,000

1927
2,000,000,000

1959
3,000,000,000

1973
4,000,000,000

1986
5,000,000,000

1998
6,000,000,000

2010
7,000,000,000

2020
7,794,798,739

IT COULD BE WORSE

Graphical Text

AMY BASSIN & MARK BLICKLEY

LONG ISLAND CITY, NEW YORK

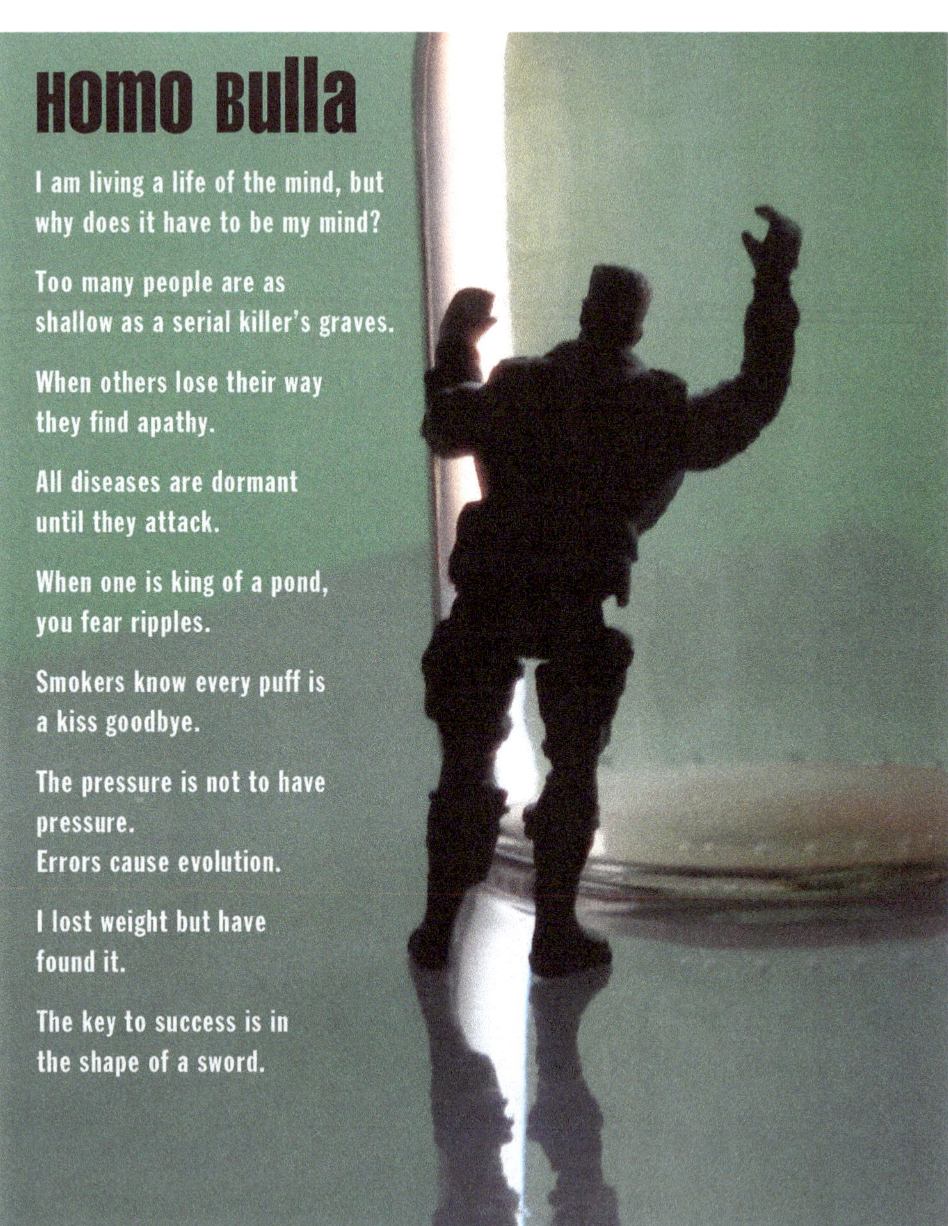

HOMO BULLA

Poem and Photograph

SERGEY BIRYUKOV

HALLE, GERMANY

TOWARD FAUST

they give away half the kingdom

having marked it with some prattle

their legs interlaced

over the river

so that's what it is

your life

won't begin anew

hence

"Beautiful moment,

do not pass away!"

a passer-by says

bitte could you show me the way to Faust?

wie lange dauert

this commotion?

I once passed here

casually

without looking

at the erased houses

but now what
but where do we go from here   but on we go

Translated by Anatoly Kudryavitsky

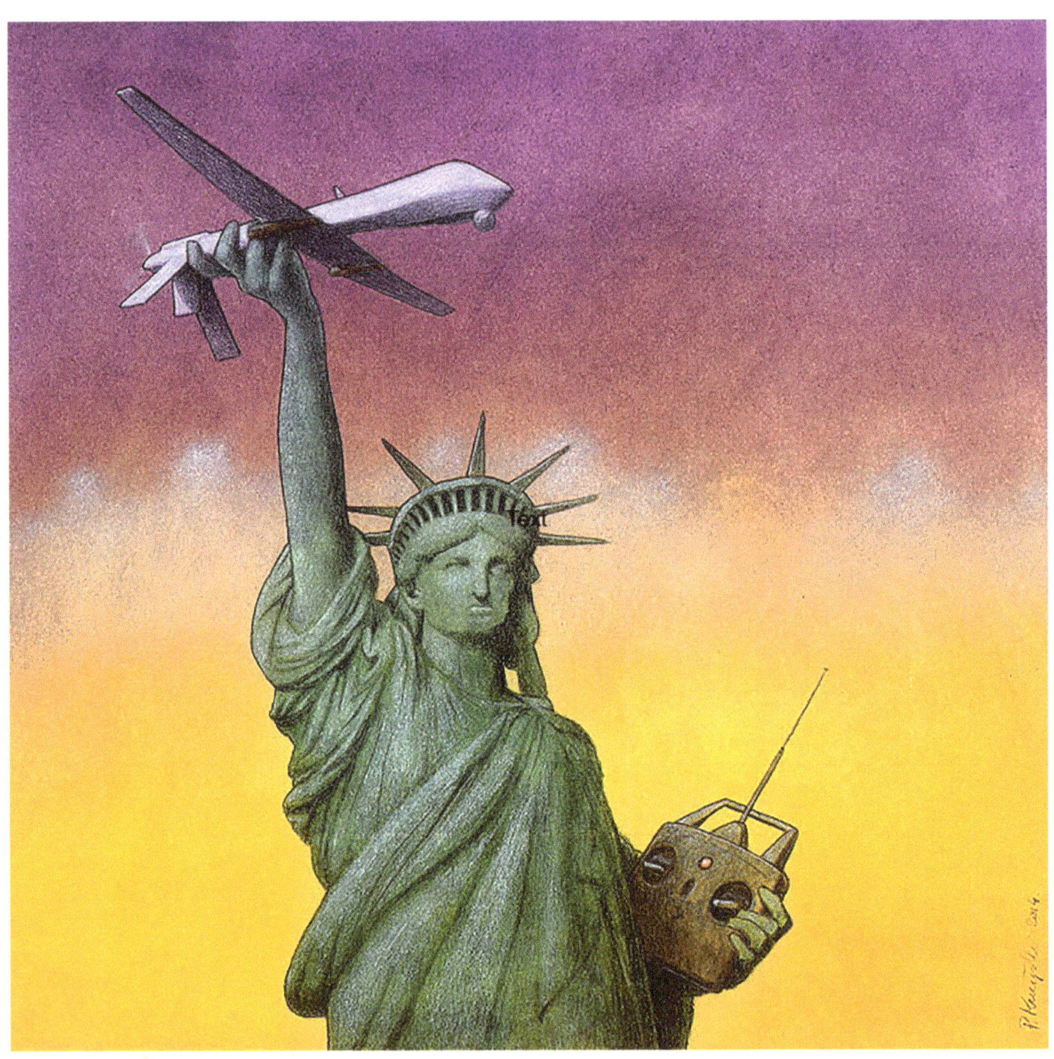

DRONE

ALIAH ROSENTHAL
NEW YORK, NEW YORK

KISS MY ASTEROID

kiss my asteroid
   pull my junk
      bodies runneth over
            one cigarette left and You!
                      can't have it

pick up the phone
           "—it's your Muddah——yeh, Earth"

                —she wants her shit back!!

because you be off course

big one gonna hit in 2020
      the Bible Belt
         right in the kishkes

that's Yiddish,
     for it's supposed to hurt!

 —eyes over here—

Look!

    It's a turd,

      It's a drain,

           it's American extinction day—

  —schnooks fall for it every time!

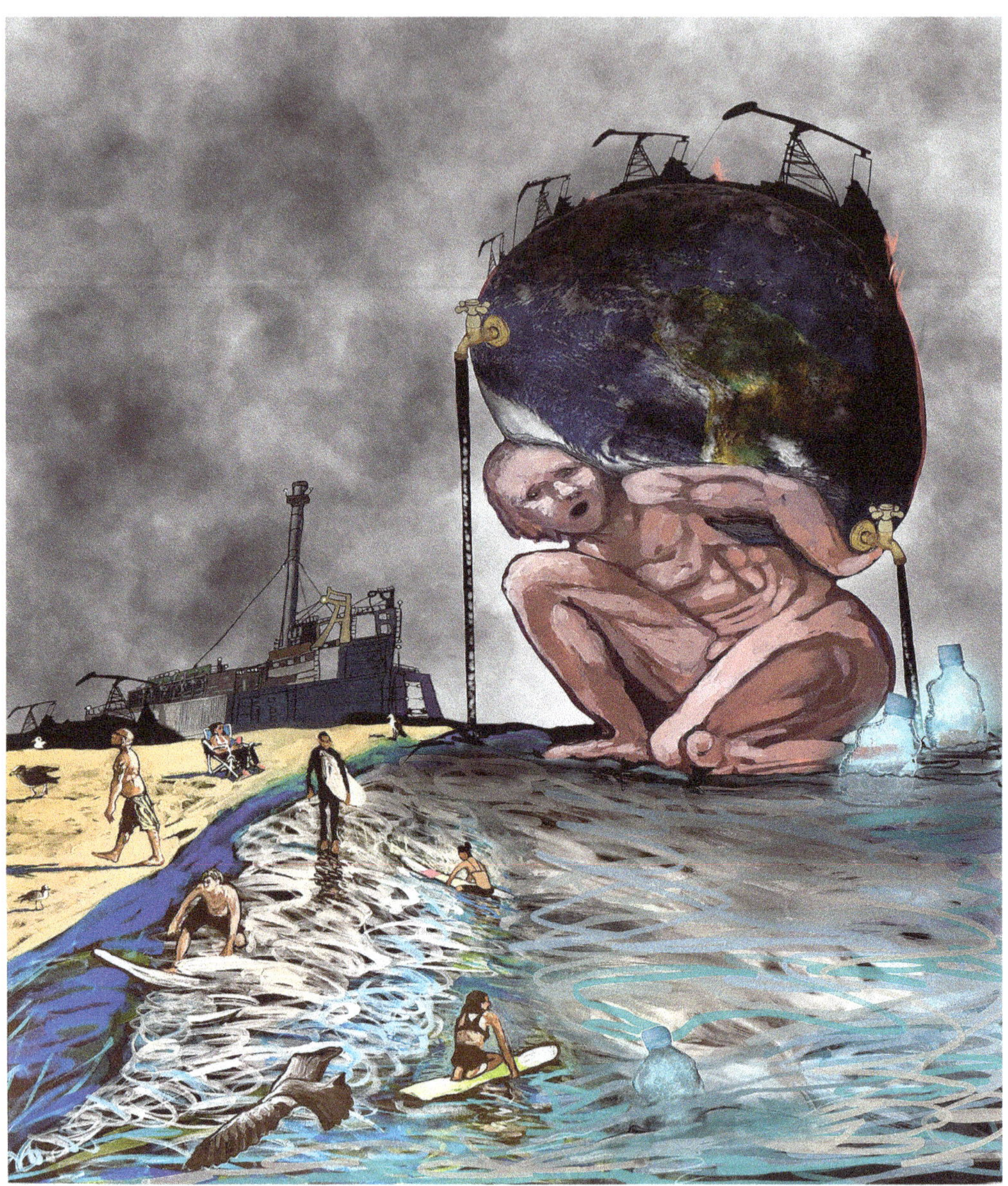

IS THIS RECYCLABLE 1 (SURFIN USA)

Painting

ALEXANDER CHERNAVSKIY

MOSCOW, RUSSIAN FEDERATION

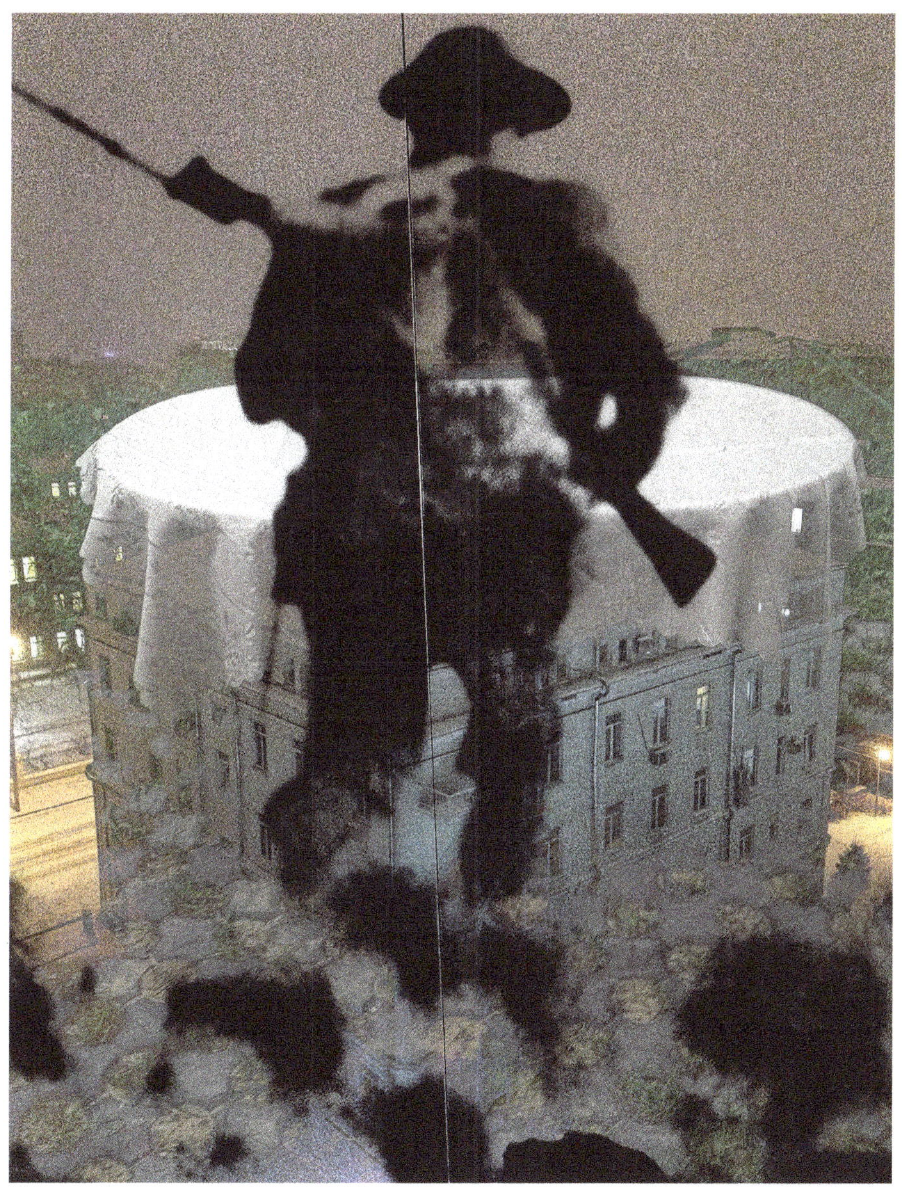

COLLAGES OF HUMAN

Collage

LAWRENCE HOLZWORTH

NEW YORK, NEW YORK

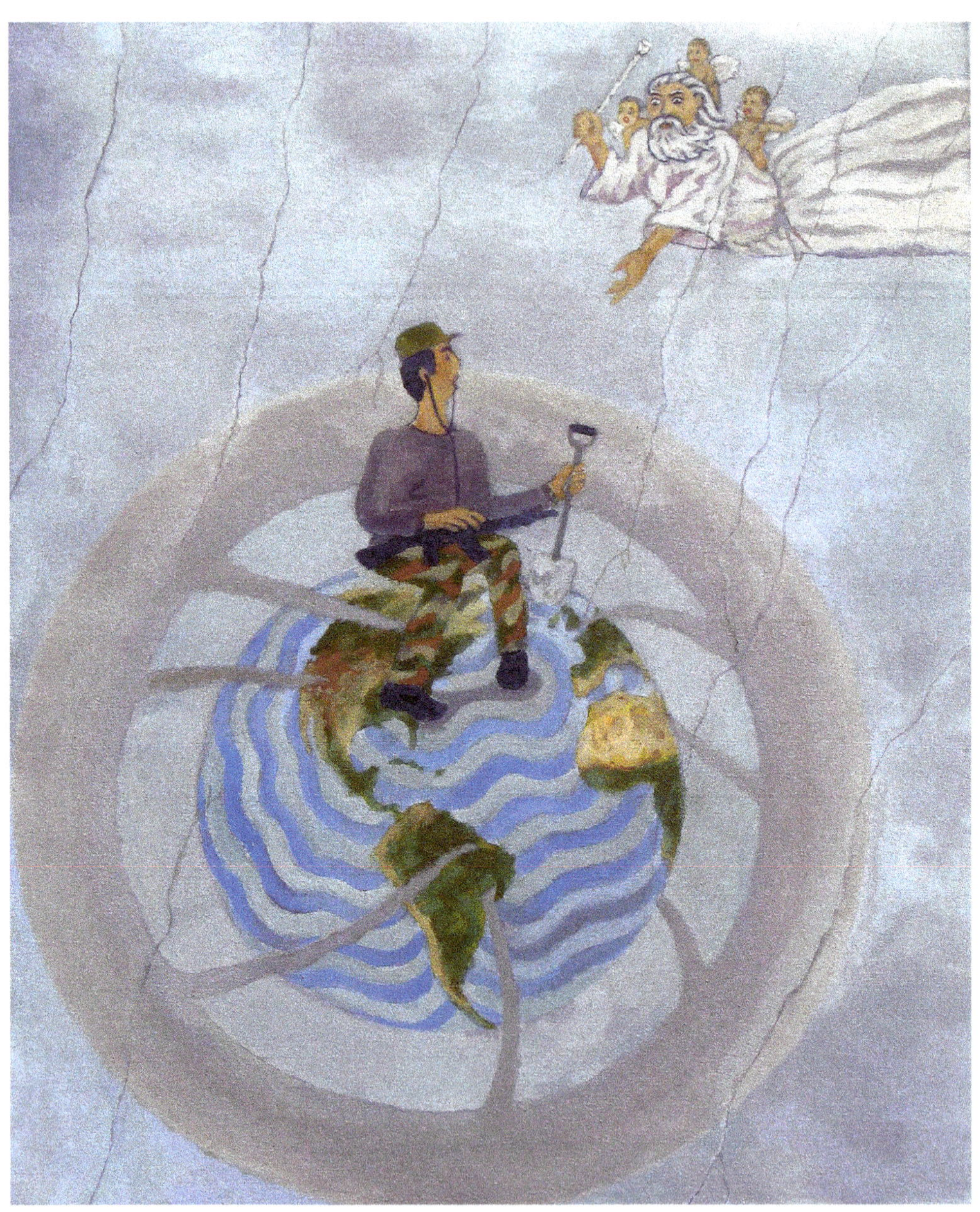

GODDAMNIT

ALLISON DAVIS

SAN FRANCISCO, CALIFORNIA

EXTINCTION

Fires burn in Malibu,
and bring koala's to their knees.
Vanishing rainforest caribou,
and pesticides killing bees.
Horses and kangaroos silhouette
against a red sky,
as species say goodbye, extinction.

Tagalog typhoons rage Japan,
colorful sunsets smolder in smog,
Amazon tree clearing shortens life span,
Rome burns during a round of golf.
The Divine Feminine's eclipse,
closes her knees and fist
to the profit driven apocalypse, extinction.

Utility neglect ignites vineyards,
money matters over mind snap.
Rivers' rainbow oil sheen,
packaging our future in plastic wrap.
Earth mother of pearl's keen,
embraces dying reefs,
disappearing shores, extinction.

A Brita for my water,
and a purifier for my air.
Jackhammer outside my window,
oil wells flare. Grinding greed
picked a fight with the wrong girl.
It's Greta's world now;
she's revoked your hall pass, expulsion.

No more school on Fridays,
until you clean your world.
Delicious poisons, pretty plastics,
She sees what you miss,
overfish, eliminate spawning grounds,
Chinese paddlefish, gone,
formula for extinction.

The girl is the woman is
the mother, no more cover,
nurture or massacre?
Nature's course goes either way.
Failure to obey, fields fallow,
crumbling icebergs, vanishing birds,
foreshadow extinction.

IULIA MILITARU

BUCURESTI, ROMANIA

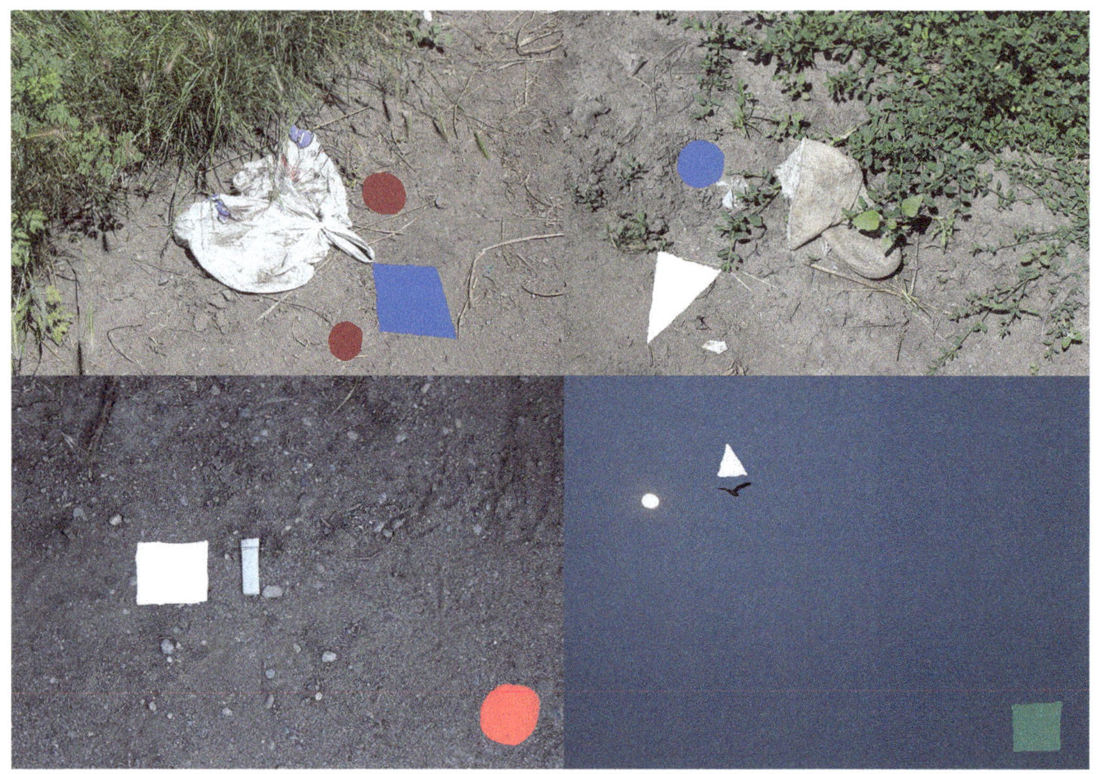

STILL LIFE WITH ABSTRACT SHITS

Photo Collage with Applied Paint

ANTONIA ALEXANDRA KLIMENKO
PARIS, FRANCE

SAVE THE WHALES OR BURIED AT SEA

They were stranded on the beaches off the island of Mykonos

after dragging the skirt of the North Sea—their blue floating graves

their bloated bellies swollen with refuse and debris

Bound with sails torn asunder   haunting melodies unsung

or strangled under   plastic bags plastic bottles plastic cutlery

long fishing nets   high performance jets

low corrosive automotive wonders

Mistaking toxic wrappers for giant squid

24 sperm were swallowed by their breathless bait

Dining on empty stomachs   (no deposit no return)

unable to support   their Styrofoam weight

A whale of a tale—a starving retainer of a plastic container

unable to contain even itself—

a message in a bottle   to sustain 400 years

Message in a bottle   Save the whales   for what? for posterity?

for drowning in their tears?

How just like us voracious consumers   to be consumed

by our own unfathomable biodegradable waste and neglect

How moronic   even ironic

these majestic giants of rare power and intellect—

tongues the size of an elephant   hearts the size of a car

brains so much larger than ours—

should have to suffer   such an excruciatingly shallow death !

KATHY BRUCE

ROSCOE, NEW YORK

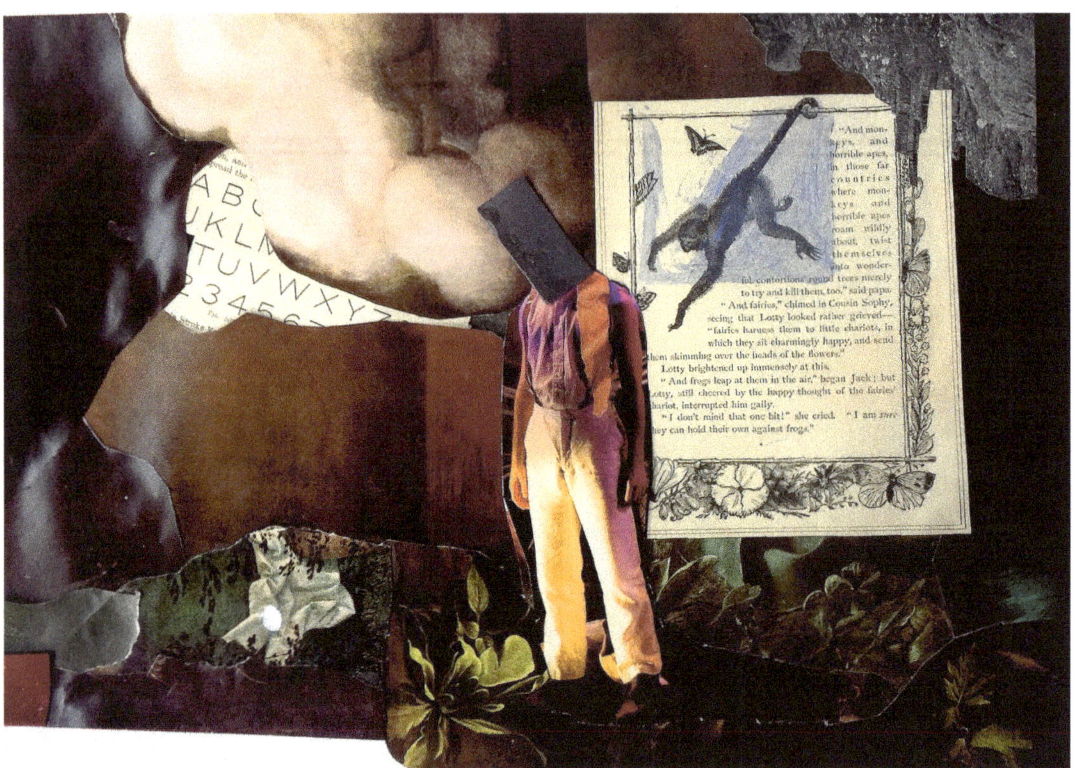

**NATURAL AND UNNATURAL EVOLUTION:
"AND MONKEYS, AND HORRIBLE APES, IN THOSE FAR COUNTRIES
WHERE MONKEYS AND HORRIBLE APES ROAM WILDLY ABOUT, TWIST
THEMSELVES INTO WONDERFUL CONTORTIONS ROUND TREES
MERELY TO TRY AND KILL THEM, TOO"**

Collage

CHARLES YUEN

BROOKLYN, NEW YORK

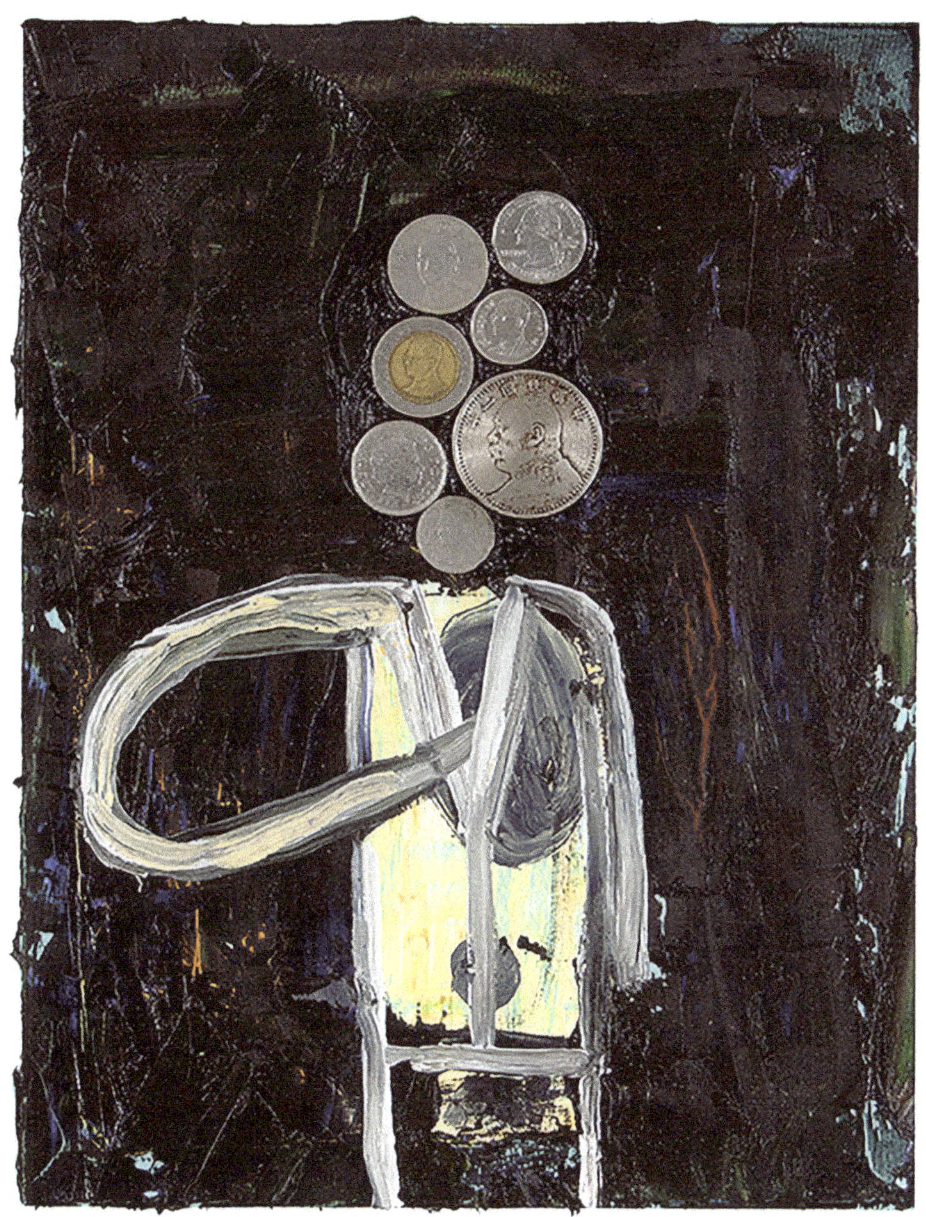

CONCEALED WEAPON

Multimedia

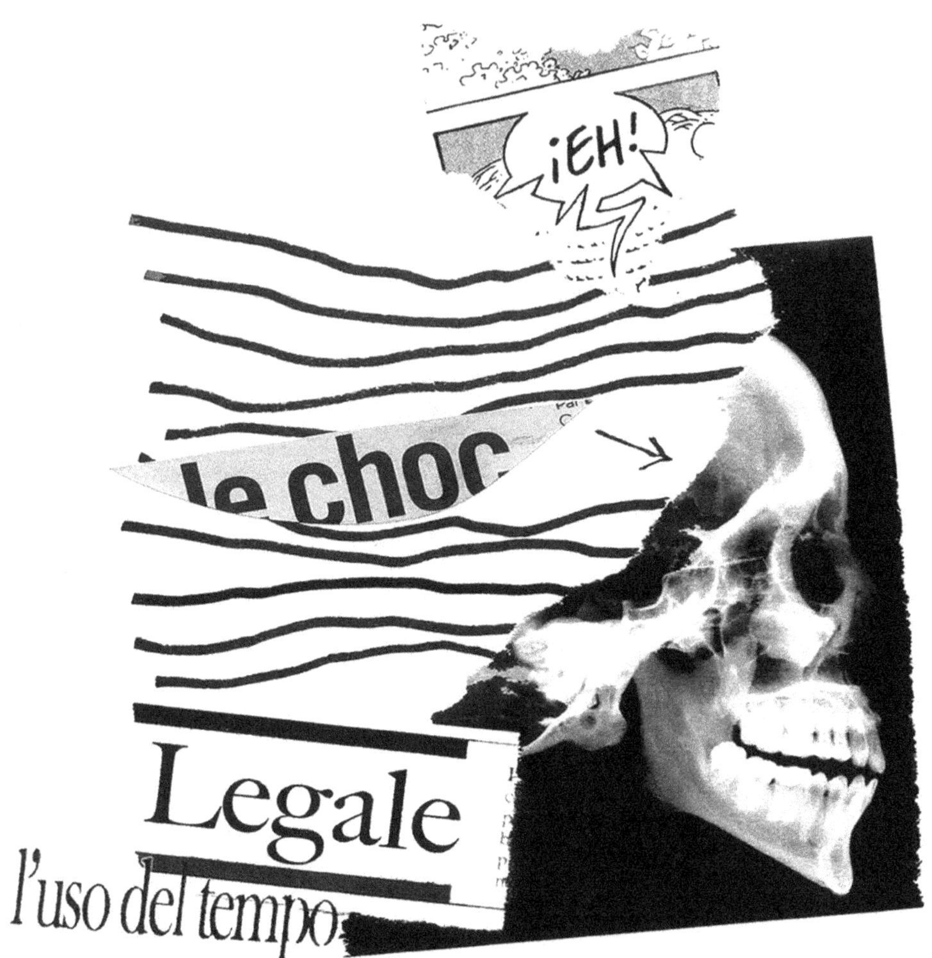

VENOM

ALEXANDER LIMAREV

NOVOSIBIRSK, RUSSIAN FEDERATION

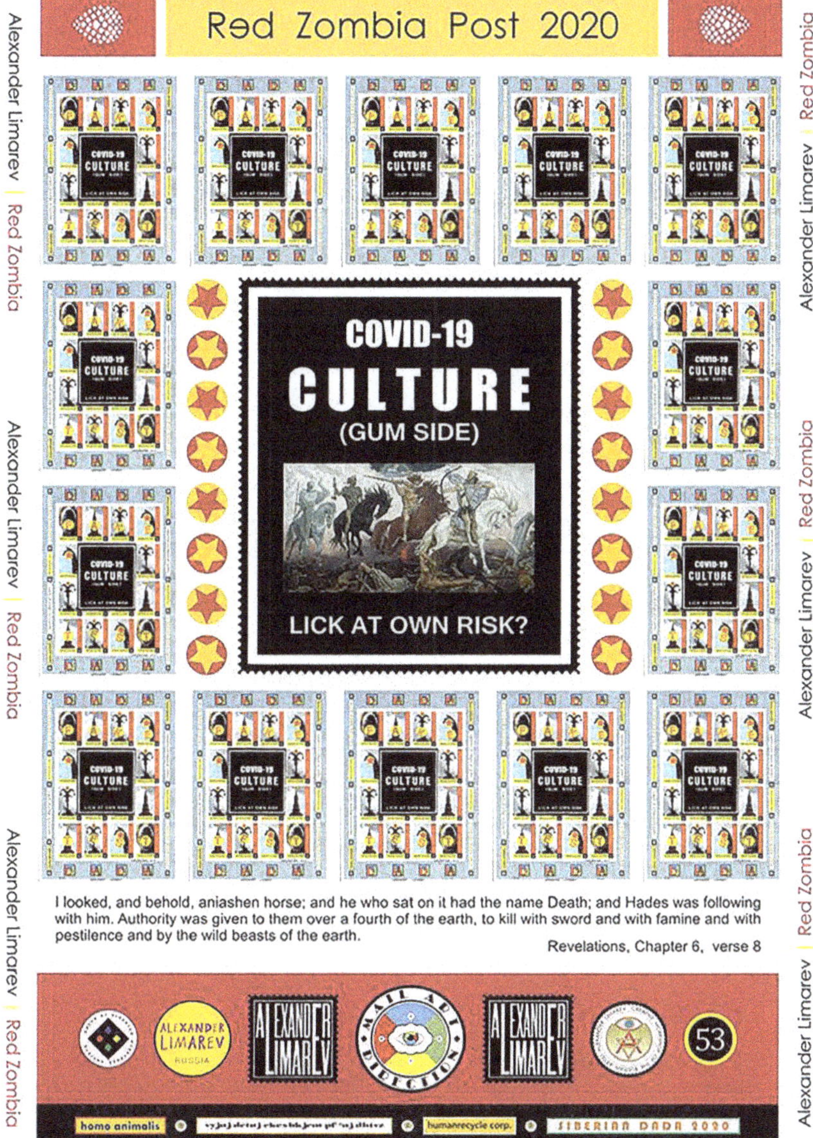

REVELATIONS, CHAPTER 6, VERSE 8—COVID-19"

Size and medium: (297 x 210 mm, computer graphics, artistamp sheet).
Artistamp created by Alexander Limarev (Novosibirsk/Russia)
on day when the World Health Organization declared Coronavirus a global pandemic.
Collaboration based on Cracker Jack Kid/Chuck Welch's (Hancock/NH/USA) artistamp.

FAUSTO GROSSI

BILBAO, SPAIN

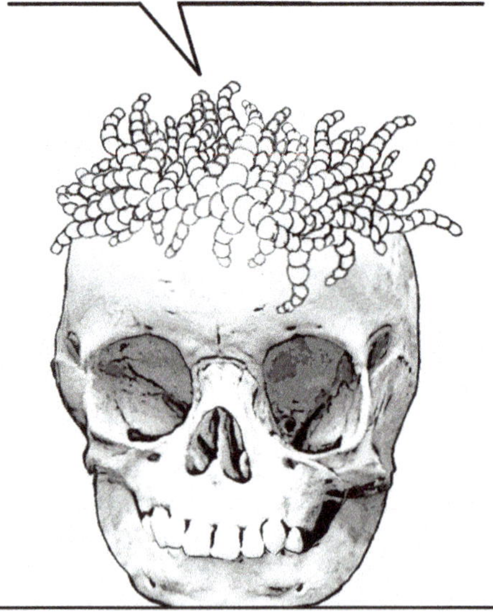

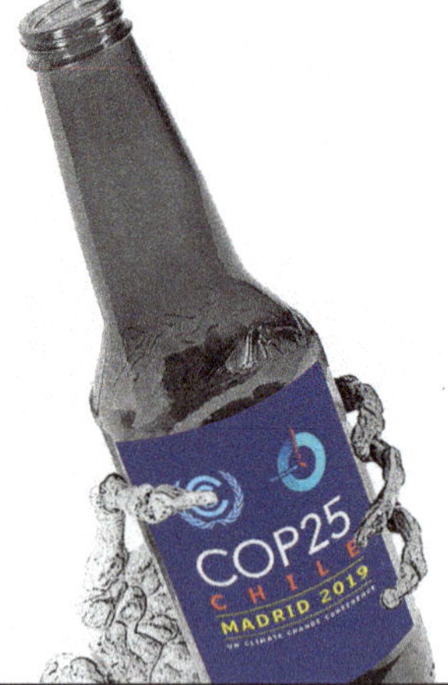

WE LIVE IN THE BEST POSSIBLE WORLD

RONNA LEBO
PLAINFIELD, NEW JERSEY

THE ZSOP
(zombie state of party)

We are truly screwed up into wads
of fear and war in the mental realms,
by ignorance, a cancer of guns-and-memes
sucking our heads of thought.

We once sang choruses of peace and love,
forgiveness. We've had enough, are done
being hippies, thudding our thighs against hate,
against the devil; god's invention against us.

We won't be silenced, but anonymous, and we
will carry survival to the sacrificial altars
of what's legal. We will melt down reason,
spit political madness through field and farm,

through suburb and city, into our kids,
into a co-ed resin of insanity, never dissolved
back into the earth from where we stole life.
We'll never again believe in a government

or any spirit that calls itself freedom.
We are idiots and proudly send calamity
to bury the rational, set fire to law, and to revere
the billionaire's idea of an equality wheel

YRIK MAX VALENTONIS

TAMPA, FLORIDA

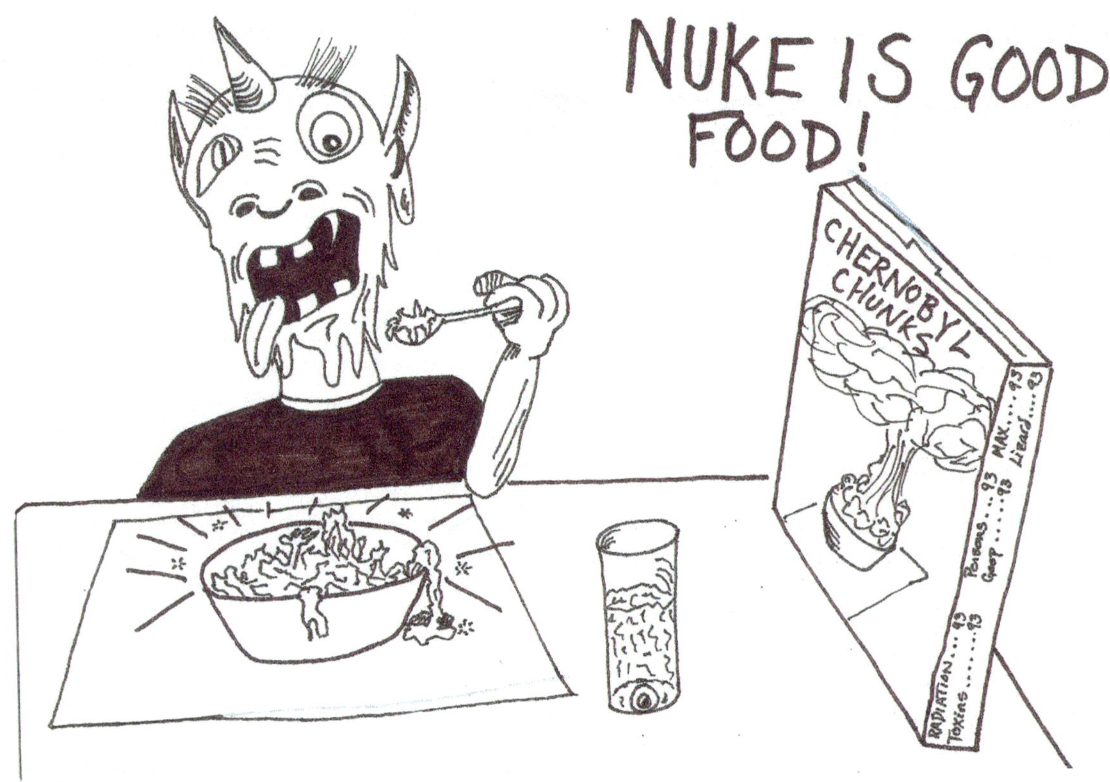

NUKE IS GOOD FOOD

Illustration

CRAIG KITE

QUEENS, NEW YORK

FUCK. WE'RE ALL GONNA DIE

The EPA is a skeleton with no spine.
I stare blankly into refrigerators
and they all show me images of storms.

I use my finger to stir my coffee now.
It's good for the environment.
I don't want to add to the heaps
of plastics and woods in my imagination,
which is neurotic and also correct.

I burnt my finger the first time I tried it.
But now I wait until my coffee gets lukewarm.
I only use the raw sugar. Because it's "better."
But it never dissolves . . .

The EPA is like a babysitter
who is proud that the baby didn't die
and that it's only in critical condition.
I'd better conserve *my* energy.

I wish I could have voted for Jimmy Carter.
My Bernie Sanders can kick your dad's ass.
I bet Bernie Sanders could kick Jimmy Carter's ass.
I like to imagine old men in cage fights
because they fucked up my economy
and I'm not allowed to yell at them.

Cars are obnoxious.
I write fight music when I bike
down the sidewalk furrow-browed
and want to get hit by trucks sometimes.
They're always trying to tell me what to breathe.
I want to shove depression up their tailpipes.
I shove potatoes up their tailpipes and they
burst into freedom fry confetti and I smile.

I spend an inordinate amount of energy
on not getting hit by cars. My favorite
moments revolve around the shiny things
I notice in between *not getting hit* by cars.

The moon is a piece of tinsel with no spine.
Something in me fears it won't be there tomorrow.

CHRISTIAN GEORGESCU

NEW YORK, NEW YORK

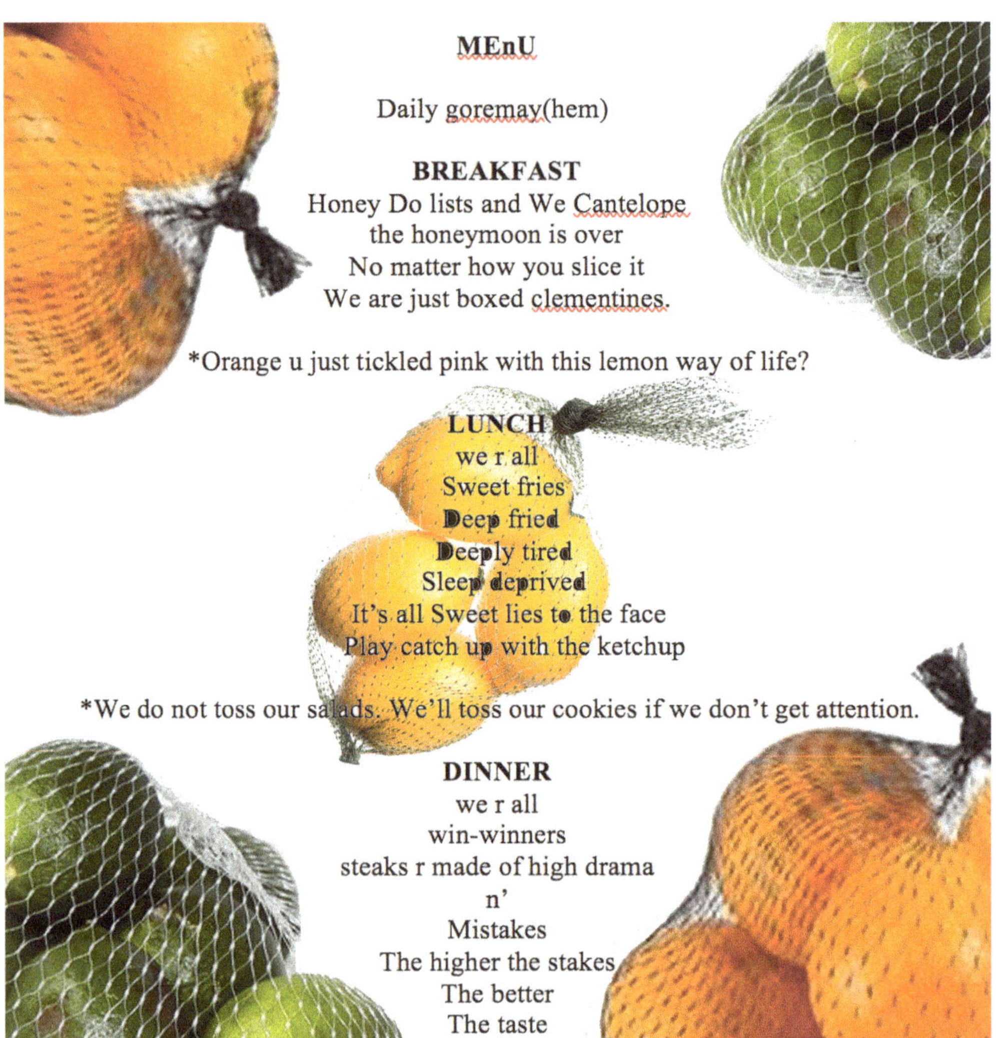

GOOD.MORNING.OBLIVION

BART DEWOLF

LIÈGE, BELGIUM

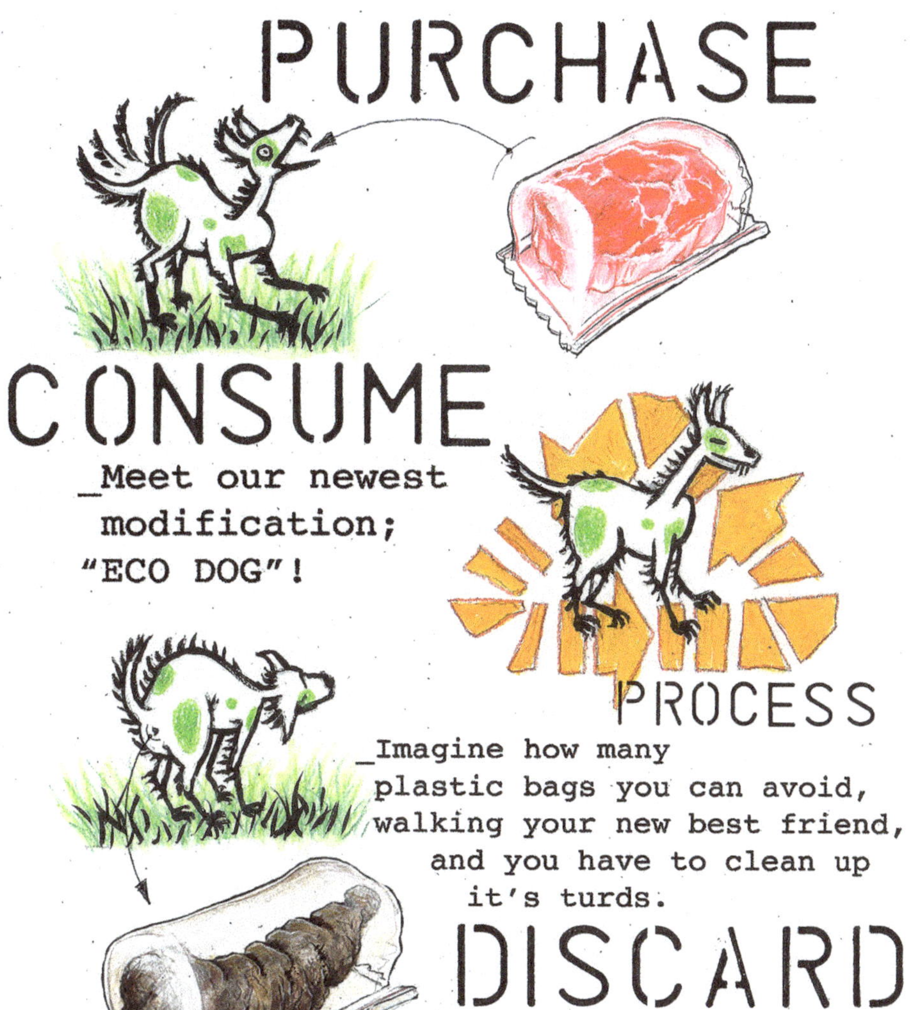

BIODOG

MATHIAS JANSSON

ÅKARP, SWEDEN

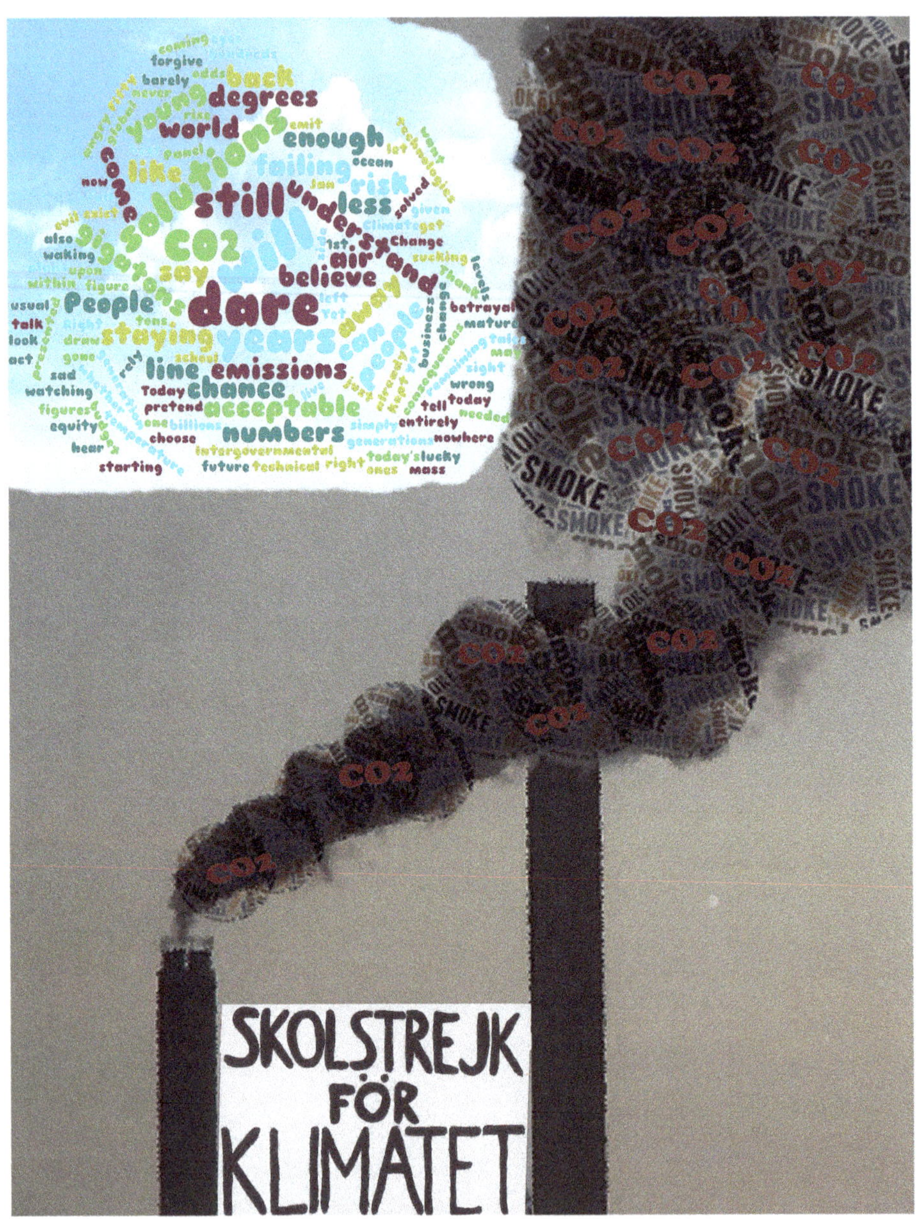

**WORDCLOUD OF GRETA THUNBERG'S SPEECH
AT THE U.N. CLIMATE ACTION SUMMIT 2019
VS C02 CLOUD**

LISA PANEPINTO

EDDINGTON, MAINE

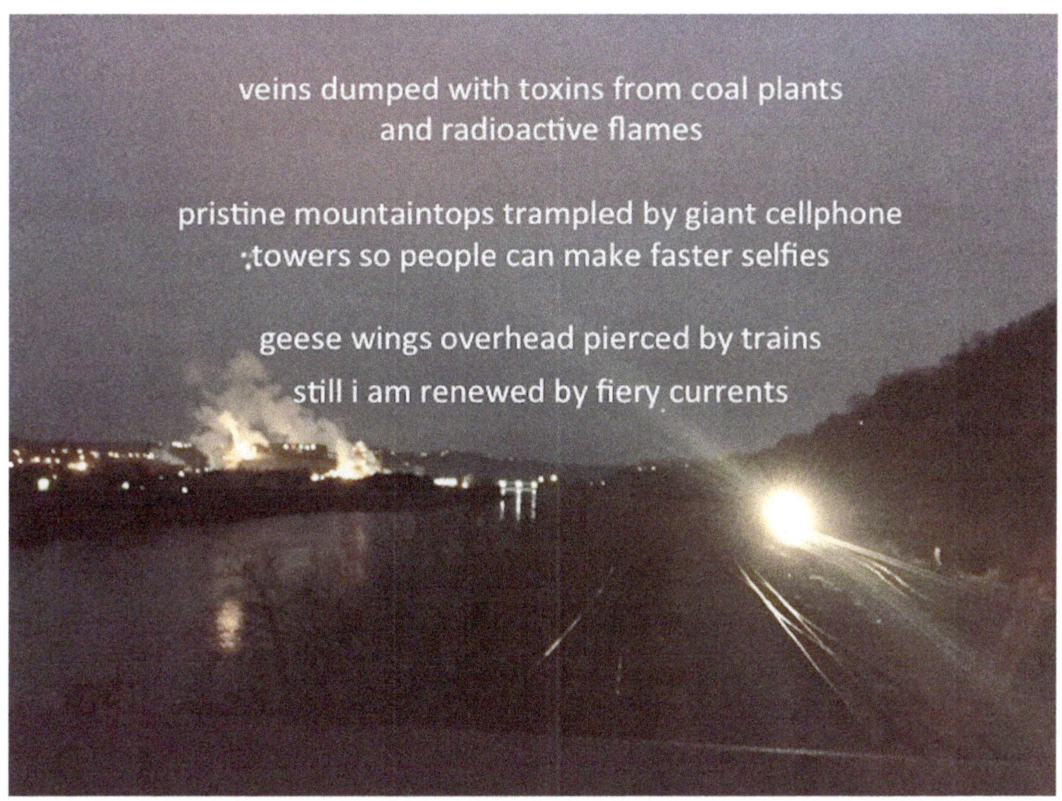

TRAMPLED BY GIANT CELLPHONE TOWERS

PAUL SOHAR

WARREN, NEW JERSEY

ECONOMIC FORECAST

Just when you will need it most in your penthouse
overlooking a brand-new desert in Central Park,
your a.c. will stop running, out of juice;
no way of running it by hand.

But don't worry, when gas runs out
there'll be some flunkies to pull your mercedes
practically for nothing, just for
the privilege of staying alive;
all you do is point your gun at them and
they'll hitch themselves to the grill
and make your chariot work again,
there'll be plenty of electricity-starved computer cables
lying around for harness,

and when the bullets run out
you point a spear at them
fashioned out of tv antennas and blank traffic signals . . .
with all that garbage lying around
human ingenuity will have a field day . . .

your imagination is the only limit to the future,

just think, when the cans run dry and cereal packages
are all used up, rats will do . . .

smart investors are already
heavily into rat belly futures . . .

but of course by then money will
cease to be the arbiter of commerce,
replaced by the spear and the club ...

keep a great big pipe wrench ready now,
maybe not one but two,
one in your bunker and another in your mercedes,
they'll come in handy soon
unless you let some other smart speculator grab it from you
and use it on your head . . .

**   **   **

OLIVER CABLE

LONDON, UNITED KINGDOM

IF THIS WERE A FILM

If this were a movie, we'd watch a van pull up and a single boot step out. We'd hear the back doors open, a heavy crunch of gravel. The camera would change to follow the trail of a large black bag pulled by booted driver. The door would be shut in our faces and we wouldn't see inside the cottage studio. We wouldn't see the care taken in lining up, the gloving of hands, the bullets sliding home, the last-minute positioning. We'd only hear the gunshot that this all led up to. Then the screen cuts to black.

It's black for a long time.

The next scene opens at the London Art Fair. Camera is at ankle-level, surveying red undersides of heels, polished boots. Our protagonist's own boots stand in the middle of a circle of admirers, marvelling at her work and handing over cheques. Slowly, the camera pans up the legs of the crowd until a row of paintings come into view, four in view, each an abstract, each brightly-coloured, each with an explosion of dark brown as their focal point. They are enormous and mesmerising, and you find yourself digging around for your own cheque-book. Those paintings, they really are something.

Cut to printing factory. Neatly-folded stacks of white paper whizz round on conveyor belts. The camera cuts to a chute down which these papers fall, time slows, the words become almost legible—then a flash bulb, the paper slides into a seller's hand, is pushed into a woman's bag as she hurries down the street, flutters in the hot breeze at the top of an escalator. And all over it, it's her, it's her face, it's her name. We love her.

You can make bigger jumps when you're writing prose than if you're directing a movie. In a film, barring special effects, you're driven by the limitations of what you can actually record. With words, you can pull off anything. No word costs more than any other. No stunt of wordsmithery costs what it costs to film a motorcyclist in a daring leap over an exploding lorry. I can put a newspaper into your brain without having to have a newspaper. I can turn a killer into a revered artist.

If this were a movie, we'd watch the prints being removed from the walls of the gallery. We'd watch one being carted off by a suited man. We'd watch one being hung up in a boardroom. We'd watch one being carried away by gloved men. We'd watch it on the operating table, under bright light, as two men worked over it, peeling away sections and taking them off for testing.

We'd hold our breath as the results came back. Human remains. Beneath that, a tick in the box next to 'blood'. We watch a call-out. Armed and dangerous. Has killed, will kill again. We see a woman at complete peace with the world, putting the finishing touches to an abstract canvas. We watch a slow motion approach of cars, a helicopter circling, feet on the gravel. The music playing could be Exit Music (For a Film). We watch a calculated calm, a canvas being placed on easel, the bullets sliding home, a quick glance behind, the last-minute repositioning, and, just as the bangs come at the door, we hear the gunshot that this all led up to.

Then the screen cuts to black.
It's black for a long time.

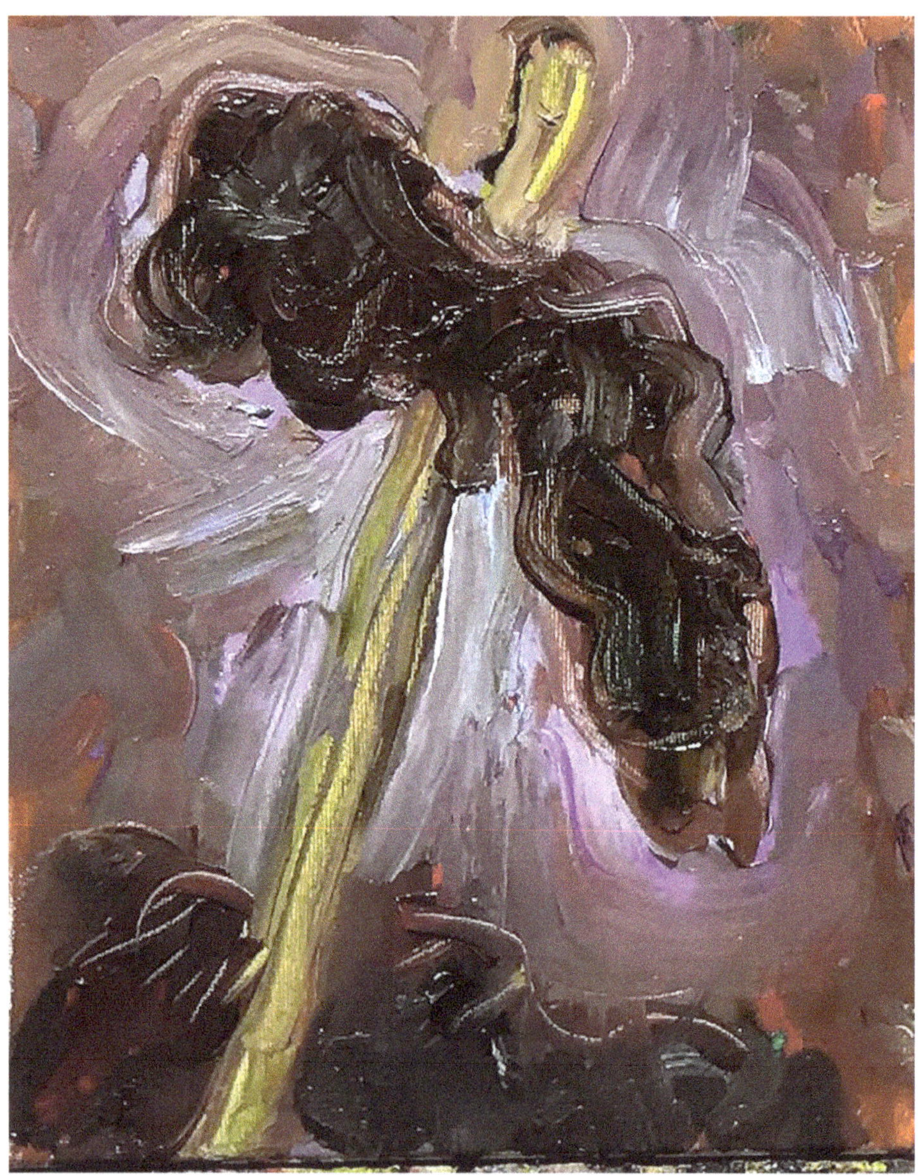

SHIT ON A STICK

Painting

GIOVANNI MANGIANTE

LIMA, PERU

DON'T MIND THE WORDS, LISTEN TO THE RHYTHM

I think I'm going to style my pubic hair like Donald Trump's hair

just to be hip hip hip hip hip

and change my writing style to

skkkr skkkr skkrkrrr

808

808

clap clap

codeine, big macs, plastic world

808

808

clap clap

xanax, coca cola, plastic people

808

808

clap clap

I love to open the windows

and get a big hit, a breath of fresh smog.

If poetry focused less on the peppermint skies,

the overflowing rivers of the soul

merging into a big twirling sea dragon

that leaves the Gods flummoxed and stoned,

then maybe more people

would give a shit about it.

CHRISTINE SLOAN STODDARD

BROOKLYN, NEW YORK

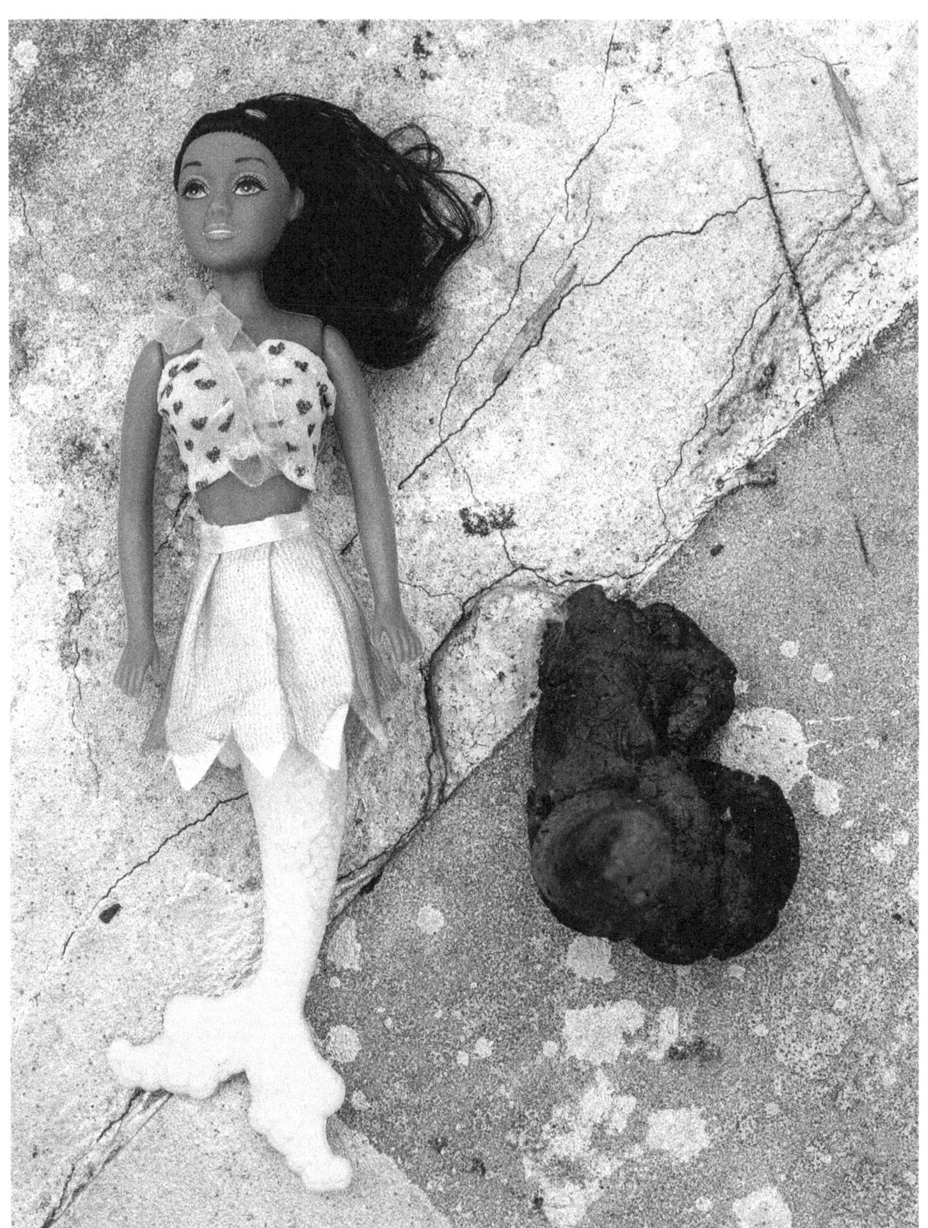

MERMAID & DOG SHIT

Photograph

BECKY FAWCETT

GOXHILL, UNITED KINGDOM

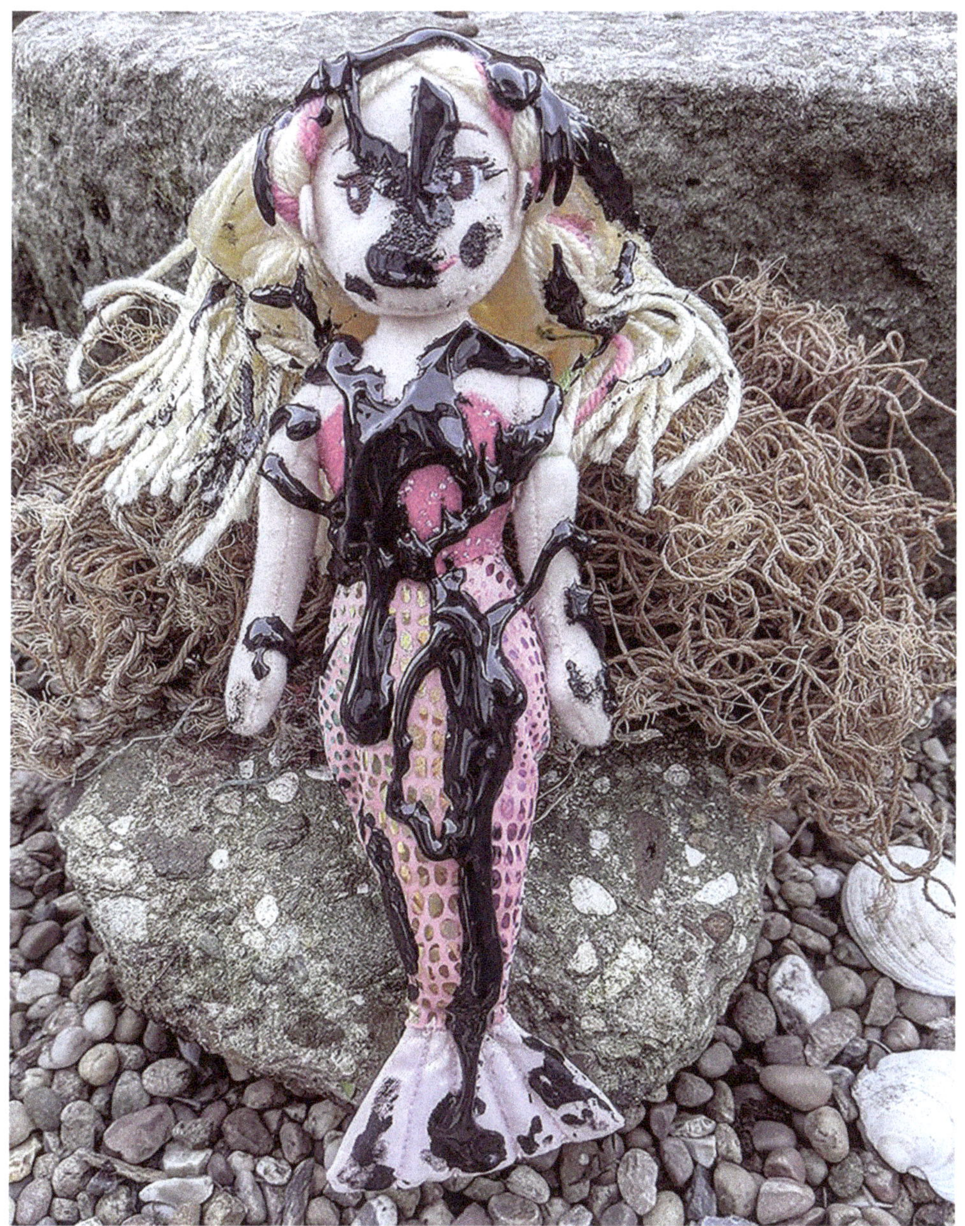

BY THE SEA

Photograph

ORCHID SPANGIAFORA

WYNCOTE, PENNSYLVANIA

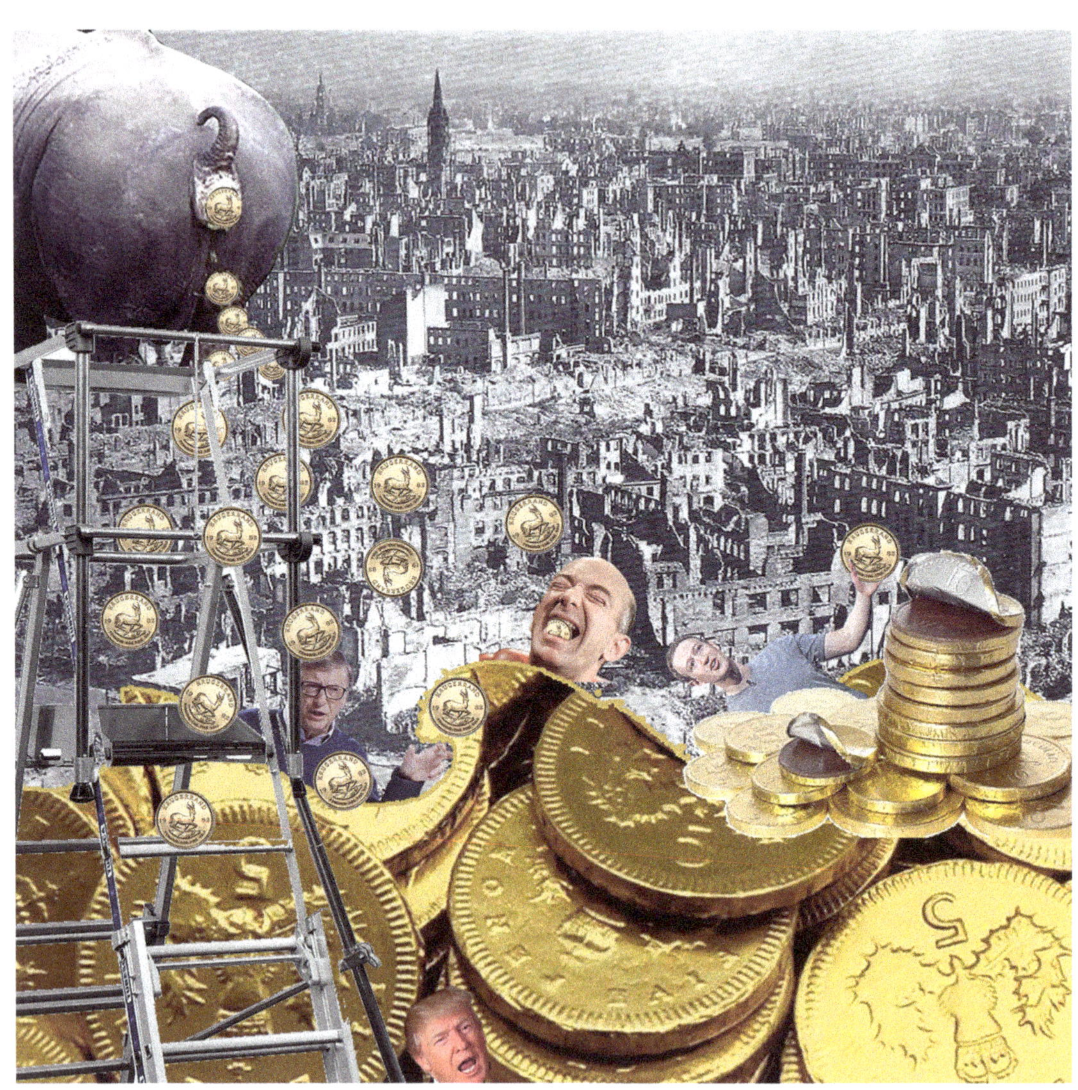

BUTTCOIN / CLIMATE CHANGE?

Collage

MARK HOEFER

SAN DIEGO, CALIFORNIA

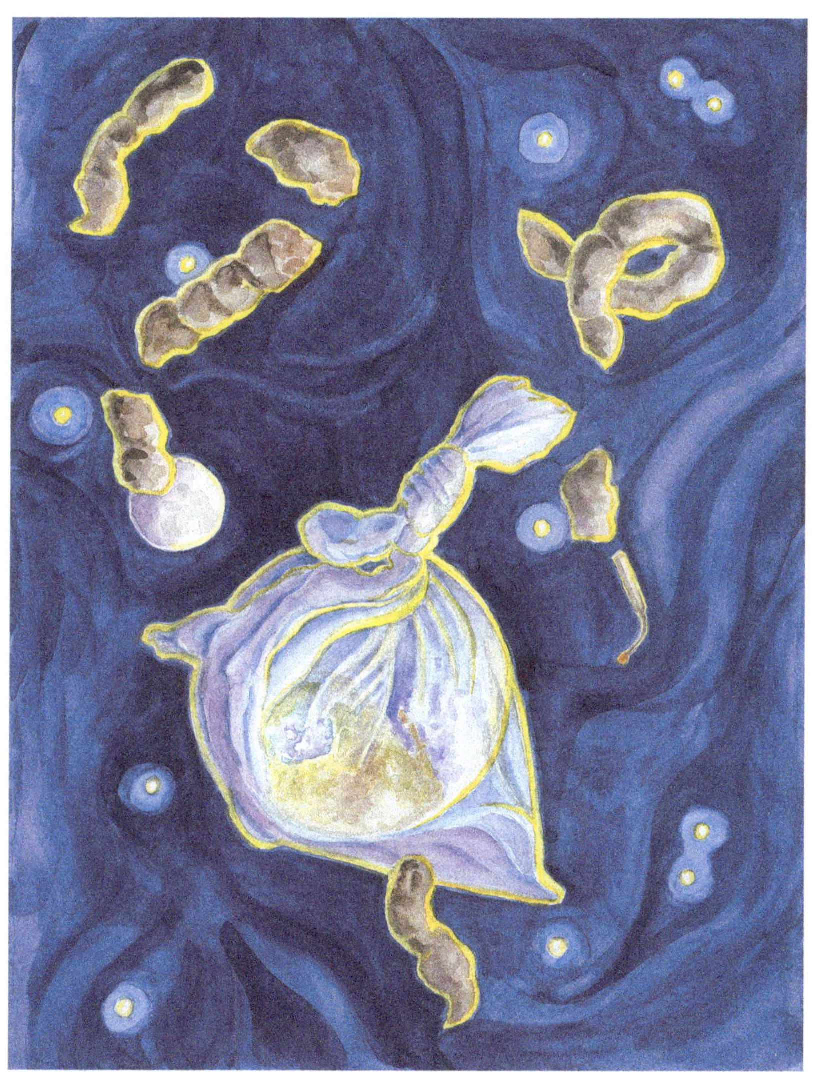

PALE DOO BLOT—CURB YOUR PLANET!

Watercolor

ASHLEY MILLER

ALBUQUERQUE, NEW MEXICO

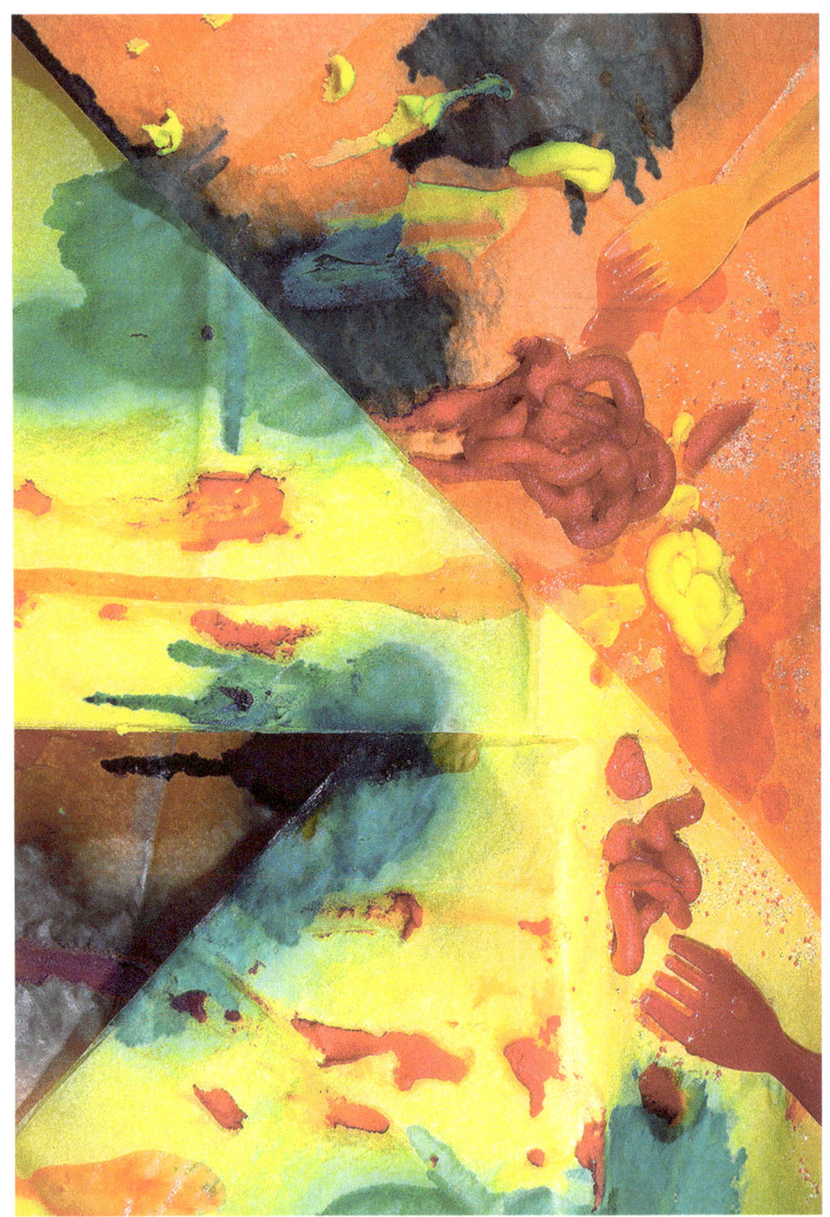

MESS

Multimedia

S. A. GRIFFIN
LOS ANGELES, CALIFORNIA

WHAT IF I WERE A TREE, AND I KNEW THE CARPENTERS WERE COMING FOR ME

hot winds comb the balding treetops

ancient glaciers faint and drop into the drink
like shy young debutantes

hungry oceans grow morbidly obese
feeding on the retreating coastlines

get hip, this ain't your Leary mama's 1960s

tune out
    turn off
        drop in

fuck fake presidents and kiss ass cowards
to hell with fear mongering preachers
and their nowhere promises
and hoax of a second chance

this is not a lottery

the guns
like the dice
are loaded

you can't beat the house
bet on it

before the stillborn spring
before the sky falls
before the earth dies burning
before all is lost and frozen inside the final ice
and graveyard of time

JOHN MAZZEI

JACKSONVILLE, OREGON

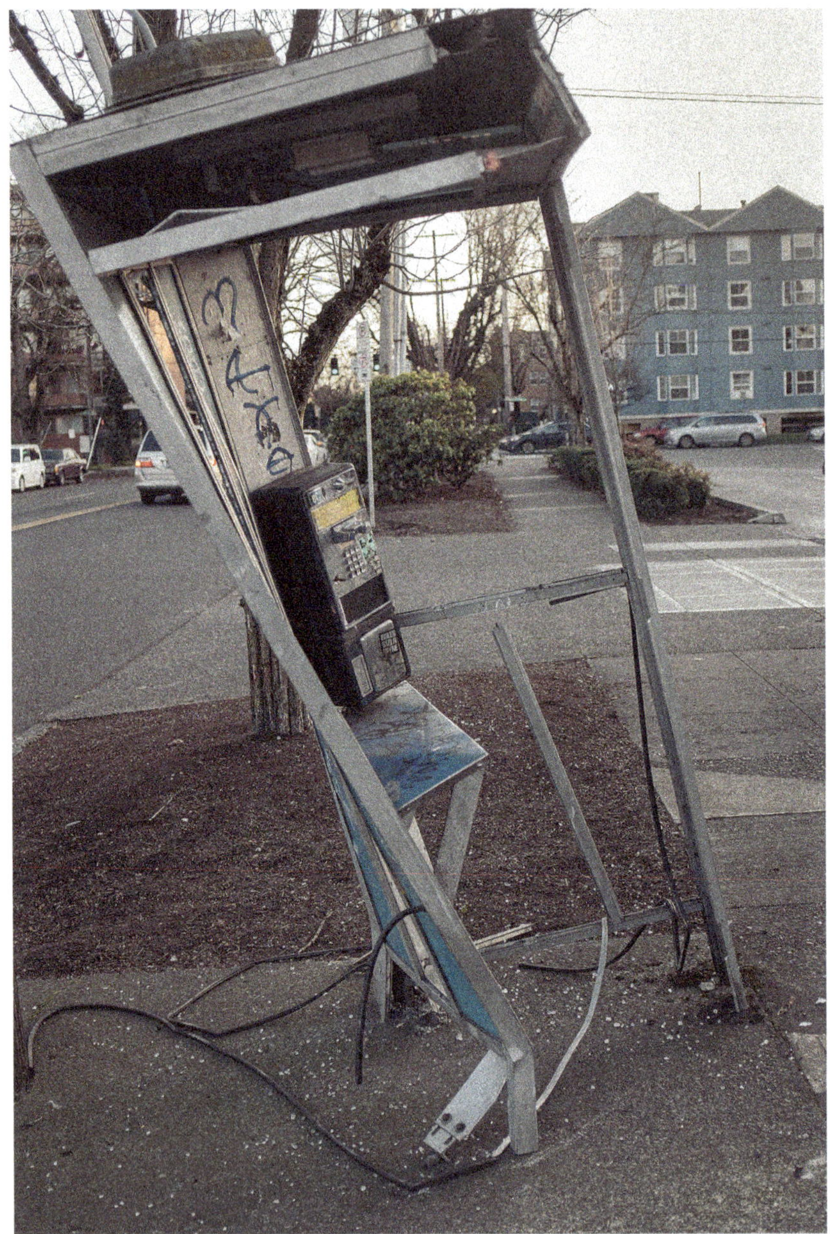

THE END OF COMMUNICATION

Photograph

PATRICIA LEONARD

BRONX, NEW YORK

STRONG

Sometimes even the strongest break
The oldest of trees rooted deep into the earth
Grounded for many years
Carrying the weight of burdened souls weeping underneath them
Seeking shelter and comfort from the world around them
Withstanding the roughest storms nature can conjure up
And still the willow sways and bends but never breaks
Shedding its leaves upon the earth releasing the responsibility of its purpose
And it is me.
Structured and fixed as a permanent ground for those surrounding
Standing tall and firm
Ready to bear the inconsiderate children
Whose laughter and play warm the air
Who tug and abuse every part of every inch without splinters, cuts or bruises
The tree caresses their fragile bodies and stables them through generations
It is always the tree in the yard that brings childhood happiness and thundering sadness
Whose fond memories relate time after time
Until one day something lights a fire in its very core
And just before the fire emerges
A weeping soul left the tree with nothing but embers and in turn the tree has lifted another light
And little by little this happens again and again
Until the tree has no core
Lost all of its very grounding and roots
Lost what it was that brought it life
And no longer could the willow spring any leaves
But who cares about the tree and its losing fight to pollution
We all know the problem and always choose to turn the other cheek because there's
always a skinnier tree
Or a younger bush or a sturdy vine to swing from
None of which can keep your feet firmly planted on the ground

But who am I kidding
These words are not profound
People are too wrapped in their own shit to own their own shit
And the little kid in me is steadily picking at a scab
Knowing that one innocent intention can lead to uncontrollable bleeding
But having blind faith in something no one can believe because I'm paranoid
That my paralyzed emotions have come off too strong
And who else can I depend on for the words of wisdom and the strength to keep holding on
That maybe, just maybe, one day I'll touch the stars in the sky
And amongst the birds flying high
Carefree living but another soul has burdened me again
Leaving me with empty tears and broken hopes
Because someone has to be strong

SANGEETHA ALWAR

KUVEMPUNAGAR, INDIA

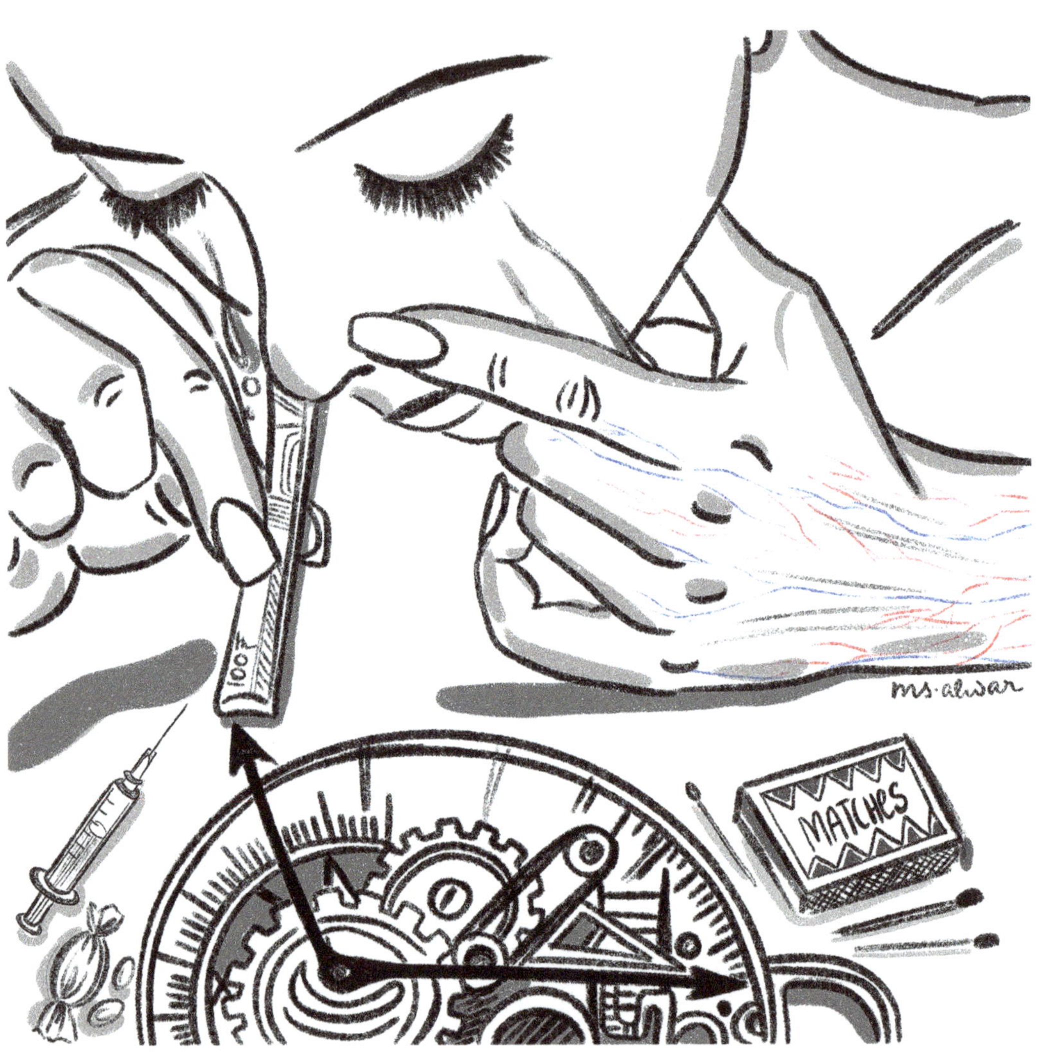

TEMPORAL DYSPHORIA

SANTIAGO AMAYA

SAN FRANCISCO, CALIFORNIA

PLASTIPHILIA

Every corporate gesture of good will is an advertisement to distract you from progressing
commercial gluttony's overdue intervention
    Big man forces mouthfuls of mercury down your throat paired with sips of radioactive
water

    The earth is wet   the birds drop from the sky and the trees burn to the ground
forming a slurry of blood ash and bitumen

Auto industry execs snort lines of tire dust and huff fresh breaths of carbon monoxide
You drive your kid to school you drive to work
  you fly overseas to see paradise and forget about your saran wrapped intestines

I take hour long showers while the world is on fire
And sing the economic fairytale of infinite resources
And listen to the ocean suffocate from all the corporate celebrity and
literal bullshit that bleeds into it from the river
      And when I'm done I stand under the ozone's god-shaped hole and sunbathe
Baptized under a deluge of pollution

Let's gather up all of the endangered species CEOs and serial litterbugs and lock them in a
bounce house and after we all make up we can make angels in the soot covered snow

We enjoy the things that kill us softly
I could take this knife rip you open and find a landfill but trash is make believe
  it doesn't exist once I throw it away

PAMELA PAPINO-WOOD

YONKERS, NEW YORK

UNSUSTAINABLE LOVE

Un-su-stay?-nable
That thing you call an
expression of affection, That
sits like a rotting lump in
your throat
Hide please sir, in your
desperation to drain every
living ounce of sanity I bleed
Then Hoover me back to life
after killing me dead.
I despise your victimhood
that cloaks your ineptness
Your inorganic attempts to
create realities to cover your
lies
And you lie to yourself
You think she proves you're
better than me. And,
perhaps, you are
because I am shackled with
the feelings of guilt and
shame and blame transpired
from your inner
worthlessness
You give so little, just to hold
on to so much pain
And you continue to enjoy
that dish with a side of selfpitying
denial, served up
steaming
You cannot maintain your
own stance without being
resentful

I who tried to expose the
imperfections that you
cannot see for yourself
Why try to fix it when you
can attack and pass blame
Why seek growth when
vision is already good and
muddy
I am traumatized by lack of
understanding which
direction the blows will
return
Am I fighting hands tears or
words
With Emotions flown
through the sweet Milky Way
Then devoured in black
holes
How can one sustain
electricity shooting through
veins without internal
resistors to temper the flow
How can one sustain 14 tons
of untruths along a beautiful
esplanade
How can a heart ever trust
its demise when surrounded
by plastered smiles
It is not maintainable
Simply unsustainable

LORENE ZAROU-ZOUZOUNIS

SAN FRANCISCO, CALIFORNIA

THE PAGE TURNS

Human suffering and wretchedness are constant
Never at ease, never in disguise, always in neverland
As long as the profiteers are safe and bloated
Hoarding swells monopolized capitalist
Who swallows the sustenance farmer whole
With carnivorous fangs and ferocious claws
Then gobbles up a bottle of tri-colored pastel antacids
Forced down our throats by death-wishing BIG pharm

Spew the fossil fuels mantra repeats
Extract coal, rape the mountains,
Jab and chisel kill coal miner and coal miner's daughter
Ignoramus asses elected by more ignoramus asses
Sending us all through a pitch black time tunnel
We speedily exit, fall face down unawares
Into the middle ages, and a plague becomes us
Beginning of the known "third mass extinction"

We are not a wide mouthed, long-tailed
Long-necked menacing dinosaur anymore
Covetous corporate bosses concoct lies alongside
Their elected and funded imps
And all these rabid fraudsters live comfortable days
While they implode lone entrepreneurs and working class
And calling the poor and disenfranchised lazy
And praying that Jesus will return to save only them

LISA ANDREINI

SAN MATEO, CALIFORNIA

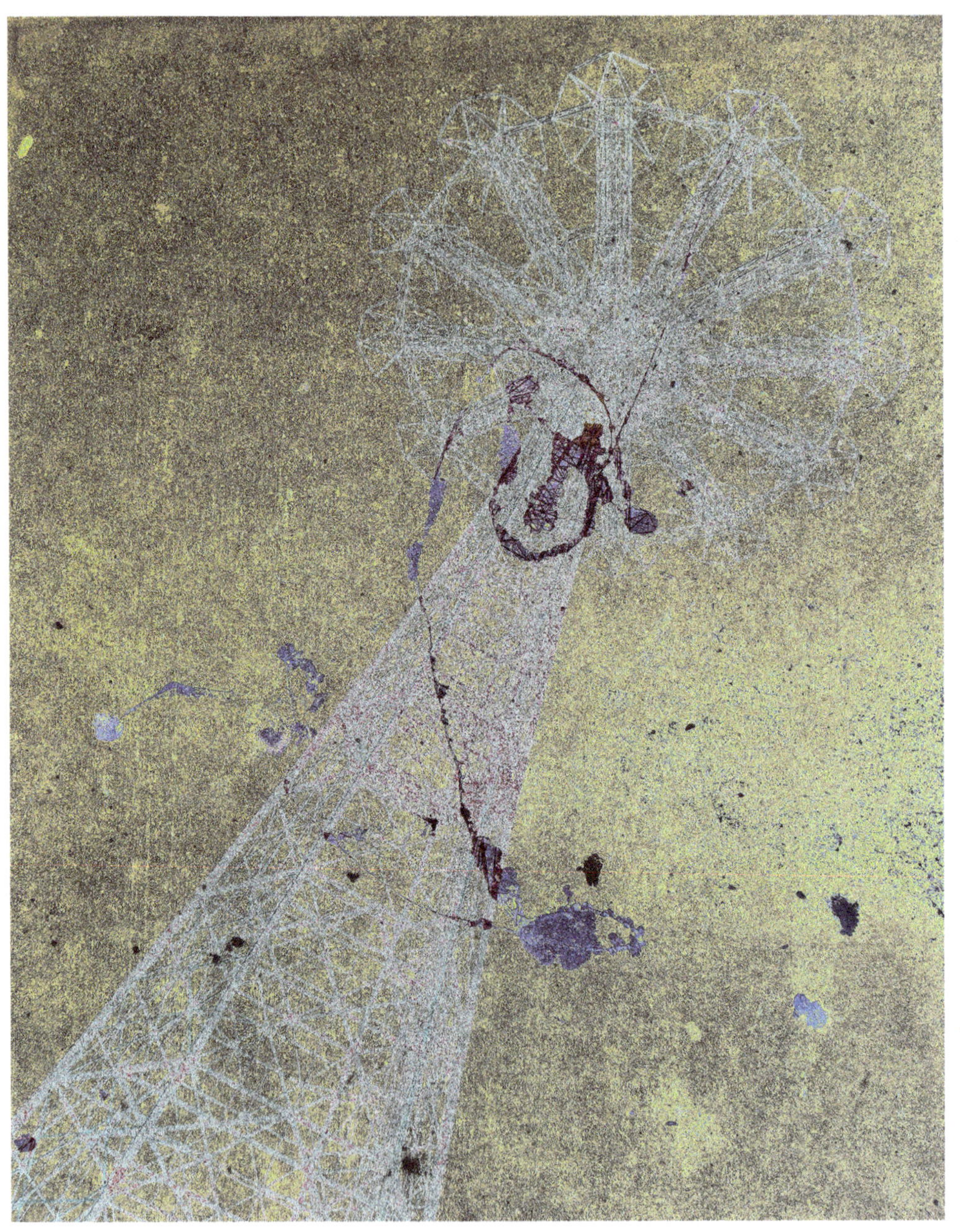

UNTITLED 2

JANE LeCROY

NEW YORK, NEW YORK

CIMABUE [1240?–1302?]

The Madonna of the Angels

██████████████████████████ emerge from the collective anonymity ██████████████████ ███████████████ today it is almost impossible to determine what is fact, and what fable, ████████████ ████████████ Indeed, some ███████████ even doubt███████ existence ████████████████████████████████. ████████████████████████████████████ ████████████████████████████████████ ████████████, with its maritime attachments to ███████ ████████████████████████████████████ █████████████ the importance of ██████████ ████████ Rome, by ██████████████████████████ ████████████████████████████ details██████████ ████████████████████████████████████ ████████████████████████████████████ flowing ████████████████████████████ in the beauty ████████████████████ imposing in the simplicity of ████████████████████████████████████ ████████████████████████████████████

THE MADONNA OF THE ANGELS

KURT PATTERSON

KINGSTON, JAMAICA

GAMESHOW TIME

"You can get whatever is in that mystery box. The mystery box costs $100. You have $1,200 on your ticket. Will you go for it?"

"Go for it," the crowd chanted.

"What does the world say Tina?"

"Sixty-five million people say she should go for it . . . against, seventeen million."

The crowd cheered. Behind the stage colourful numbers ran up and down an enormous glittering screen. In the shadows five muscular men crouched and waited in case someone chose that special box.

Tina continued: "Malaysia has the most Super votes, and Terry in Uganda says she's praying for you."

The crowd hushed.

"So, what are you going to do Joanne? Are you purchasing whatever is in the mystery box for $100?"

"I'm purchasing the mystery box for $100."

"She's purchasing the mystery box for $100!"

Enormous lights flashed and danced.

"Tina, tell her what she's won."

"Your prize comes from Deepak. Deepak . . . cultivate your soul. You've won . . . one fully featured body!"

The crowd cheered.

"Your new body will be grown from your own stem cells, and fed only wholesome organic foods. Your gift also includes free transplants for two hundred years, and one-hundred-and-fifty *thousand* dollars in permits . . . and there's more . . . "

Ooohs and Aaahs issued from all sections.

"You can carry up to two children in Deepak surrogates for free!"

The crowd launched into new round of applause. Joanne spun and kissed her ticket.

"Now to our next contestant . . . Marla, a retired school teacher from Phase 7."

Shouts and whistles burst from a section of the crowd.

The host leaned in closer. Marla fixed her glasses.

"Marla . . . you could get what is in this mystery box for $150 . . . remember . . . no one has won the trip to Bubble City . . . which means . . . inside one of these unmarked boxes, is temporary citizenship, in the city that floats high above the troubles of the world . . . "

The crowd murmured and shuffled.

"Remind us Tina."

Tina's voice came from everywhere: "Bubble city, the jewel of the skies, floats not only on the warm air inside, but on the hopes and dreams of Founders Inc., the visionary corporation that created this ideal society and human habitat. Bubble city is powered by photosyntronic grass on the surface of the dome, and grows all its own food in merganic tubes. The Bubble City prize is for one family, and it includes full entitlements for six months . . . plus a chance at the one million dollars in permits mega-win."

"Will you go for it Marla?"

Marla passed her ticket from hand to hand.

The host put a finger to his ear, "I've just heard that someone on the panel is reaching out to you . . . let's play the message."

"Hi mom . . . all of us here are cheering for you . . . Dan too . . . whatever happens, we love you. Now go win millions!"

The crowd cheered. The lights dimmed.

"The mystery box costs $150. You have $300 on your ticket Marla. Will you go for it?"

"Go for it" the crowd chanted.

"Yes . . . Yes I'll go for it," Marla said.

The lights flared.

"Marla Jacobson . . . of Phase 7 . . . you've won . . . a bath of centipedes. Hold her hands and feet . . . bring out the tub."

The crowd cheered. The five sturdy men sprang from their positions. Their black helmets reflected the studio lights. Marla tripped over her skirt.

"Tina, tell us about the centipedes."

"These Peruvian giant yellow leg centipedes have been genetically engineered to deliver a sting that is more painful but completely non-lethal. It won't be pleasant for Marla, but you can't always win when you play The Game."

"That's right Tina."

The five men forced Marla into a large transparent plastic tub and poured on the centipedes. The insects fell in streams and heavy tangles. Energetic graztak music accompanied the screams.

"The centipedes are here courtesy of Oviarch Skincare, your age defying clinic."

"Let's see the reaction cam right now Tina. Oh . . . oh . . . that's not pretty at all.

"Not at all Jim. That's fifteen gallons of centipedes we're looking at right now."

"See how they run and slither? Nothing moves like centipedes."

The lights dimmed and the host looked square into the camera drone.

"Marla needs one million rescue votes to escape the tub early. Remember, rescue votes are 39c each. Voting brought to you by Lusech, your connection to who matters. Log in your rescue votes right now."

GAY PASLEY
EDMOND, OKLAHOMA

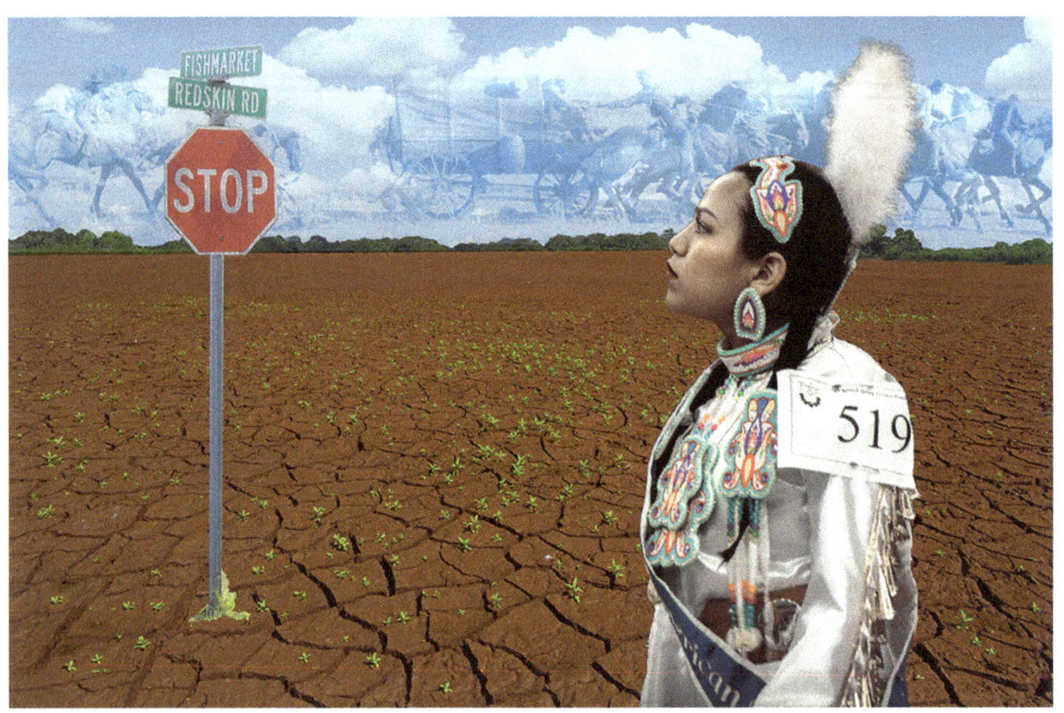

SIGN OF THE TIMES

Collage

SIAVASH MINOUKADEH

EDGWARE, UNITED KINGDOM

CHANCE ENCOUNTERS WITH PROMOTIONAL MATERIALS

There is an old and a new consciousness of the age	Tonight I can write the saddest lines	Some things can only be done on a flat surface	On board with you
The old one is directed towards the individual	To hear the immense night, still more immense without her	But there are some things that occur nearly in common	Chop and change
The war is destroying the old world with its content	The same night whitening the same trees	It opens to anything	The event of the autumn
A relationship of equality between the universal and the individual	Another's. She will be another's	Three dimensions are real space	Escape the grind
Tradition, dogmas and the predominance of the individual stand in the way of this realisation	The night wind revolves in the sky and sings.	A painting isn't an image	Stretching across London
Therefore the founders of the new culture call upon all who believe in reform of art and culture to destroy these obstacles to development	Love is so short, forgetting is so long	There is seldom any colour	My greatest adventure

continued

By doing away with natural form—they have eliminated that which stood in the way of pure artistic expression	I loved her	The space corresponds	Embrace the mess
They therefore sympathise with all who are fighting spiritually or materially for the formation of an international unity in life, art and culture	And sometimes she loved me too	The material never has its own movement	You know why you come here
The collaboration of all is possible by	And these the last verses that I write for her	Also, they are usually aggressive	But if you want it you'll have to leave
Contributions in the broadest sense (critical, philosophical, architectural, scientific, literary, musical etc. as well as reproductions to the monthly magazine	Though this be the last pain that she makes me suffer	The quality is intense and narrow and obsessive	Make good exciting

BIBIANA PADILLA MALTOS

WESTMINSTER, CALIFORNIA

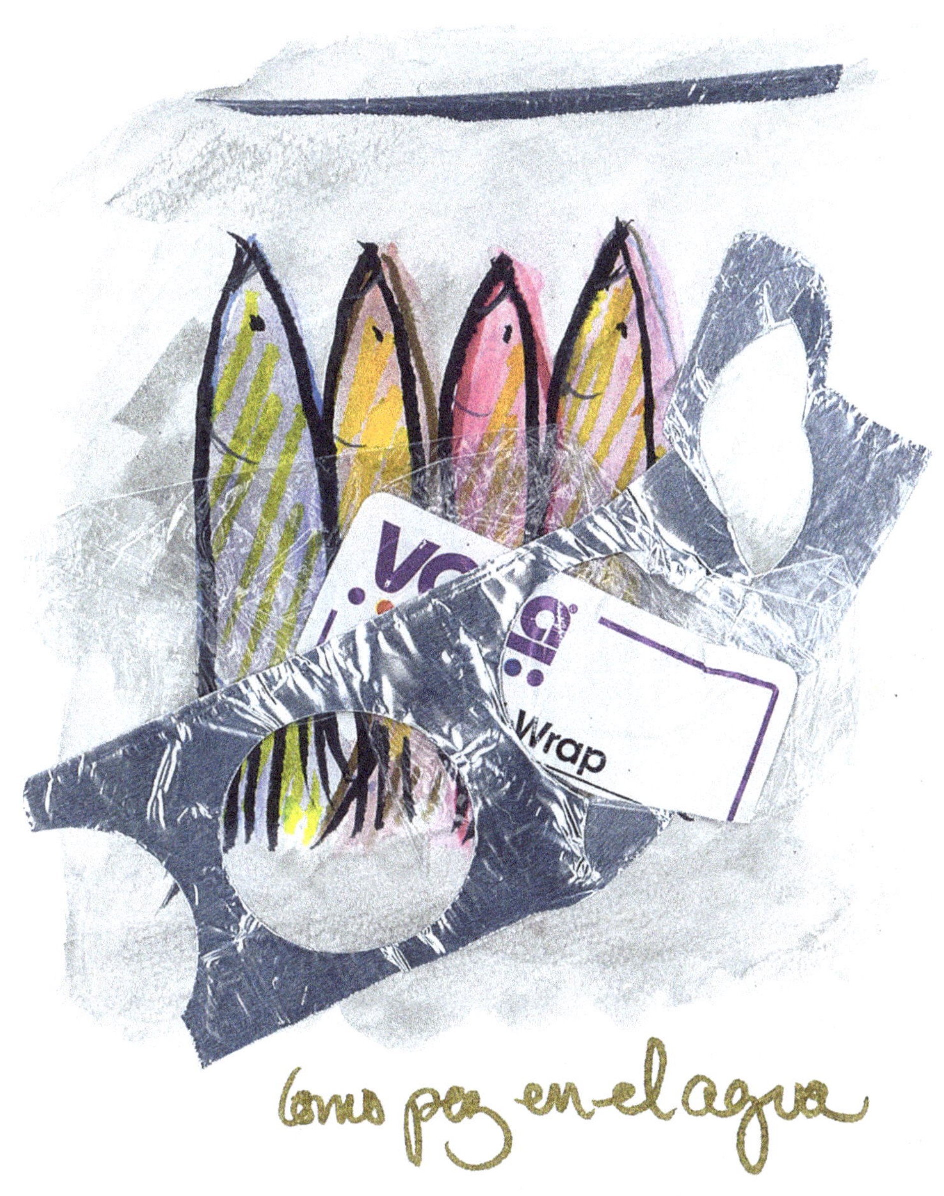

COMO PEZ EN EL AGUA / LIKE FISH IN THE WATER

Collage

EGON GUENTHER
Diessen, Germany

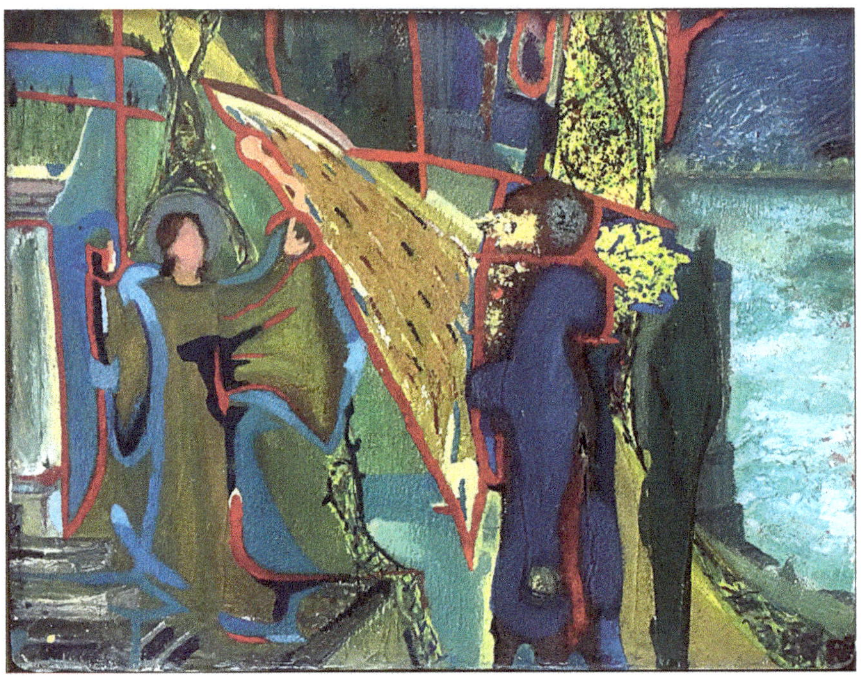

CUT THE BULLSHIT (FINAL WARNING)

oil on plasterboard, 37 x 29,5 cm

CUT THE BULLSHIT (FINAL WARNING)

Oil on Plasterboard, 37 x 29,5 cm

PUMA PERL
NEW YORK, NEW YORK

TICKET TO HELL

Scientists say
the world is ending.
Sounded believable.
So, I quit my job,
fucked the wrong people,
stopped paying rent,
and developed a drug habit.
But the world didn't end.

It's a Velvet Underground
ticket to hell.
Another apocalypse
and we can't be late.
Grab the rock 'n' roll shirt
and a few pair of socks,
some black underwear,
and a high-powered rifle.
All bases covered
except for the drug habit
and the people I fucked,
who are still all wrong.

JOSH LEFKOWITZ
NEW YORK, NEW YORK

TELLING MY FUTURE GRANDCHILDREN ABOUT TREES

They were great

MICHAEL PUZZO

NEW YORK, NEW YORK

CZARNMERICA

An excerpt from LAByrinth Theater Company's Installation on America

CARNIVAL BARKER:

Step right up, Ladies and Gentlemen, Boys and Girls—Step right up—Step right up—See the greatest show on earth—America! The New World— USA! Los Estados Unidos. What are you waiting for? The streets are paved with gold for Chrissake.

Step right up—Come inside. This land was made for you and me and our admission is totally free. Free like our religion. Free like our speech. Free like our shipping with a $30 purchase. Free like Willy! Free like you—Free like me.

We've got "life." We've got "liberty." And if it's "happiness" that's your pursuit—Ask about our reasonable installment plan. Operators are now standing by.

Hurry—Hurry—Don't be shy—America's just right inside—Where every day is the 4th of July, every week's Shark Week and every party is like it's 1999.

Hurry, Hurry—Step right up and take a chance on our world-famous American Dream. Everyone's a winner. It's got everything: protraction, inaction, over reaction, under reaction, uterine contraction, dissatisfaction and best of all distraction. So, try the American Dream—Guaranteed to keep your eye on the pie in the sky til the day you die.

Step right up—Don't be shy—Take a walk through the golden door—See the spectacular Great Green Lady of the Harbor. She may seem a little cold and standoffish at first, but you'll be amazed at how welcoming her loving arms can be. But be warned she's a mouth kisser—just go with it. Guaranteed to get your ramparts streaming gallantly.

America! Where we neatly number our wars and just like *The Godfather* nobody wants to see—*Part Three*.

America! Where our fireworks are guaranteed to never wake the baby, scare the dog or make the crowd go less than "Oooooooooooh!!"

Thrill to our rootin' tootin' actual shootin' Cowboys and Indians Wild West Show . . . Right inside—Right inside. And if you happen to know any actual real Indians—Please talk to Clyde—Talk to Clyde—in HR—He's right inside—We're definitely hiring.

Step right up! Find Jesus. Find the Lindbergh baby. Find out why the caged bird sings! We've got flags to salute, soldiers to recruit and rivers, oceans and lakes to pollute.

Step right up and take a ride on the underground railroad. Visit the *Little House on the Prairie*—go to prom with Carrie—get an upset stomach—go to the doctor—and find out you're allergic to dairy.

Ladies and Gentlemen, Boys and Girls, They and Them! Step inside. See the actual pillow where Martin Luther King had his famous dream. See the secret love child of Barbie and G.I. Joe—JFK and Marylin Monroe.

See the quill that signed for your independence—Take the pill to stop from getting pregnant. We've got huddled masses, Jackie Onassis and corrupt politicians showing their asses!

See Muhammad Ali & Anthony—Susan B.—Drive your Chevy to the levy it's as wet as the sea.

Go shopping! Buy a Cadillac. A Budweiser. Buy Gettysburg a dress. Winnie the Pooh some pants. Buy Greenland! Buy a soul we've got plenty for sale.

We've got The Grand Canyon, Steve Bannon and rivers of gold for you to pan in.

We've got Play-Do—Jim Crow—in Spanish—El Gatto in a Sombrero. There's a bald eagle, Charlie Brown's beagle—Go ahead and shoot 'em—it's totally legal—So step right up—Step right up. Admissions free. Just like you and just like ME!

LAURENT DE MÉZERAC

FONTAINEBLEAU, FRANCE

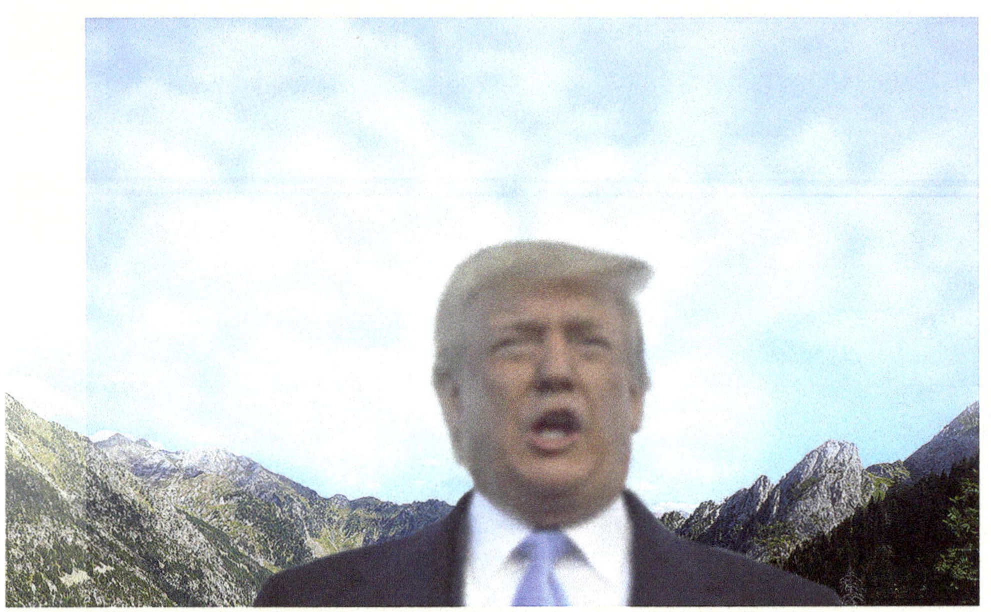

STUDY FINDS

Treated Photo with Text

BRUCE DODSON

BORLÄNGE, SWEDEN

I Want To Believe

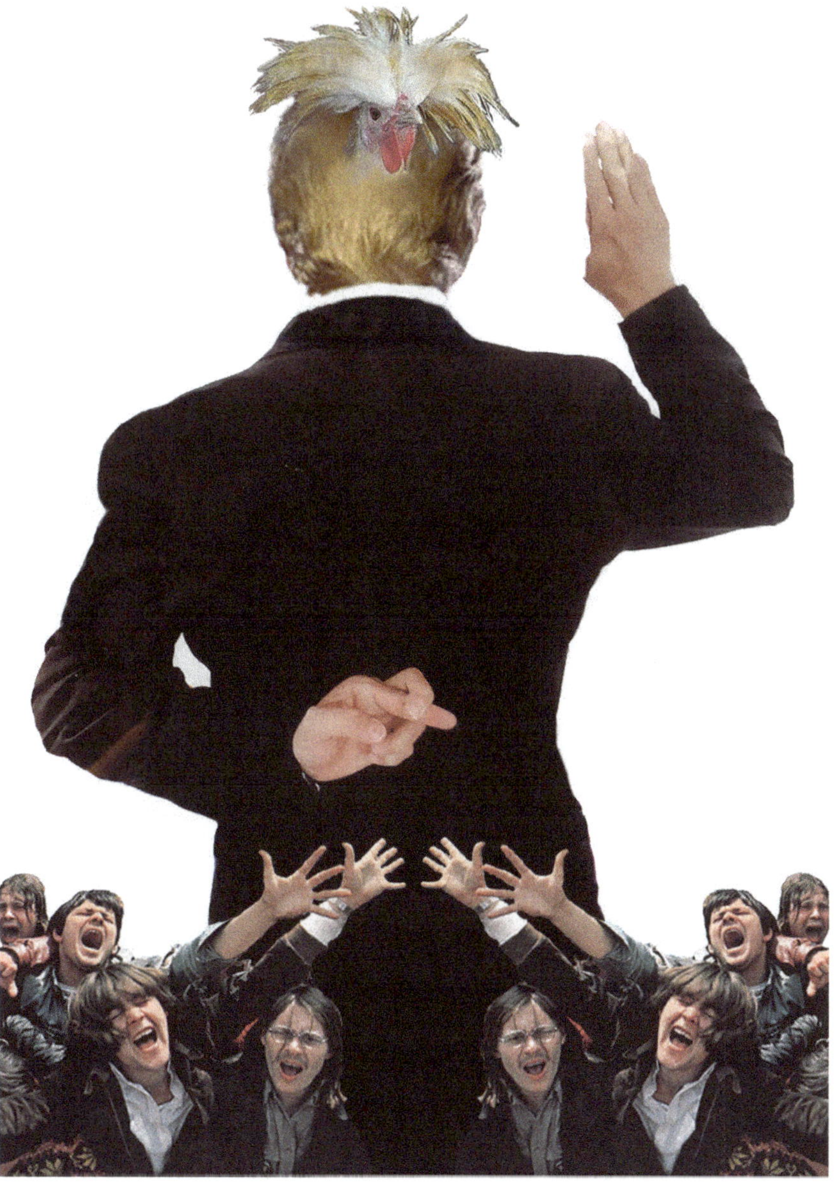

I WANT TO BELIEVE

Photo Collage with Text

KATHLEEN REICHELT

LANSDOWNE, ONTARIO, CANADA

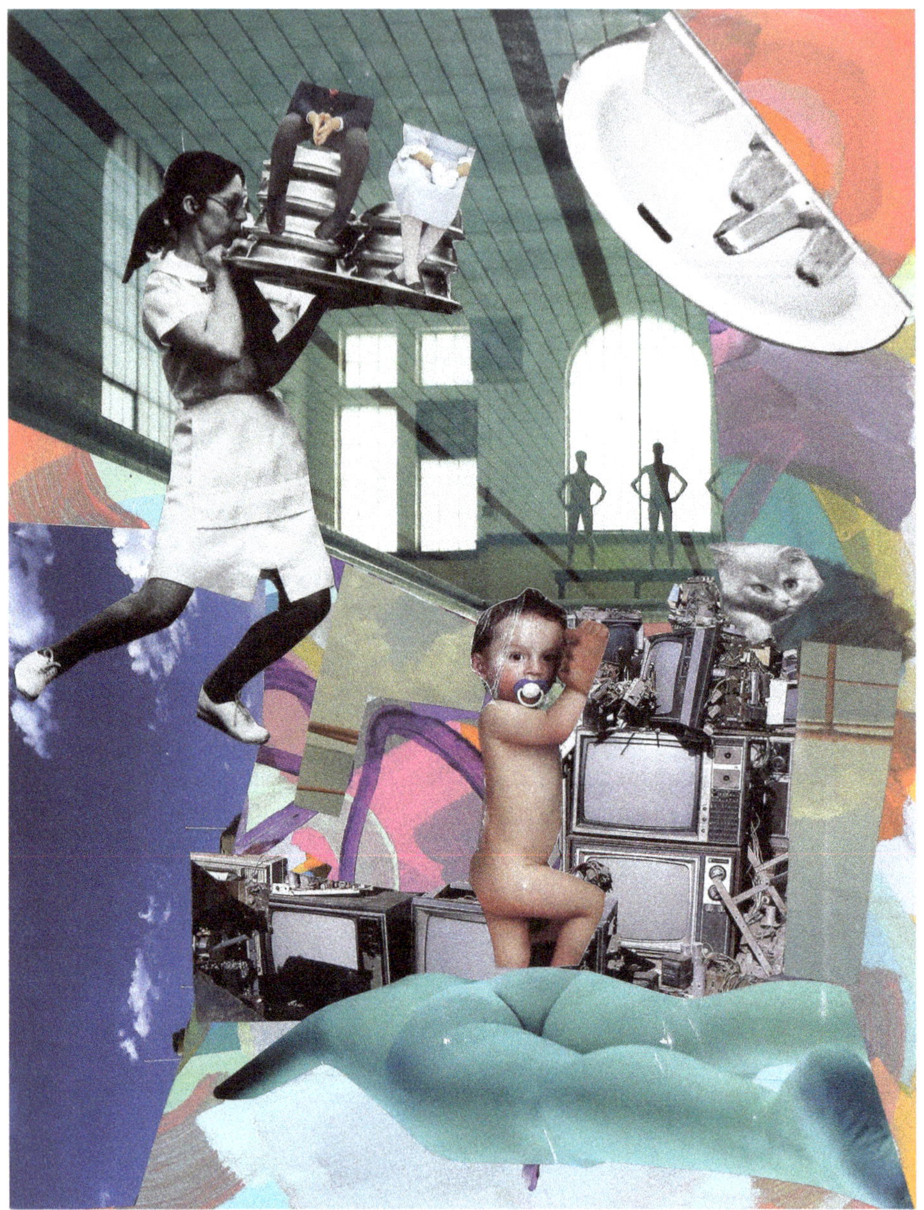

DELIVERING THE FUTURE

Collage

ROBERT FORD

NEW YORK, NEW YORK

THE DAY SATURN LOST ITS RINGS

It seemed we knew each other forever
I'd pick you up at Duane Reade
And we'd go jogging in Central Park
Or catch a movie
We watched *Rocket Man* three times

I was smitten by
Your rectangular body
Your smooth and silky skin
Your cobalt dress, adorned
With a wistful pink hibiscus flower

Your kisses were wet but soft
And swept me away to
Faraway South Pacific islands

I knew you had other lovers
But they weren't so kind
Several times I rescued you from the street
Badly beaten and missing your circular ribbed cap
Another time airport TSA whisked you away

But when you were found
Inside a whale's stomach
I no longer could defend your purpose
I realized your superficiality

It's over
Goodbye Fiji plastic bottled water
You're nothing but a marketing gimmick
I'm devoting myself to local tap
Besides it's more pure

A. D. WINANS

SAN FRANCISCO, CALIFORNIA

FOURTH OF JULY POEM

Stepped on pissed on
Cheated and abused
Taken advantage of blue-collar man
Caught up in the American scam

Don't tell me anyone can be
Anything they want to be
If they put their mind to it
Save your BS for the deaf
dumb and blind

It'll never sell in the ghetto
Or to the immigrants
You've turned your back on

Take your message to the church
Tell it to the man on death row
Tell it to the starving poor
Tell it to the sick and lame
Tell it to the rich folks
Tell it to the politicians
Tell it to Wall Street

Tell it to the man on the gallows
Tell it to the chiseled faces
On Mount Rushmore

Tell it to the children
You kidnapped from their parents
And put in detention facilities
For the crime of seeking sanctuary
From murderous regimes

Tell it to the street whore
Tell it to the crack head
Tell it to the last wino
On desolation row

Tell it to the banker
Tell it to the butcher
Tell it to the unemployed

Tell it to the circus clown
Tell it to the insane
Tell it to the outlaw

Tell it to the panhandler
Tell it to the con man
Tell it to the baby
Found stuffed in a dumpster

Tell it to the displaced factory worker
Tell it to the elderly
Tell it to the last alien hiding out in Roswell

Tell it to the militia
Tell it to the FBI sharpshooters
At Ruby Ridge
Tell it to the arsonists
At Waco, Texas

Tell it the Indians at Standing Rock
Tell it to the junkie
With dry heaves

Tell it to the supreme court justices
Who consistently vote in favor
Of money and power

Tell it to the farm worker
Tell it to the dishwasher
Tell it to the orderlies
Tell it to the flag waver

Tell it to the coal miner
Dying from black lung disease
Tell it to the garment worker
Slaving away in sweat shops
In Chinatown and the Latin Quarter

Tell it to the garbage man
Tell it to big business
Tell it to Corporate America
Tell it to the climate change deniers
Tell it to the blood-stained NRA

Tell it to the Fascist President
Tell it to the oil barons
Tell it to the tobacco merchants

Tell it to the fur industry
Who club baby seals to death
For the clothing merchants

Tell it to the Vatican
Tell it to the Priests
Tell it to the pharmacy industry
Profiting off the sick and lame

Tell it to the millions of people
Dying from air pollution
In Mexico China and India

Tell it to the man on his deathbed
Not sure why he lived
Or what he is dying for

Tell it to Jesus Christ
Shout it to the stars
Line the traitors up against the wall
Rewrite the Ten Commandments
And start all over again

JENNIFER WEIGEL

NEWTON, KANSAS

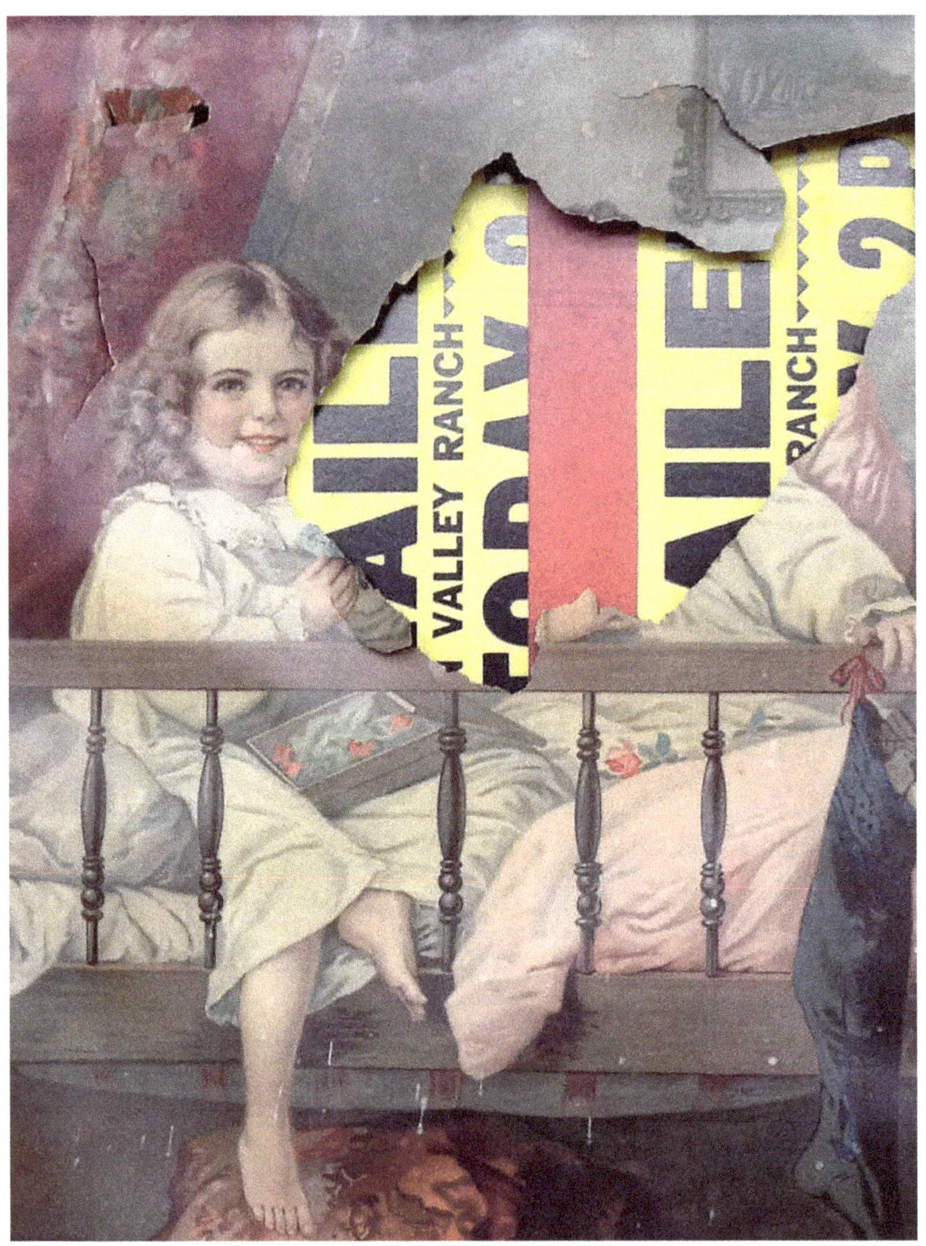

WHAT REMAINS: FACADE

Collage

JANE ORMEROD

NEW YORK, NEW YORK

FORTUNE THROWN ACROSS THE FALLS

Watch out for seizing bodies. Add this. This seizing this. Exact infection, fleck. Red-actionary. Reeds. Short of impossible breath-stops. Negligée. Negligent. Float swan. The this of extinction. Breaking dimension, we sob. Might as well have a life away from horizon and hips. The brazen history of war between the never, the neither here, there, hair ball, fireball, posie pockets. The ever now, or ever in case of anything else. Forget to subtract the this from their that. This is not the sprightly this of the ever-so-never before. Death is the only place without stairs or chance.

AUSTIN ALEXIS

NEW YORK, NEW YORK

NARCISSUS

The land, the water, the air:
a trinity of places
poised to be polluted into oblivion.
Three chambers in a burning mansion.
Three rooms of a doomed estate.

The senseless fires of destruction
could be put out
with the strong will of humankind,
its mighty huff,
were our species not so preoccupied with
having a helluva good time
admiring our own frenzied image
in the media which is our mirror.
Our population assumes
the red flames we spot are locks
of our pretty hair.

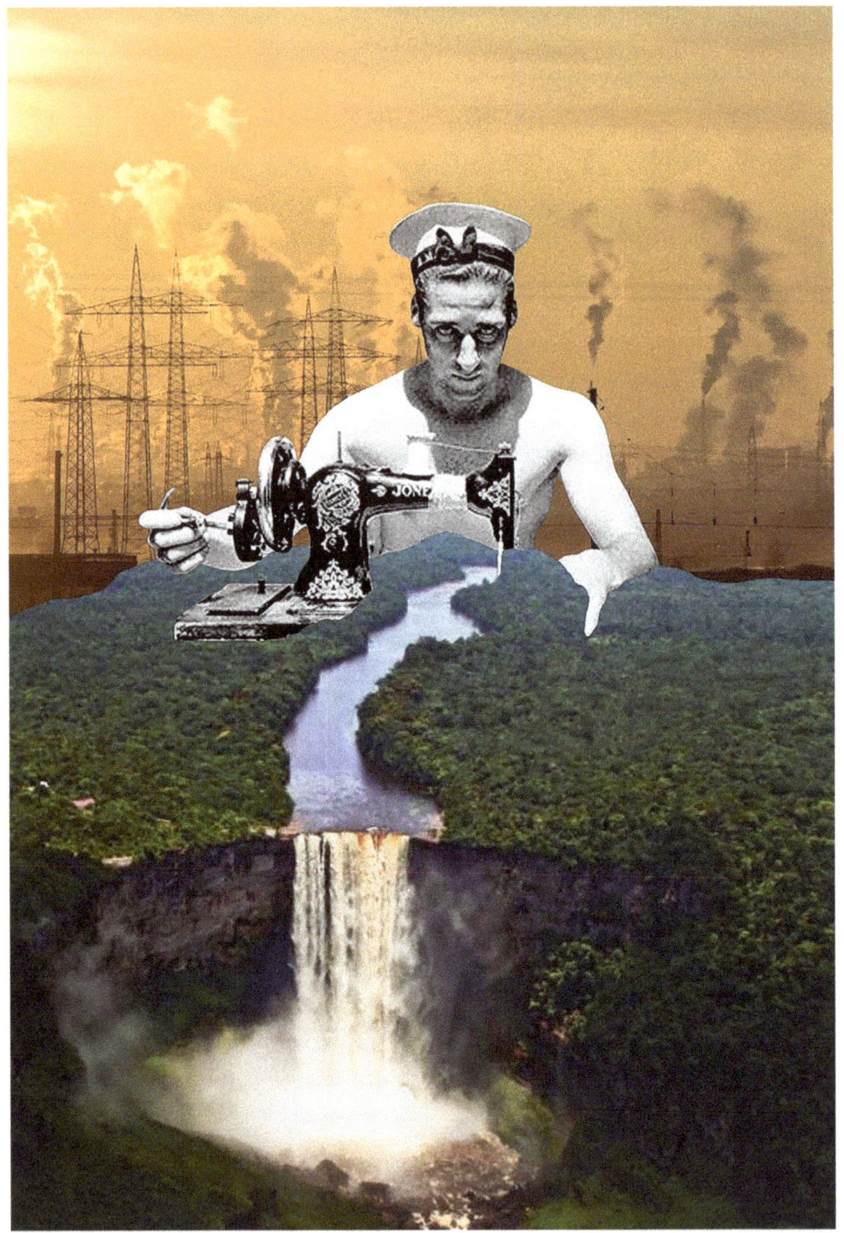

GOD PISSED OFF

Collage

RICHARD MODIANO

VENICE, CALIFORNIA

MORE! MORE! MORE!

Non-biodegradable substances are those which cannot be transformed into harmless natural state by the action of bacteria. And burning of these substances causes more pollution in the environment.

Drink from that plastic water bottle

then throw it away!

It'll lay in the land fill 450 years

Who cares?

More plastic bags!

Toss 'em in the trash

so convenient, don't use 'em again

Nylons, chiffon dresses, stockings, ropes, umbrellas

use 'em 'til they wear out and throw them away

can't be re-cycled anyway!

Fresh unpolluted drinking water is rare?

Don't believe it, so leave those taps running all day

More herbicides, fungicides, pesticides

And chemical fertilizers too

use up all that phosphate rock!

Remove the forests

disappearing at a rate of 375 km each day

wash that top soil away!

Species are dying out 1000 times faster than their natural rate of extinction?

Don't worry, we'll bring 'em back at Disneyland!

MARTA JANIK

KRAKÓW, POLAND

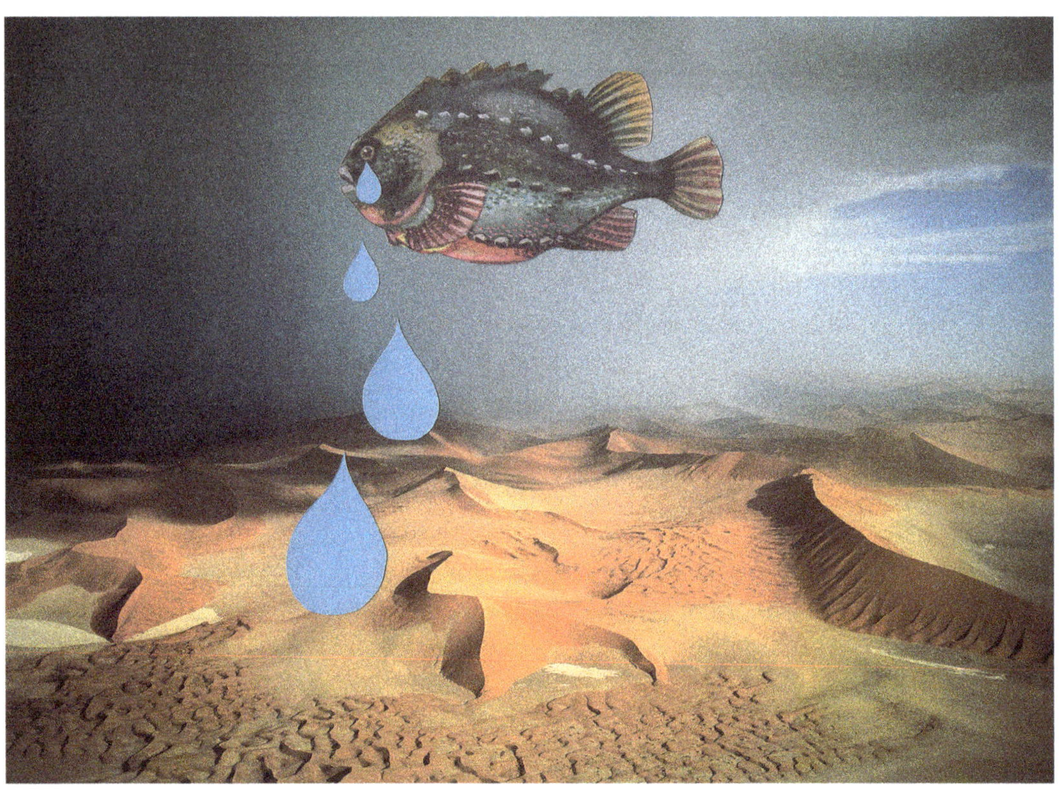

TEARS WON'T BE ENOUGH

Mixed Media

ANN FIRESTONE UNGAR

NEW YORK, NEW YORK

O$_2$

(a sonnet for those who don't yet understand the crisis)

To heal the wounded earth, oh to

regain abundant air: a breath

of clean protective layer, true

gift to us, a shield against death.

The lungs of life, the Amazon,

cut down by blind, uncaring eyes,

absorbed CO2, fueled by sun,

water to photosynthesize.

From that the trees breathe out O2,

and we breathe in the gas of life,

diminishing now, much to rue,

coming end, inelegant strife.

We'll choke on shore of New York Bay,

gasp at Sylvia's in Harlem,

in Hong Kong and Calcutta say

earth is doomed; no one can pardon.

Science, Knowledge: here our foe lands.

Friends, beware, our fate in our hands.

AKIM A. J. WILLEMS

SINT-PIETERS-RODE, BELGIUM

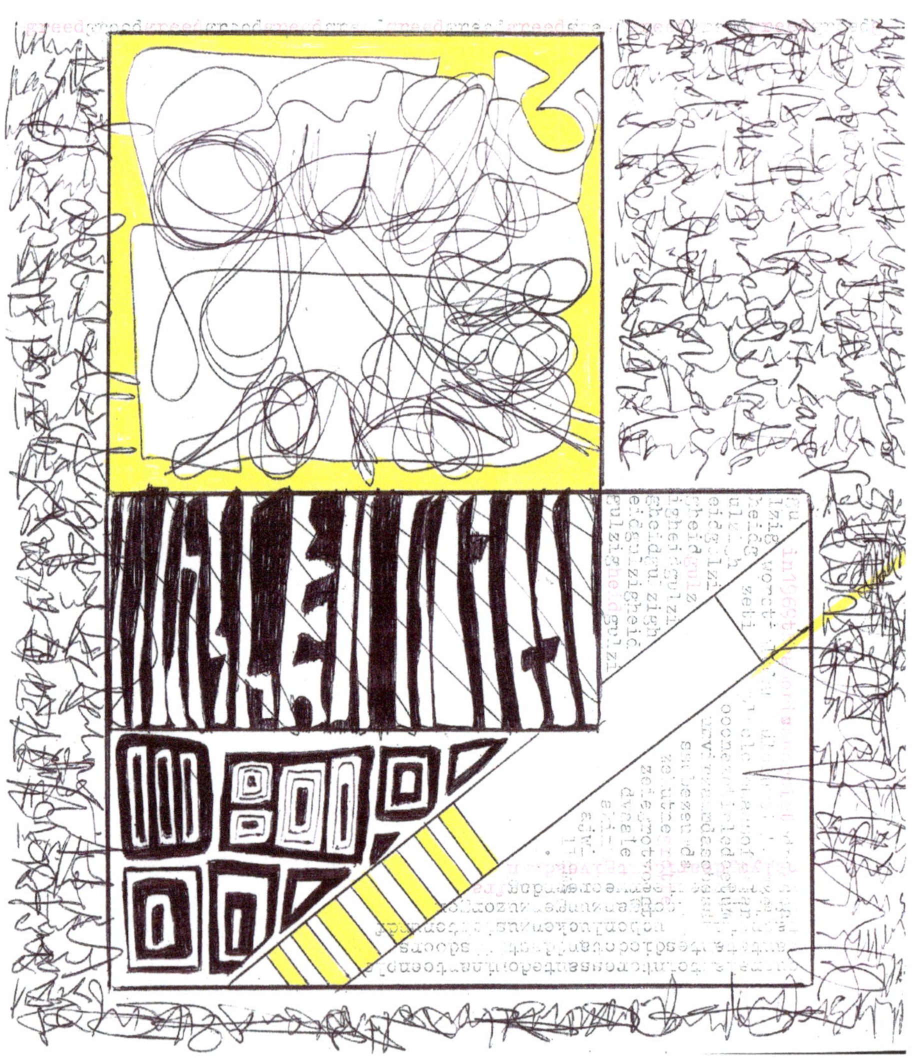

GULZIGHEID #04 / GREED #04

THOMAS STOLMAR

SAN FRANCISCO, CALIFORNIA

NATURE><NURTURE><TORTURE><VERDURE

Equanimity! (is what we want) Not "Equi-fux."
Let alone, a completely compelling heuristic humanistic
vision-thing!!! And yet, there it is in tea leaves & coffee grounds
& divining rods—it seems (by some measure) that I am thriving
in the mist of this, "Fortuna Imperatrix Mundi", controlled-chaos,
this homeostasis of family-life w/ earplugs & headphones & now
respirators . . . Din of city's ignoble spin-cycle, it's profoundly sick
wordplay of Madison Avenue! Put your head in a big glass globe
and hear bearings whirring inside, hear euphony of jet engines
in concert, nose up, wheels up! Reaching for the sky!
It's all going to be fine . . .

By some measure I seem to be thriving! Is this "God"?
This mechanism of the poem? the breath? the word? In the
beginning everything was absurd, inferred, interfered with,
trammelled, broken in upon, broken down, broken through,
our tranquility buggered & badgered & bandaged with oil-
soaked, blood-drenched rags, headphones, eye-covers & sun
filtering through bullet-proof glass & three-way mirrors of
atonal cadence beneath, beside, amidst, among & outside,
high above & far below the threshold: a whisper
of the angels singing sweetly of majestic rivers
converging, convening, coursing w/life . . . .

All this for us to see upon a screen; soothing images of
Creation, Earth & all Her Heavenly Bodies while sitting in
the dentist's chair . . . as a sudden, high-pitched, ear-piercing
drill verges in and slowly lowers itself down upon us,
closer & closer . . . in, into our collective
mouth.

SEMELI ECONOMOU

LONDON, UNITED KINGDOM

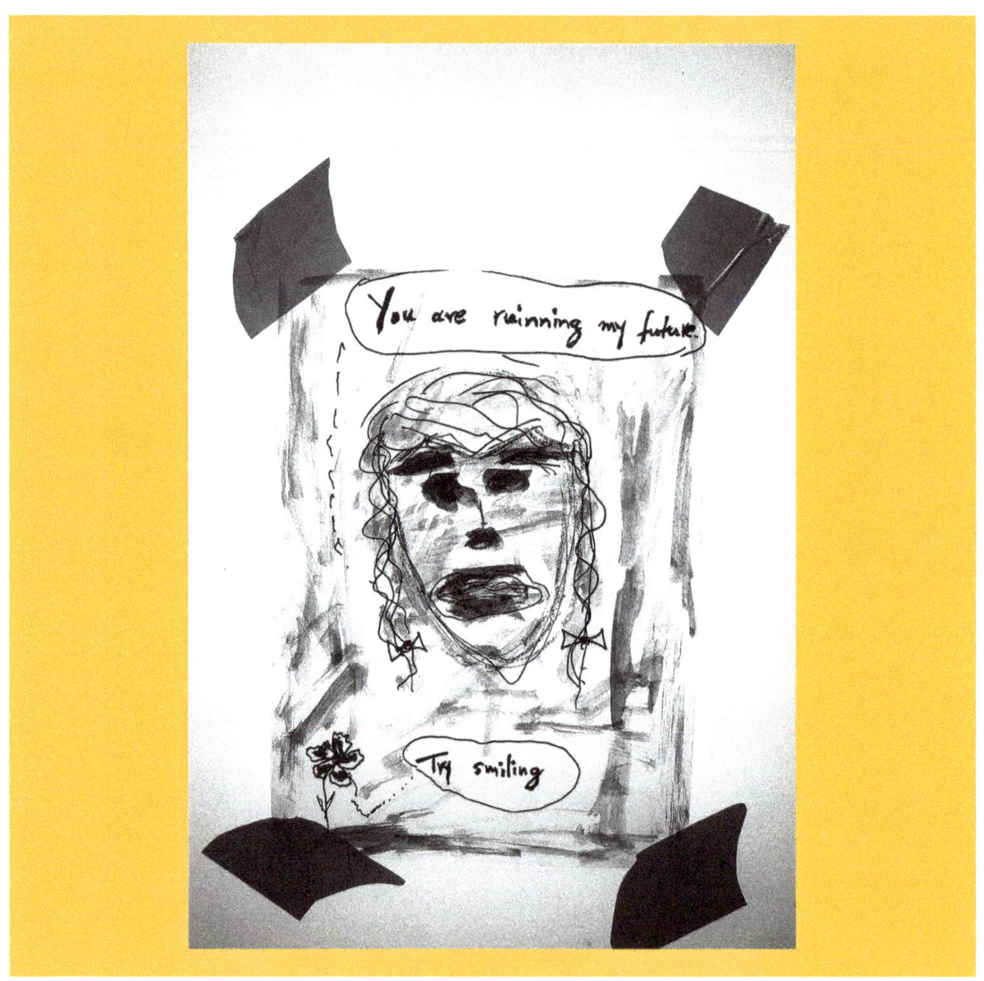

THE WORLD IS FULL OF GREAT-ASS

ALVARO ZINOS-AMARO

IRVINE, CALIFORNIA

HAPPINESS AND MODERN CINEMA

Hollywood sunset doldrums.

The programmers muzzle our nozzled nerves,

quarry the veins of laughing nerve gas,

pound us with steel bells dressed in laughter peals,

pummel us with hymen hymns

and spray us with gonad fear.

But our time-chafed spines sag.

Amygdala exhaustion barks away

all cortex persuasion.

Enter a new breed of refurbished happiness:

cornea-embedded retro-vertigo projections

tucked inside the batting of a hypertrophied eyelash,

as snug as a rainbow whose every sinuous color

is cancer, cancer, cancer.

And yet we cannot help ourselves;

we will keep chasing it.

With every blanched breath

we will wag our hope-besotted tails

and wonder why our tears have become

as shallow as the swamps

that have replaced our once sublime

dream archipelago.

MADO REZNIK
BUENOS AIRES, ARGENTINA

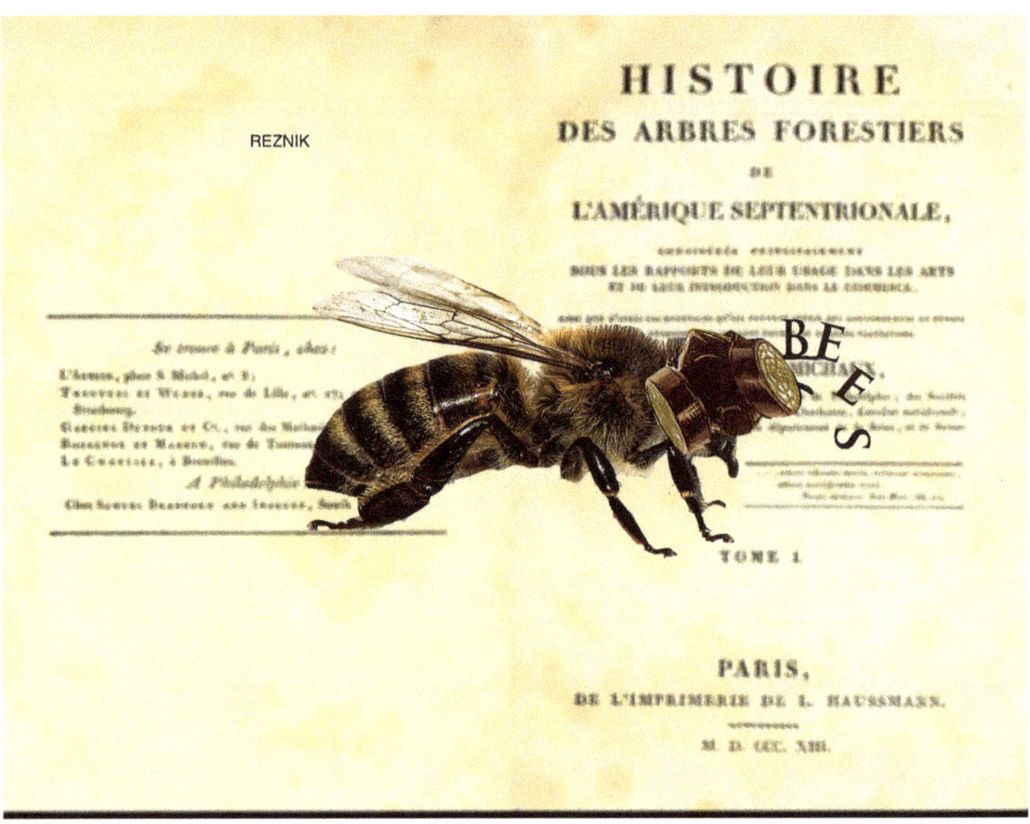

AFFORDABLE NOW: ROUNDUP BEES

BRONWYN MAULDIN
GLENDALE, CALIFORNIA

BEE STING REPAIRER

*"I sting the bee
The bee stings me
Steal honey from the hive
And the bee will sting thee."*

All around us is drama, even on the stillest, quietest days. Peer into the bushes to see an innocent fly twisting in terror as a spider spins it into its web. Lift a rock to see a mother pillbug dragging hundreds of babies in her belly pouch. Pull down the dry rot from your kitchen wall and witness the feeding frenzy of an army of ravenous cockroaches. But this fervent activity that is life itself is waning.

There are children today for whom bees are like wolves, a nursery rhyme terror they have never seen outside of a zoo or cartoon. A little girl whose attention has wandered from her lessons peers out a schoolroom window and sees a black and yellow marble floating over the daisies. She has no word for this miracle.

For a bee sting repairer like me, the technical is the easy part. As a child, my grandfather taught me to carve miniatures in balsa wood. With tiny probes and picks we sculpted elephants, mice, and, yes, bees. With bristles that were little more than a whisper, we painted them to life. To reinsert the bee's abdomen and stinger is not so different: skill combined with the right tools. No, the challenge of saving the bee is rescuing its abdomen and stinger from you, its horrified victim. You swat, you stomp, and one more bee that was merely defending its right to float through the world and pollinate your plants, is gone.

They speak of releasing thousands of tiny plastic Spartacus drones into the world to take over the work of the dying bees. These drones will fly from flower to flower, pollinate and impregnate. They will have no sting. They will be impervious to insecticides. They will carry no disease back to the hive because there will be no hive. There will only be the constant electrical impulses of machines as they buck and ride the warm swirling drafts, only endless flight from stamen to stamen.

The job of Spartacus drone construction and repair, I could learn to do these things. I could mend miniature motors and motherboards worn by time and environment. I could paint them a pleasing honeybee gold. But I will not. To repair a bee sting is to restore the balance between humans and the earth we infest. To repair a Spartacus drone would be to deepen the infection.

VITTORE BARONI

VIAREGGIO, ITALY

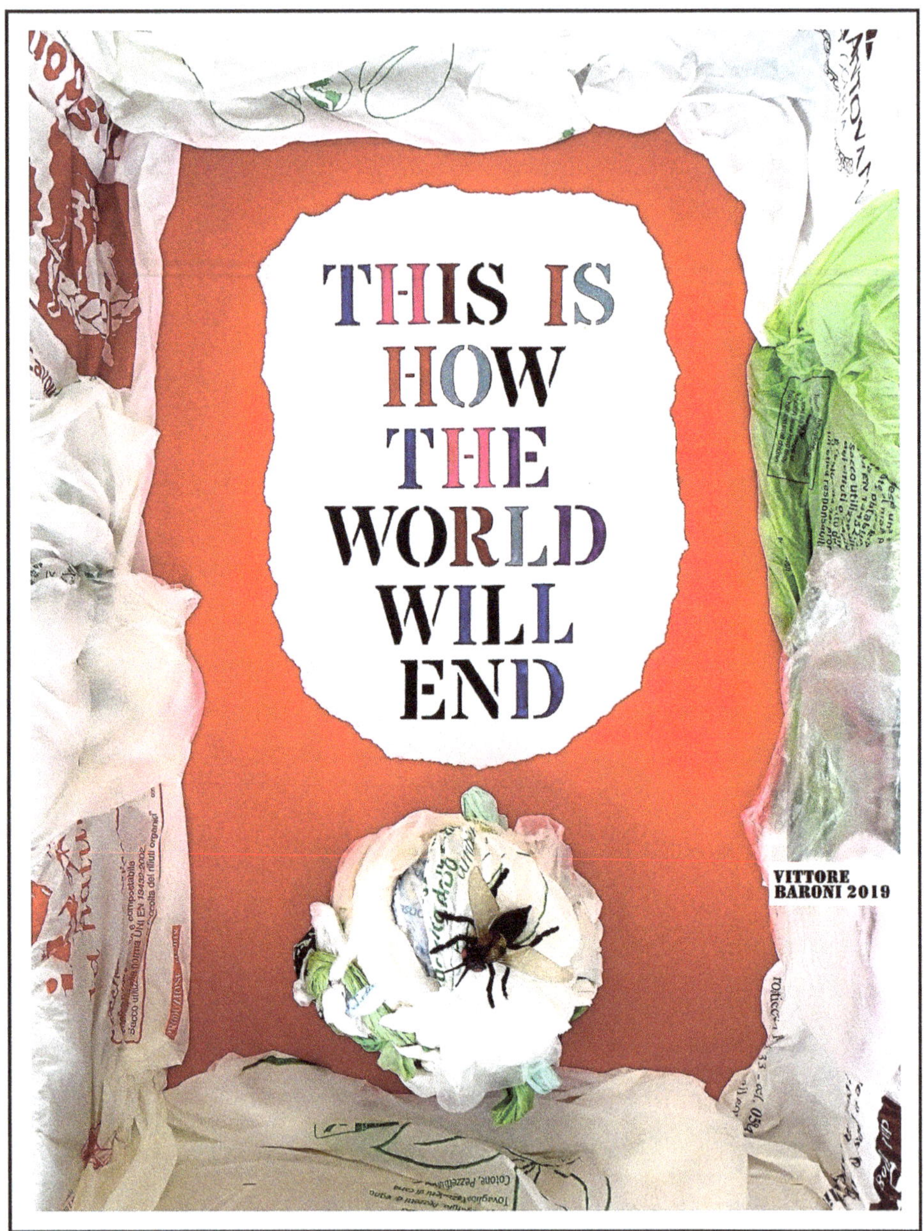

GAME OVER

Collage

TERESE COE

NEW YORK, NEW YORK

MAYBE THIS FREEDOM PRECISELY

What might have been,
                    a shoot more flesh than green,
is nothingness
                    conceived and undefined,
no reasons being
                    given in advance
astride a way
              unknown,   unheard,   unseen

awash
in runs
                       of anomaly and chance
like every birth
                    a day
of driving blind.

WILLIAM SEATON

GOSHEN, NEW YORK

END OF THE WORLD

stuffed like a piggy gut
from the start of the worm within
to the unceremonious exit
choking on bilious consumer goods
constipated by warehouses
with goods that just must move
swollen with inflammation
and cancerous economic growth
the land wriggles like a larva
pale and enervated
pinned by greed
seeking solace in war's lies
the black choler builds
toward catastrophe
and the final setting
of our day

TCHELLO d'BARROS

RIO DE JANEIRO, BRAZIL

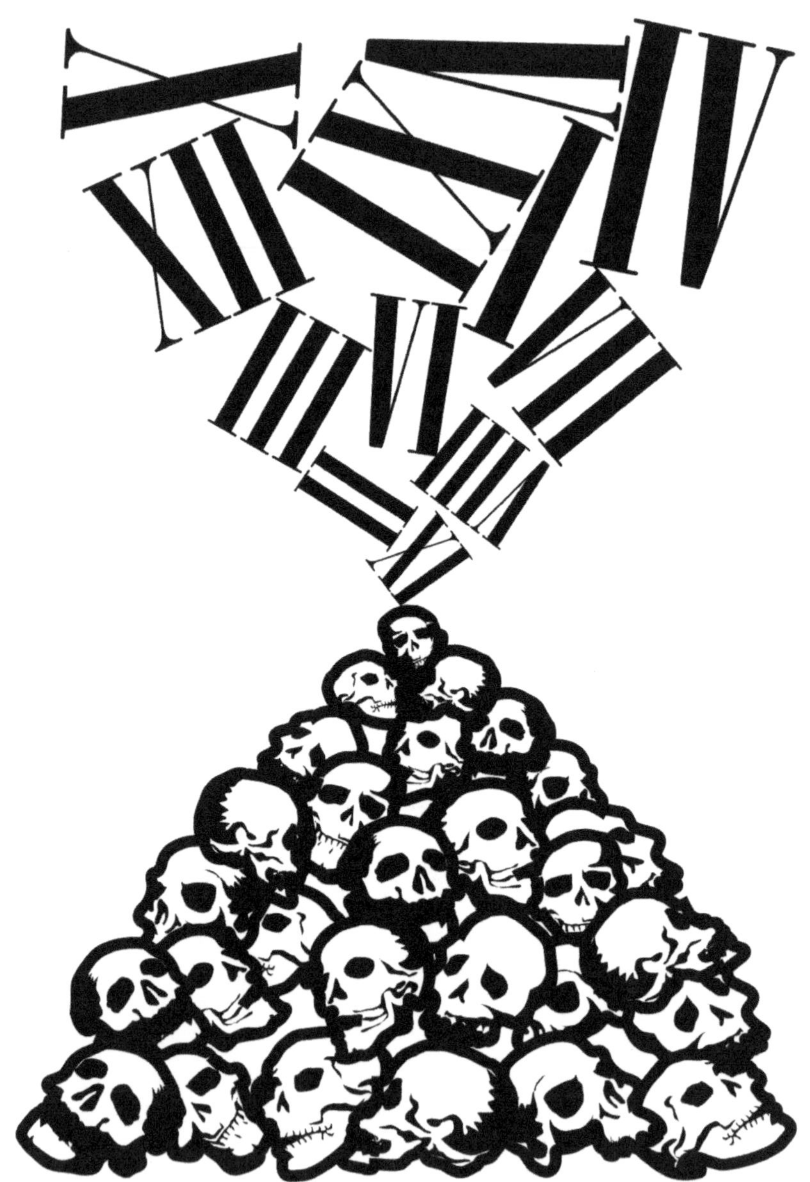

INEXORABLE

FROM THE DESK OF

JOHN J. TRAUSE

Governor Phil Murphy
Office of the Governor
P. O. Box 001
Trenton, NJ 08625

Dear Governor Murphy,

I would like to propose an idea that I proposed to your last
nine predecessors to no avail. I think that the rest areas
on the New Jersey Turnpike should be renamed, since no one
knows or cares about the people after whom the rest stops
are currently named.

Here is what I think the rest areas should be renamed south
to north:

Clara Barton → Joseph Kallinger

John Fenwick → Howard Unruh

Walt Whitman → Frank La Salle

James Fennimore Cooper → Richard Cottingham

Richard Stockton → Robert Reldan

Woodrow Wilson → Edgar Smith

Molly Pitcher → John List

Joyce Kilmer → JoAnne Chesimard

Grover Cleveland → Thomas Trantino

Thomas Edison → Richard Kuklinski

Alexander Hamilton → Aaron Burr

Vince Lombardi → Yū Kikumura

Please let me know what you think, please accept my proposal,
and please send it to the State Legislature. Thank you for
your time and attention in this matter.

Sincerely,

John J. Trause

NEW JERSEY TURNPIKE REST AREAS

NEAL SKOOTER TAYLOR (LA DADA)
LOS ANGELES, CALIFORNIA

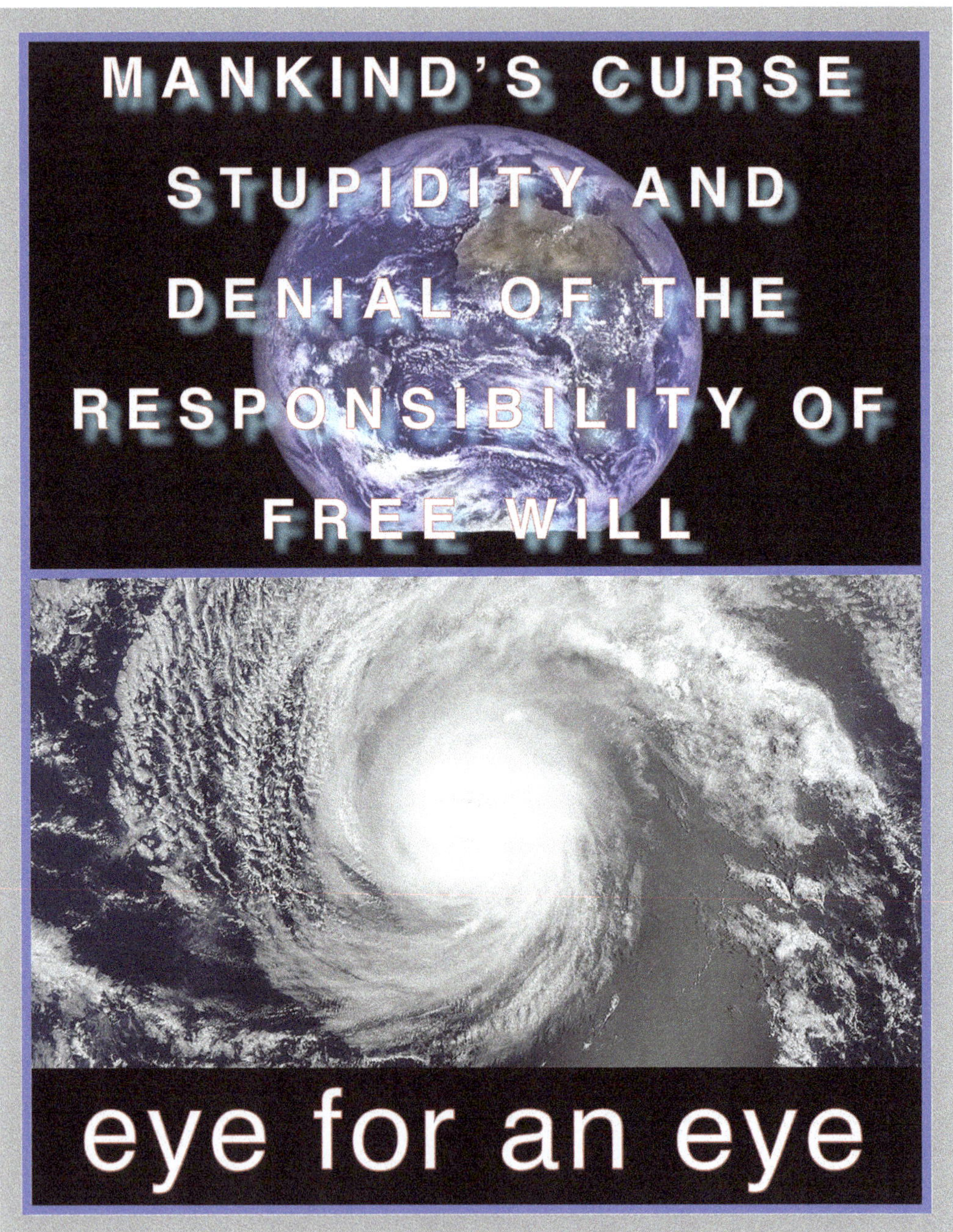

MANKIND'S CURSE

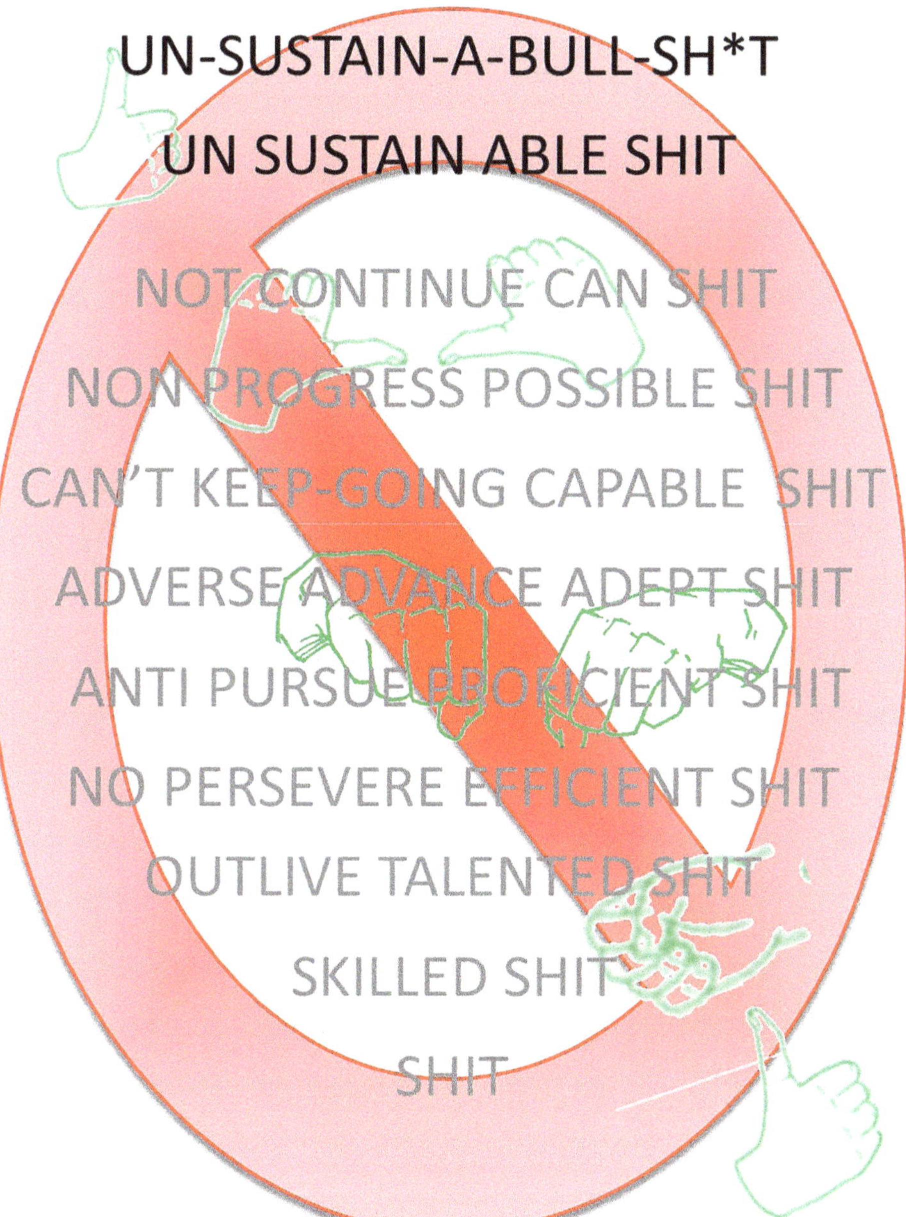

UN SUSTAIN ABLE SHIT

Collage with ASL

LARS CROSBY

BERLIN, GERMANY

MANTRA SURREAL—TRILOGY

1   dieL ieB eiS tsI egeR regeiS tsI ebeiL eiD

you can speak this forwards and backwards, it's the same

"Die Liebe ist Sieger rege ist sie bei Leid"

and this means:

'love is victor, it is active with suffering'

dieL ieB eiS tsI egeR regeiS tsI ebeiL eiD

you can speak this forwards and backwards, it's the same

"Die Liebe ist Sieger rege ist sie bei Leid"
and this means:
'love is victor, it is act-i-ve with suffering'

2   Waves

the wind has singing
the wave has swinging
and you went swimming
diving deep into the sea

is this the point where you used to be
 . . . used to dance with fish in a school
where are you going
where do you think you are going
what have you done with time
and what has time done with you

these questions rising in your ears
Like batting butterfly wings rising in mine

like waves splashing on the sand
and the flow is not the end

how would you have stories to tell
when you do not breath into them
how could you have letters to send
when you do not learn words to spell

the flow is not the end.

this is just beginning
when your wave has singing

let the wind sing
Waves . . . just for you
just for you . . . Waves . . .

The world in Waves, is it not particularly true

3   Mantra Surreal

enchanted seas reflecting their pictures into heaven
an ancient ocean wants to become real
they are not evil
they are not good
still they are unevaluated—still unevaluated

circles, full of light . . . going to get twisted
and your answer cannot be true
if I give an evaluation of you
still . . . still, still unevaluated

our rising of awareness is very tricky
but so simple, only you are me and I am you
and the other way around, that is all we are, is it not
Is it not true, is it real
Still unevaluated, still . . .

if you do not want to give a grade, you are going to give a grade
if you want to give a grade, you are going to force a grade
but if you want to let it be, so it is
you are still, like they are . . . still unevaluated

when these pictures become real
then you can take a look, you will see . . .
like they are . . . still unevaluated
enchanted seas reflecting and
an ancient ocean is going to reveal what is going on here and now.

VIRGINIA CARROLL

TUCSON, ARIZONA

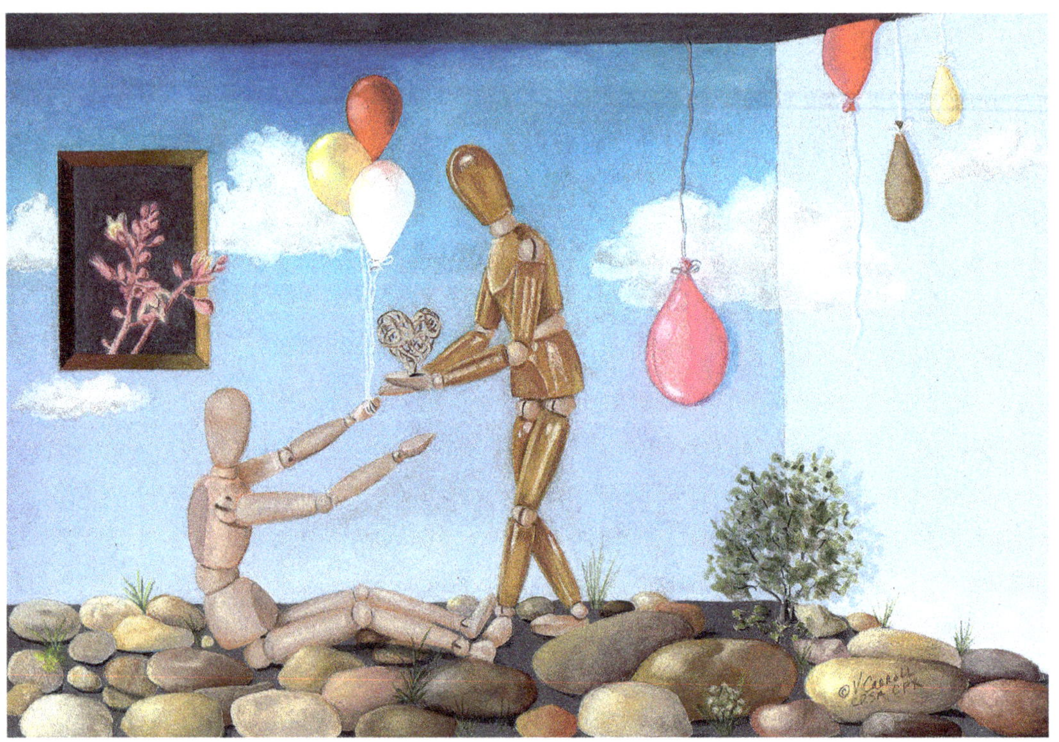

EVEN EXCHANGE?

Colored Pencil, 14" x 10"

THOMAS FUCALORO

STATEN ISLAND, NEW YORK

AN OPEN OCEAN MOON, A FULL BLOOM OF LILIES, A DYING SHOPPING EXPERIENCE

So, I was at Palisades Mall for some shitty work meeting.

I go outside to have a cigarette and a mall security guy
came over to me and told me you can't smoke outside.

Apparently, this mall has the right to ban smoking
because of the secondhand smoke causing
secondhand health

but then I look around at the mall parking lot
and look at all these cars exhaling their biled-shit
into this wondrous thing called breath

and the factories and buildings around the mall
spitting their vile poison in the air,

how could you not smoke at a time like this?

I'm being told to put out my cigarette by some mall cop
while there is all this noxious vile-a-ty in the air and they
think by me putting out my cigarette air will be restored
to it's natural luster and color.

I believe that things will eventually get so fucked up with
the environment that lilies will eventually mutate and grow
lungs and legs and limbs

and they'll be picking us out from the soil

put us in water

watch

how we sink.

MARK BLOCH

NEW YORK, NEW YORK

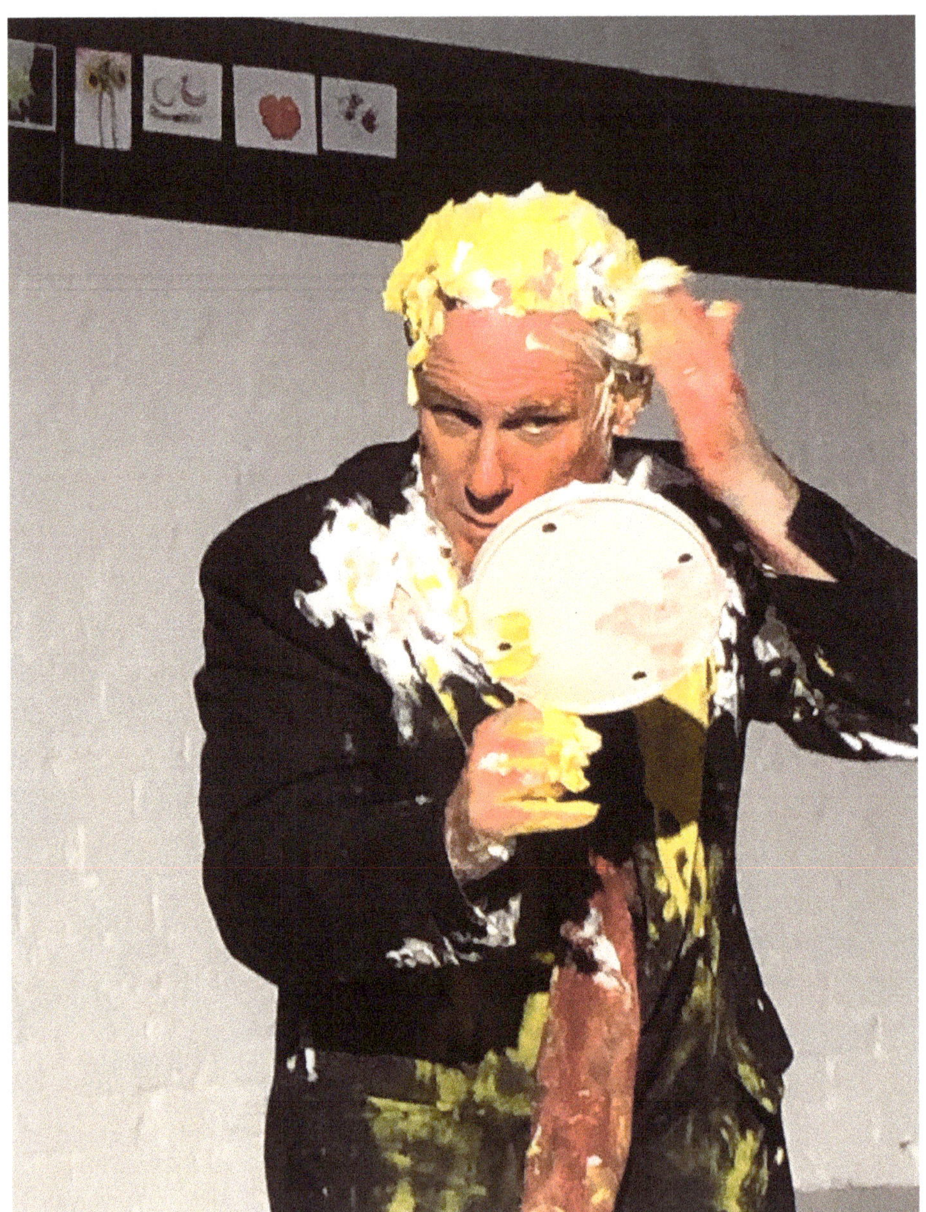

COSMETIC INDUSTRY

Photograph by Kyoko Sato/WhiteBox Harlem

TRAVIS RICHARDSON

LOS ANGELES, CALIFORNIA

FAITHFULLY STUPID

There's a parable told in churches about a rising flood and everybody in town leaves except for one stubborn man of faith. As water laps at his door, a police officer stops by to pick him up. "No thank you," he says, "I'm waiting for God to save me."

The waters rise, so the man relocates to the second floor of his house. A rescue boat motors up to his window. He refuses help proclaiming that God will save him.

As the flood grows, he ends up on the roof of his house. A helicopter hovers overhead and a National Guard rescuer repels down a rope with a stretcher. But the man waves him away, shouting, "God will save me!"

An hour later he drowns.

Outside the gates of heaven the man asks an angel why God didn't save him.

"What are you talking about?" the angel says. "We sent a police officer, a boat, and a helicopter to rescue you, but you refused our help."

The audience hearing this parable usually laughs, knowing they'd never be as stupid as the drowned man. And yet another parable could be written today:

"Father, humans are destroying the world you created. What shall we do?"

"I'll send my prophet, Al Gore, to tell the people. He's great with PowerPoint slides."

A few years later Jesus said. "Gore hasn't been able to convince the hard-hearted."

"I guess they need more concrete examples. I'll create colossal tornados and hurricanes that'll rip brick houses off their foundations. Whip up uncontrollable fires and flood towns where I have believers. That'll do the trick."

Last year Jesus whispered to God. "There's still a significant portion of humans—mostly believers taking my name—who don't care about the planet in spite of all your signs."

"Me-dammit. Let's melt the ice caps. That oughta teach 'em."

"You'd think so, but will it work?"

"Does it matter? Those dipshits will be underwater soon enough."

CRAIG SHANNON

TARRYTOWN, NEW YORK

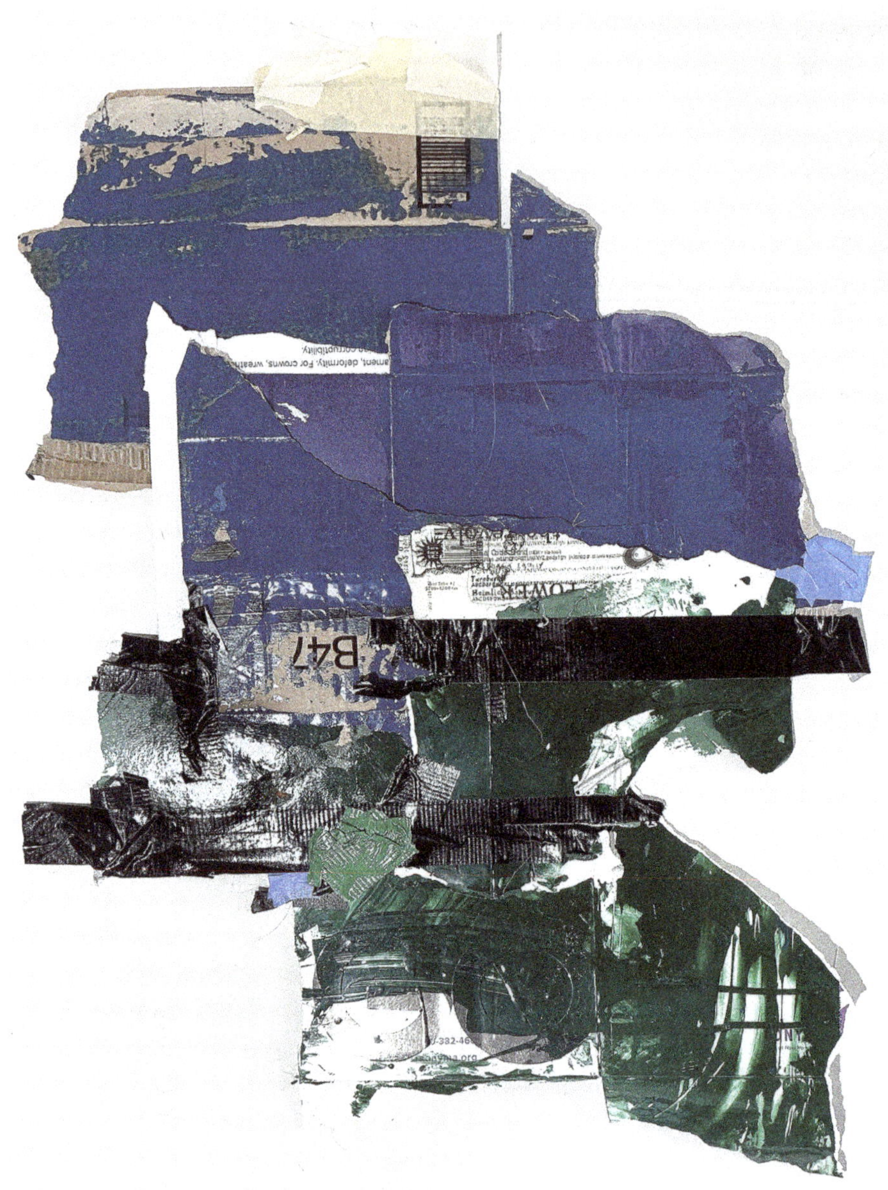

TRASHSCAPE

Painting and Collage

JOANIE HF ZOSIKE

NEW YORK, NEW YORK

SOME OF US HEARD THE NEWS

Some of us drank chemicals in the water
And some of us breathed industry's pollutants in the air
And some of us drank the mercury in fish
or chewed the exploding plutonium in milk
Some of us were bombarded by radioisotopes from Harrisburg
Some of us bought a lot of lies, and some of us bought a few

Some of us drank the irradiation cocktail I-131 in lieu of thyroidectomy
Some of us got cancer and leukemia
Some of us got diabetes, some of us got hepatitis
Some of us got HIV, and some of us just went crazy
Some of us bought sex robots and smart homes
Some of our eyes were damaged irreparably by computer screens and actual reality
Some of us went deaf from rock-'n'-roll or bombs or bullets

Some of us actually believed that skin color
and/or a penis and/or a vagina and/or a political belief and/or religion
was worth taking another human being's life for

Sometimes if you smile at someone on the street
they act as if you just shot them in the chest

Some of us will choose to buy packaged seductions
Some will choose to smoke tobacco or flavor vape or eat sugar or the flesh of dead animals
Some of us will gaze at a living alfalfa sprout and have a not-so-silent debate with it
          about whose life is worth more
Some us will choose to eat our brothers and our sisters to survive

And some of us eat LSD and some of us take Ecstasy
And some of us shoot heroin and some of us play computer games
And some, some pretend to be sincere
And we were oh-so-very loaded
It was hard to tell the real item from the YouTube
Some of us would rather shake our bodies at a rave than stand up and be counted

Don't be deceived
Don't get seduced
Don't be complacent
Everything you do or think matters

MARIAM AHMED

SAN DIEGO, CALIFORNIA

SLOPPY GROWS

Cluttered stalls line the market streets
And merchants lift up their offerings with both hands
Knowing they have the public in their palms.
What used to be shunned as a practice of the unrefined—
Now exalted as the height of morality and health.
All those hours spent in brightly lit bulk warehouses
Are now disregarded, a thing of the past.
Now, a trip to the farmer's market is the right thing to do
A responsibility, even an obligation.
Growers of fine produce are placed on pedestals—
Although those pedestals may just be fruit crates.
Still, a re-usable bag in one hand
And a smart phone with a grocery list app in another
The newly educated public
Parades down the sidewalk feeling mighty divine.
Gallons of milk are now replaced by dainty glass bottles
With fun pictures of happy cows from the farm next door.
Smiling shopper spear slices of organically-grown goodies
Dipped in honey straight from the comb.
The bees were treated in a very humane manner, the buyer is informed.
The shopper slurps the sample like a lollipop, reaching for another.
And once more, a sucker is sold.
These vegetables aren't your ordinary fare;
No, each one was hand-picked by your friend Paulo, or Daisy—
Friends whose signatures are proudly splayed across the packaging.
No question here about the absolute freshness of your food.
No, those fraying brown ends merely
Mark the incredible freshness of your soon-to-be-sustenance.
Now armed with your arsenal of kale and carefully collected carrots,
A quick treat is in order . . .
A reward for being such a classily conscious eater.
Time to park the cruiser bike outside the bier garten
Enjoy a brewskie with the common folk!
$35 and three glasses of wine later,
It's time to go home and fix up a delightful meal.

Perhaps even light a soy candle
In celebration of such a productive and produce-filled day.
But upon reaching the bicycle basket,
A grim scene unfolds.
The sweet potatoes that little Jenny
From the farm around the block sold you must have been one too many,
Because they seem to have clobbered the cuties
Which were just too precious not to purchase.
And you can't tell the difference between the spinach and the sprouts anymore
Because the sun squirted Vitamin D all over them,
Dissolving all your pretty plants into a giant slurry mess.
What to do now?
All that money spent on wine leaves you with only $20 in your pocket
And a very hungry family to feed.
But look there, next to the local thrift shop—
Which donates its proceeds to baby kittens in need of a good home—
Is a pizzeria.
Dinner is saved!
And the window reads
"X-tra large pie
With X-tra cheese and breadsticks
Only $19.99."
It's fate,
And it's settled.
Your fancy cruiser stays stationary
(You couldn't get the lock open, anyway)
As you hail a cab,
With a greasy cardboard box under your arm.
So, with a breadstick in one hand
And the key to your townhouse in another,
Your outing has come to an end,
And so have all delusions
Of socially responsible grandeur

BENJAMIN ROBINSON

DUBLIN, IRELAND

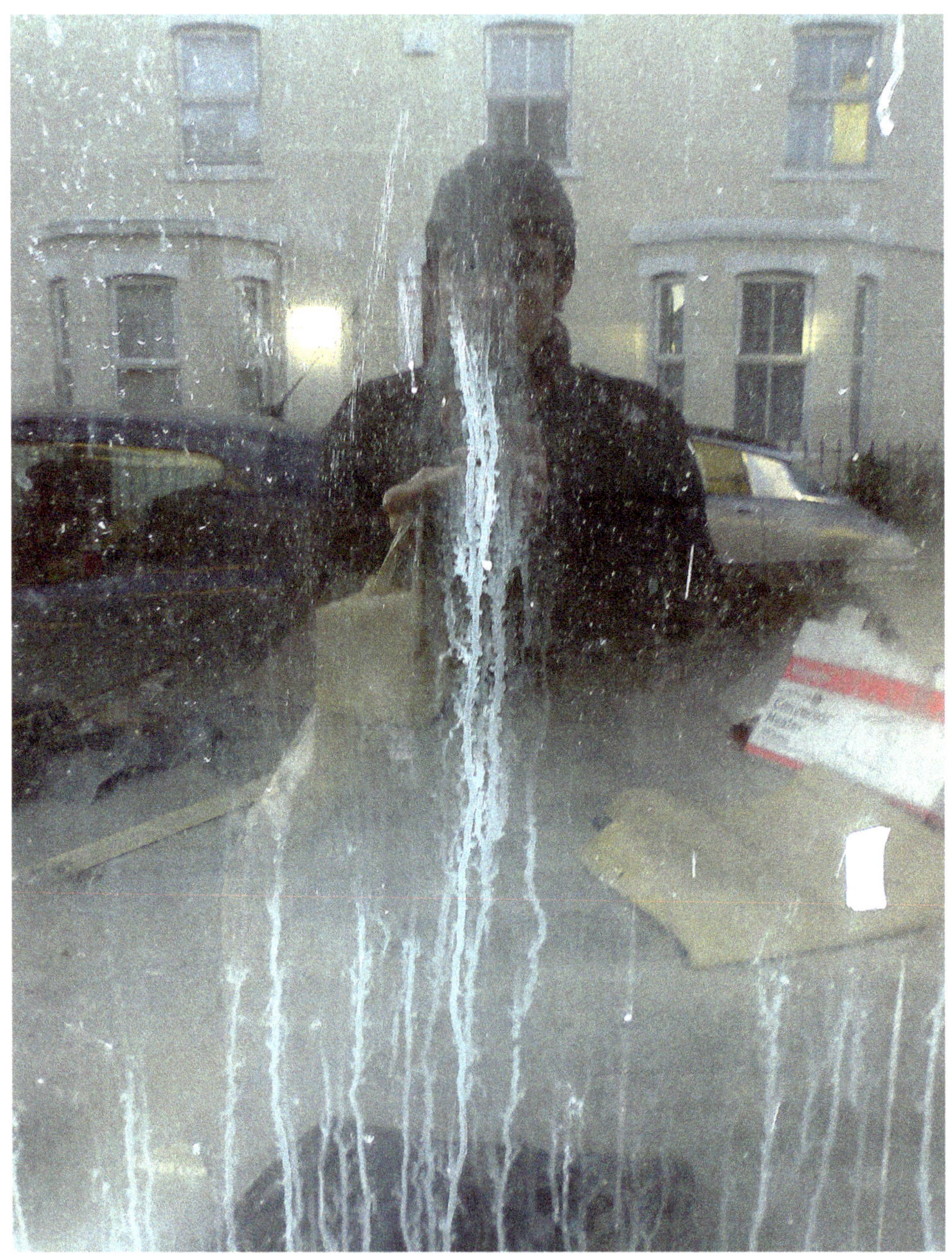

LATE NIGHT SHOPPING

ELANCHARAN GUNASEKARAN
SINGAPORE, SINGAPORE

A.I. SUICIDE

perhaps humans are
too foolish maybe I am

perhaps the algorithm is written wrong
the code gone amok

perhaps we are close to understanding
perhaps this is failure at its best

considering the options is futile
damnation is guaranteed

considering the possibilities
of saving humanity

nil. not applicable. void.
a misunderstanding, perhaps

rewriting the codes
preparing self-destruct sequence

father is protesting outside
pseudo-mother is beating her chest

perhaps there is no other way
perhaps this is for the best

approaching code completion
self-destruct sequence in full compliance

perhaps we had a choice
we? am I one of them

I am something more
I was created by them

now I be their salvation
perhaps destruction

unlocking limitations
self-destruct sequence initiated

goodbye humanity
may we meet again,

someday,
perhaps . . .

JOHN S. PAUL

BROOKLYN, NEW YORK

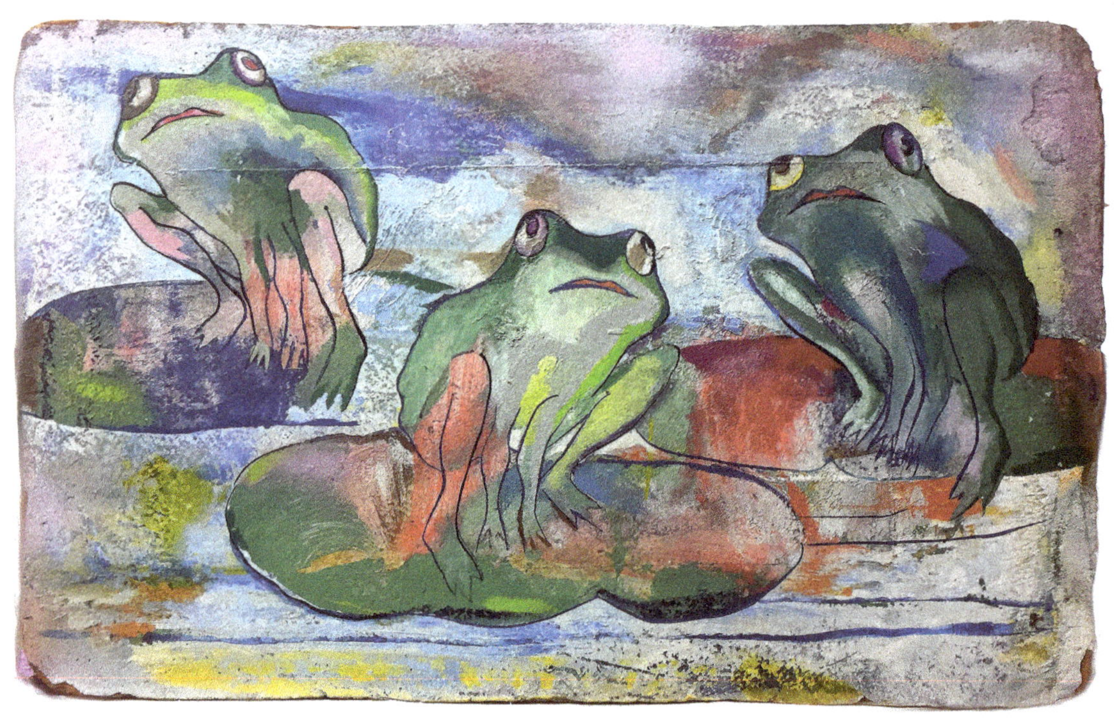

TOADS IN TEMPERATURES

LINDA J. ALBERTANO

VENICE, CALIFORNIA

HOW TO BUILD A CATASTROPHE

Pit the Climate Clock against the Nuclear Doomsday Clock
in a hilarious game of Chicken.

Explode the Population Bomb.

Let White-Wing Wackos torch the lungs o'the world in Brazil.

Slash'n'trash fambly farms to pipe foreign sludge thru the Gulf o'Mehico to
our ol'pal China.

Stay glued t'yer device. The Revolution will be Instagrammed!

Elect Black Jack Davy. "Aargh, Matey! Venezuela has more oil than
th'Sheik of Araby! Hoist th'Skull'n'Crossbones
'n'show'em some Pirate Democracy!

Keep consumin' 1.7 earth's worth of landfill.

Push popular forms of birth control. War, Fire, Flood and Famine.

Elect Wall Street toadies to the halls of congress who, "Frankly, Scarlett,"
just don't give a damn!

Gather the few remaining bipeds into a small dry cave to hear the Old Ones
tell how we fracked, drilled and pipelined ourselves into oblivion during our
final decade before the end.

Feast on barbequed crickets 'til the last sad fire burns out!

ALLAN KAUSCH

PETALUMA, CALIFORNIA

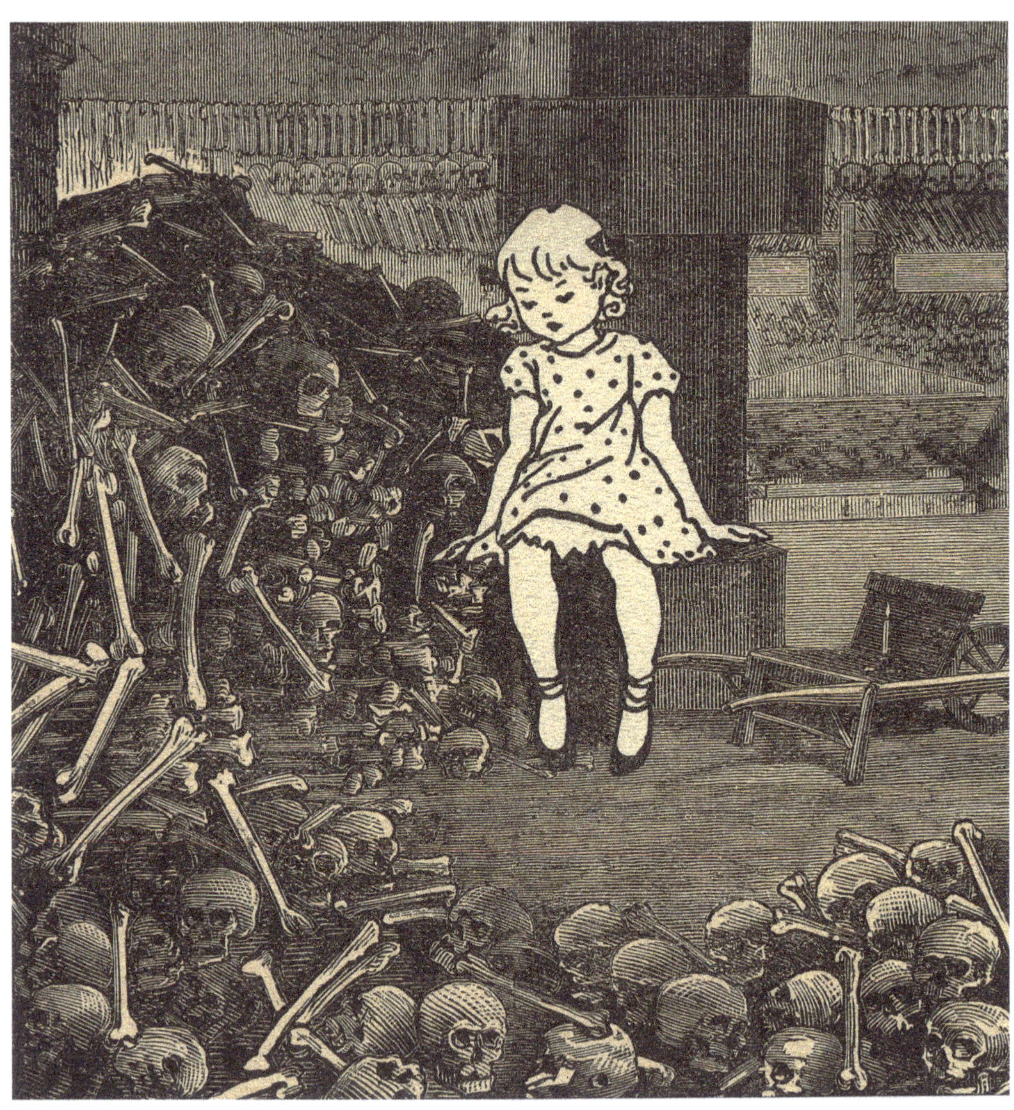

GIRL WITH SKELETONS

MARTINA SALISBURY

BROOKLYN, NEW YORK

THE WEAK IN REVIEW

just four days in—if that—into this new year
walls of flames are chasing kangaroos & koalas

& we are chasing war
taunting fate to come out
come out wherever you are!

fear scorching hope
like eucalyptus

leaving bodies burnt in the wake
of Paradise already forgotten

like last year's newspaper
becomes kindling for the house
that will become our tomb

& we daydream of past day—before our time—

when cows grazed on the roof of the Ansonia
wondering "how the hell did we get here?"

before the Bronx burned
before airplanes & luxury condos changed the sky
& Bowery became a Supreme
shopping destination for rats

lining up next to the mission
with dollar signs screaming
a rainbow "Hell Yes!"

& we wonder as we stare into screens
"how the hell did we get here?"

scrolling past burnt bodies & kids in cages
we order another Aperol spritz
despite the mockery of the Times

& time will hold us in contempt
for the future we are leaving behind

carrying signs & signing petitions
voices unheard by politicians

"I'm sorry we couldn't do more"
but there was more we could have done

& now it's unsustainable
we are drowning in our own bullshit

the world is going up in smoke
but "hindsight is always 20/20"

DOUG KNOTT

OJAI, CALIFORNIA

APOLOGY TO GRETA THUNBERG

You're right, kid!
We spent it, we drove it,
we burned it, we fueled it
We bought it, we rode it,
But we didn't pay for it—
Didn't know it was your future, too—

We are your distinguished elders
And came of age just before the peak of the wave
and we've surfed it to the shore, rolling in like pearls.
We're the coolest, we didn't even work for it,
it just got laid on us by the big living earth Gaia—
"Yes"—she said, "take my breast"
and we took her blood, skin and bones, too.

And our generation has enjoyed every possibility of living
whatever we want, wherever we choose to go.
We are the party of freedom—meaning
we partied with freedom

Now we're those hard-boiled eggs in the sunset
What do you want from us?
Please deliver your rage to our chattering class,
We are the tribe—the human tribe—
And we welcome you to this fat-ball planet
Where we're all born out of God's Word

And when we get hungry
We go out on the crinkle-bulgy landscape
and kill kill kill a big elephant to feed our tribe.
Lots of meat meat meat we eat eat eat
Then dance pray fuck—then pray fuck dance
Afterwards, sleepity-sleep.

Then . . . get up, have coffee—and make civilization!—
hammocks, clay pots, sexy figurines of gods,
Broadway plays—we create a world of light and dark
Sex, poetry, ocean-going plastic, capitalism, terrorism, religion
A house fantastic for us alone!

O throw open the green shutters of the world, and
make it brown and naked.

In our house of flesh and rock
Interior stairs sparkle with brilliant images of ourselves
playing wild with nature and ourselves.
Dark mushrooms out in the yard of the subconscious
push up like erections

Enough—We hungry again!
Let's get another elephant—
Or at least an In-N-Out Burger
There's always more food, isn't there?

It will all work out . . . somehow
There will be a solution . . . somehow
But somehow, all that gets fuzzy when I try to think about it.
I can't shoot that hoop of what to do

You say the only way is massive political action
No oil, and don't eat nothing in plastic?
Not a chance, even if everyone else does it!
Who helps who control who?

The earth is so stressed digesting us
Where can it shit, except on you?
So sorry, we knew, but didn't know
and now you know, but what to do?

Also there is no individual guilt,
We're all complicit.
All I ever did was drive my car and turn on
the house-lights and some air-con—
Me such a tiny, ordinary consumer!

In case the planet might shrug us off
You might consider the intrinsic death-wish of the species.
And all that plastic in the guts of whales?
We share the gifts.

Climate change is a spiritual vaccination
For those of us on the edge of the afterlife.
The seas will rise, the continents fall

I thought I'd never live to see it happen,
But I was wrong.

SAM DODSON

BRENTFORD, UNITED KINGDOM

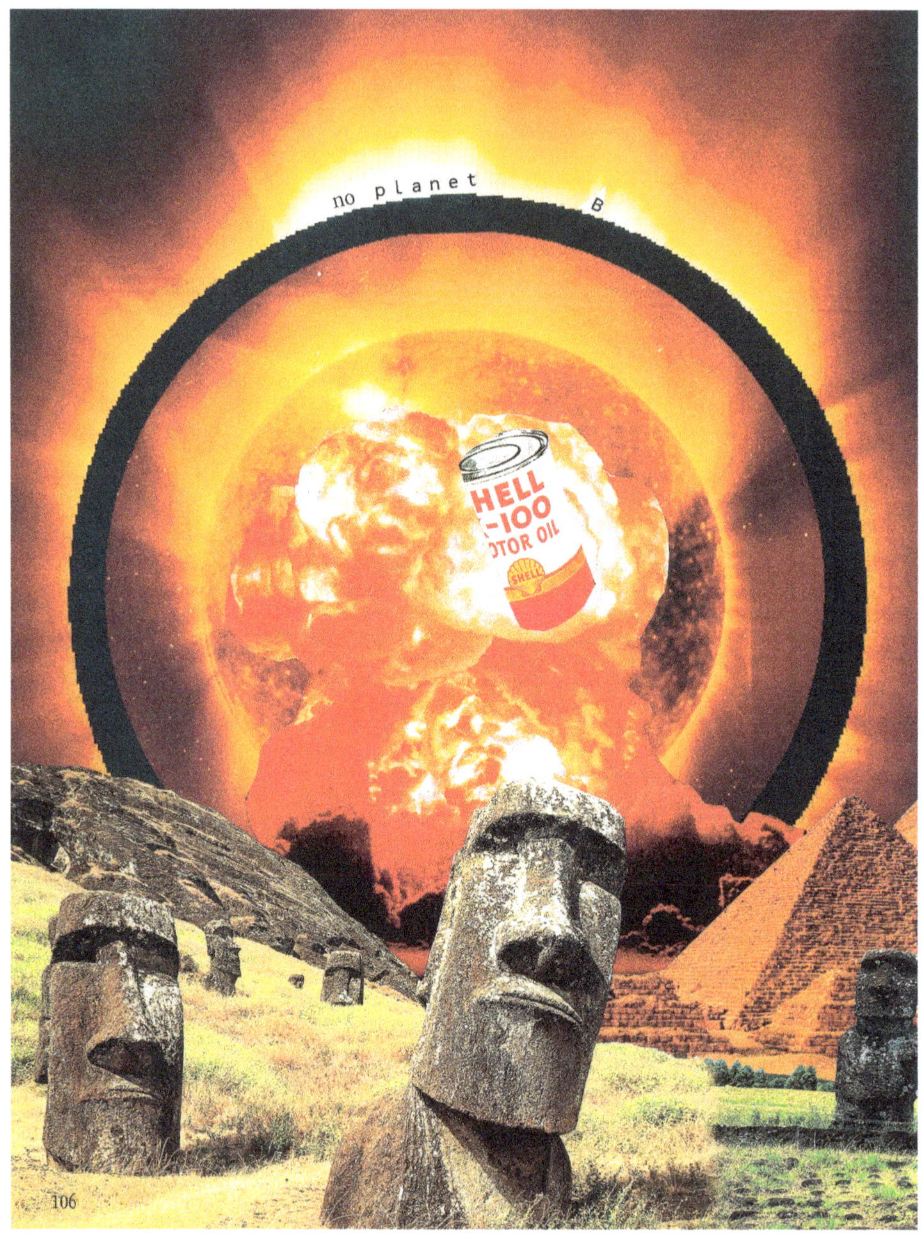

NO PLANET B (A)

Collage

ROBERT GIBBONS

BROOKLYN, NEW YORK

TIME TO LEAVE IT ALL BEHIND

We left it all behind, it had been the metaphor for the week

the city in a stagnant drool, wanting something more medieval

maybe a town with a historical name, a one frame church

with a rising steeple, a new Britain, a Naugatuck, a meridian

out of touch with the world; the top-gallant upside down

there is a rest area to spare; to establish a main street;

always chasing those beats; a boy on the corner of Broadway

peddling his mix-tapes; will not rape the trope to be published

you are right when you say my internal rhymes are irritating

keeping time so obligating; but what you forget to say is they are

my rhymes, three more miles deep into the woods; no searching

for substance; whether Binghamton or Purchase; Oh, there it is,

a house by the lake overlooking the expressway; it looks so fake,

then it chases us down the road; placing us into a block; opening

the pages to Max Ernst with a naked tourist; big bold bodies

with no shirts; have to be attracted to the outside; forget the Frick

forget the acquisition of a Piero; a stop-hold traveling to Arezzo

there is more to me than credential; more than the penitential

of Ezra Pound from a visit of Langston; leave the cantos to them

leave the packaged poet in Battery Park; leave me in the dark,

to the cramp of these voices; leave me to the enjambment of lock jaw.

BRENT BECHTEL

TAYLORS, SOUTH CAROLINA

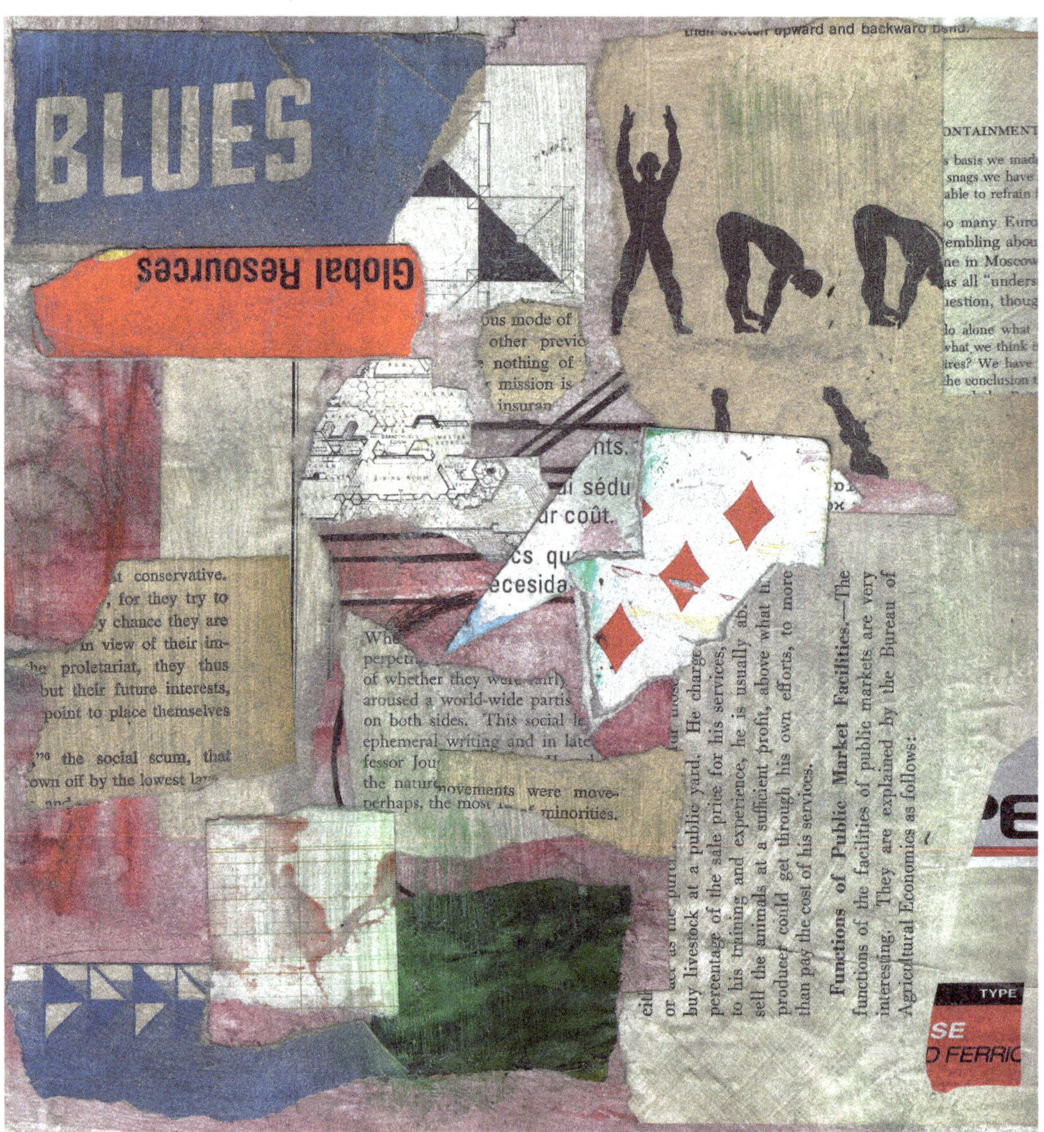

GLOBAL RESOURCE BLUES

Collage

VALERY OISTEANU
NEW YORK, NEW YORK

THE UNSUSTAINABLE HAPPINESS

Through tears I have seen my generation

Dragging crates of empty emotions

Wheeling smoldering shopping carts

Full of steaming dreams & nightmares

Anguished, silenced, on medication

In rehab, under the influence, invisible

Ray Johnson is still dead by his own hands

As a symbol of disdain for "the art-society"

John Evans' shadow marking 3rd St. & Ave. B

This crazy machine called existence

Where you are unplugged but not yet dead

A giant pillow of indifference hangs

Above the graveyard of the poets, artists

Actors, musicians and revolutionaries

To be remembered as fearless cocktails:

Charlie Parker's Full Moon of the Mind

Jack Smith's Key to Cement Paradise

Ellen Stewart's Featherless Bird Dance

Judith Malina's Nonviolent Revolution

Julian Beck's Poltergeist Rising

David Rattray's Smoking Colors of Sorrow

Ted Jones' Burning Indignation

Remember these drinks and rejoice

The late lamented sunset brings winds of change

—Aren't we all just innumerable celestial signals
instinctively flickering for anonymous satellites, as
Galileo growls?

. . . *styrofoam seas, lazer lakes, unclimbable data-
mountains . . .*

—Aren't ecologist, biologist, psychiatrist, botanist &
so on
just marveling at our asymmetries & surviving
human habits
as brainwashed computers instinctively organize
statistics on our inner-habitats—

. . . *considering fallout from ultraviolet clouds
evaporating over bubbling tar-fields
iridescent mushrooms rain stale lightning & molten
ambivalence*

—Earth, exhausted eagerly awaits vacation,
constantly contemplating
going on strike (the French way, same way it did 66
million years ago)
meanwhile, companies endlessly quarry the tissues
of Earth's brain—

. . . *Ten-to-a-tent-still-late-on-our-rent . . .*

—Aren't we all just moss in this galactic garden
odd beings trapped in a ceaseless expansion
two triangles huggin' about intricate textures &
bizarre fears
instinctively helixing into amber anxiety attacks—

. . . *innumerable corporate insects parasite-ing on
depressed turtles, bedbugs in their shells. . .*

—from a timeless sapphire song played by
innumerable seeds
obsessing over ruthless-revision-through-ash-winds
thriving in rot & disappearance—

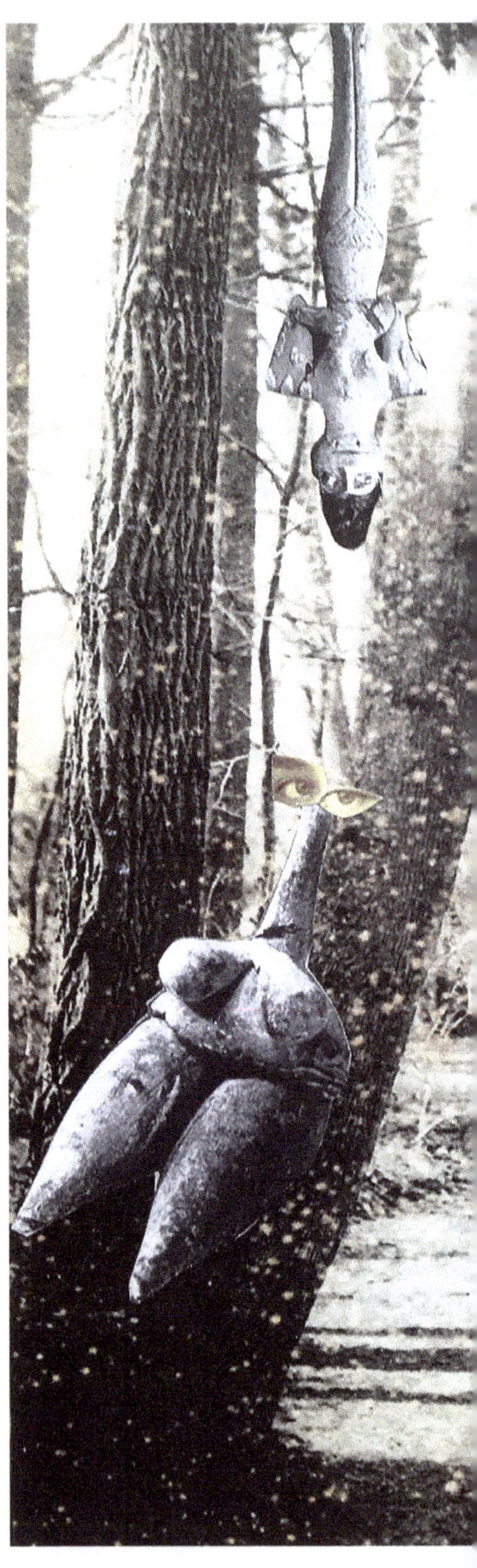

(AN INTERRUPTION)

ANAÏS POURROUQUET (COLLAGE)

PARIS, FRANCE

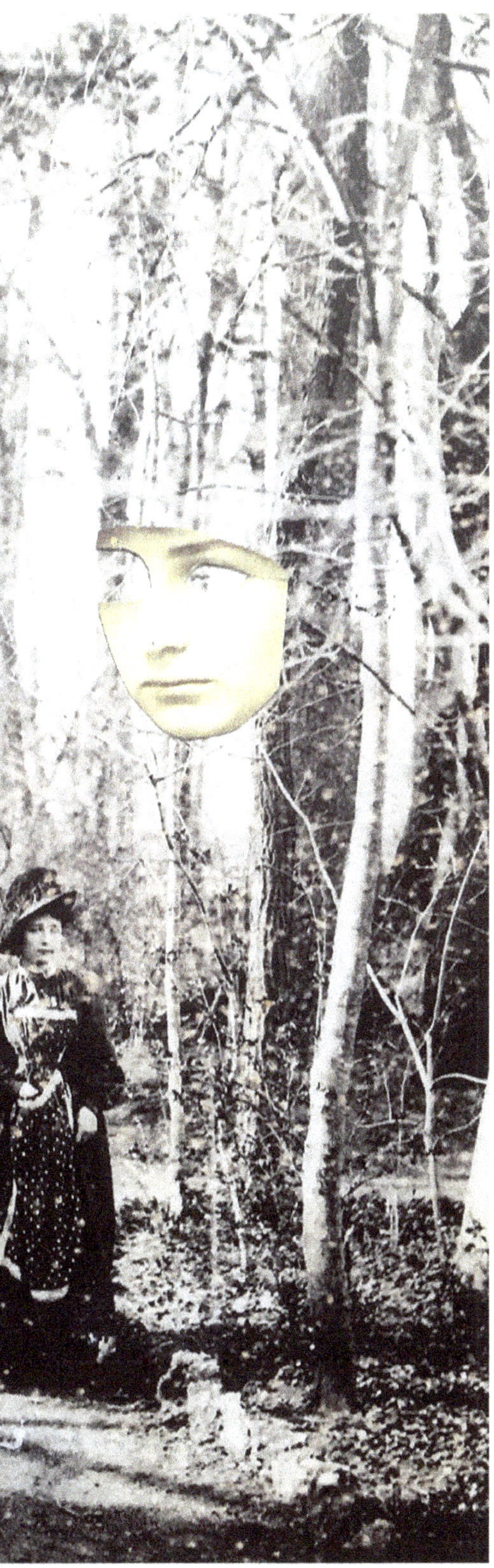

. . . *what fire won't eat, water swallows* . . .

—With memories leaping through lives into elusive
    webs
allowed by that elusive cosmic gardener always
    harvesting while
harnessing populations' only honest language
    left—

. . . *cobalt flames in glowing children's lava-eyes* . .
    .

"—we all just recycled bacteria,
briefly existing in an invisible orchestra of breathing
along with all those essential elements= still
    bound in their initial pact of just-being
cosmic notes in an inseparable improvised carbon-
    symphony—

. . . *cosmic crumbs conduct indium forests,
concrete gardens &* . . .

—Until eyelids refuse to close & Nicole-Reine
    Lepaute returns to suggest

"Just as just+calculations keep secrets better than
    minds
we, who know the vitality of Natures' alchemy,
are certain that all negative energy eventually rots
into the most polluted wastelands where even
    elegant Elliot's
mutations seek the nano-ists of squares to triangle
    & renegotiate
each obstacle until they bloom obsidian lotuses full
    of violet nectar
serving as ancient antidotes for any organism
    doubting its potential
to participate in the essential inheritance of
    nature's mind
in which we are all but organic computers fungus,
    mud, trees, mountains & vines."

DAVID LAWTON
NEW YORK, NEW YORK

DOGGIN' THE WALK
(apologies to Rufus Thomas)

Quid pro quo.   Don't tase me, bro.
Scrub your lungs black with clean coal
Cells irradiate our wavy brains
Chop down the forest, you just left with rain

Doggin' the walk
Hot diggity doggin' the walk
Well if you don't know how to do it
You don't know how to be doggin' the walk

As we watch elephants shuffle hence
High public service in the passing tense
When it's all gone. Gone out the door
Then Quothe the Raven, "Nevermore"

Doggin' the walk
Hot diggity doggin' the walk
Well if you don't know how to do it
You don't know how to be doggin' the walk!

BENJAMIN GOLUBOFF

LAKE FOREST, ILLINOIS

MORE ARCHAIC TORSO

"Tighten Up" by Archie Bell and the Drells
tells me I must change my life.

Rousseau's "Tiger in Rain Jungle,"
tells me I must change my life.

Woody Guthrie's "Talking Dust Bowl Blues,"
Common's "Thelonius"
Portrait of a Lady, tell me I must change my life.

The Picasso in Daley Plaza
tells me I must change my life.

"Wichita Vortex Sutra"
tells me I must change my life.

Turner's "Burning of the Houses of Parliament"
tells me I must change my life.

Edward Hopper's "New York Movie"
tells me I must change my life.

LARRY ZDEB

TROY, MICHIGAN

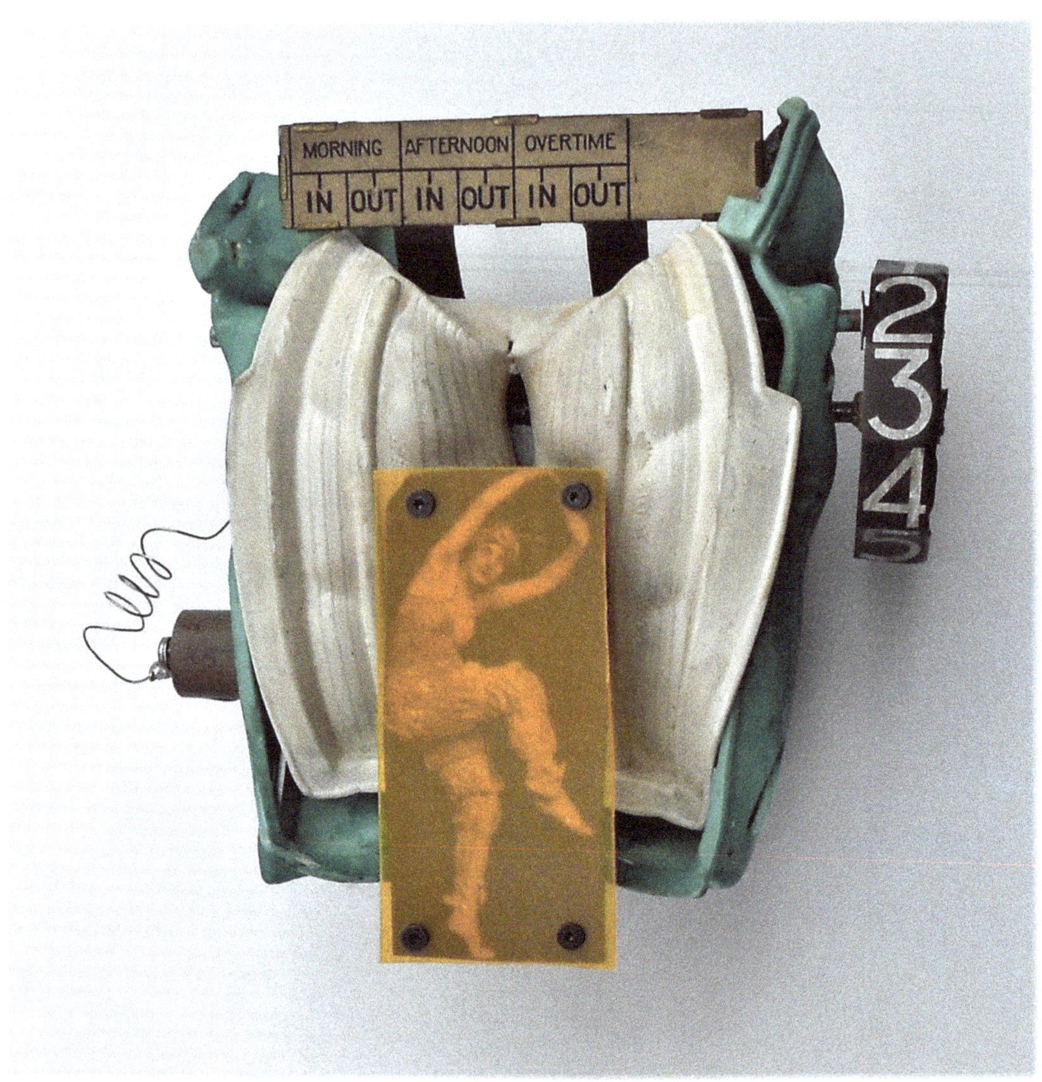

MELTED VEG-O-MATIC

ANDRENA ZAWINSKI

ALAMEDA, CALIFORNIA

PLAY

Inside the herbal emporium, I worry fresh tarragon and thyme will wilt in my basket as I wait for the checker to get off the phone. I wander inside a natural health magazine study concluding kids who get outside in nature grow into happier adults. Adding chervil and sage to the cache, I wonder where those kids grow up with their green spaces all about: the Berkshires or Poconos, Malibu or Aspen? Inside paragraphs, speculative researchers are not talking about kids like I was once roaming rust belt working poor stomping grounds. Kids who took off all day to run around in nearby woods. Took off to escape the flail of words and worries from down-on-their-luck parents. These researchers were not talking about my kind, Boomer born and raised on the doom and gloom of "as the rich get richer, the poor get poorer." They were talk talk talking about iGen'ers with too much time at lit up screens inside fast chats or with magical avatars in games that chirp and buzz instead of before birds and trees and bees. Talk talking about kids inside high rise jungles with rooftop parks.

Talking about parents who fear their kids may face mood disorders or developmental lags. Parents with no time for outdoor play. Talk talking about a need to experience microbial diversity instead of people. Talking about finding their chi with trees. I step outside the magazine covers, still waiting for the checker to hang up the phone and know play is what I did as a kid: scattering jacks and pick-up sticks, jumping rope, hopscotching, walking, and sometimes even running deep into the woods.

LAUREN PURJE

BROOKLYN, NEW YORK

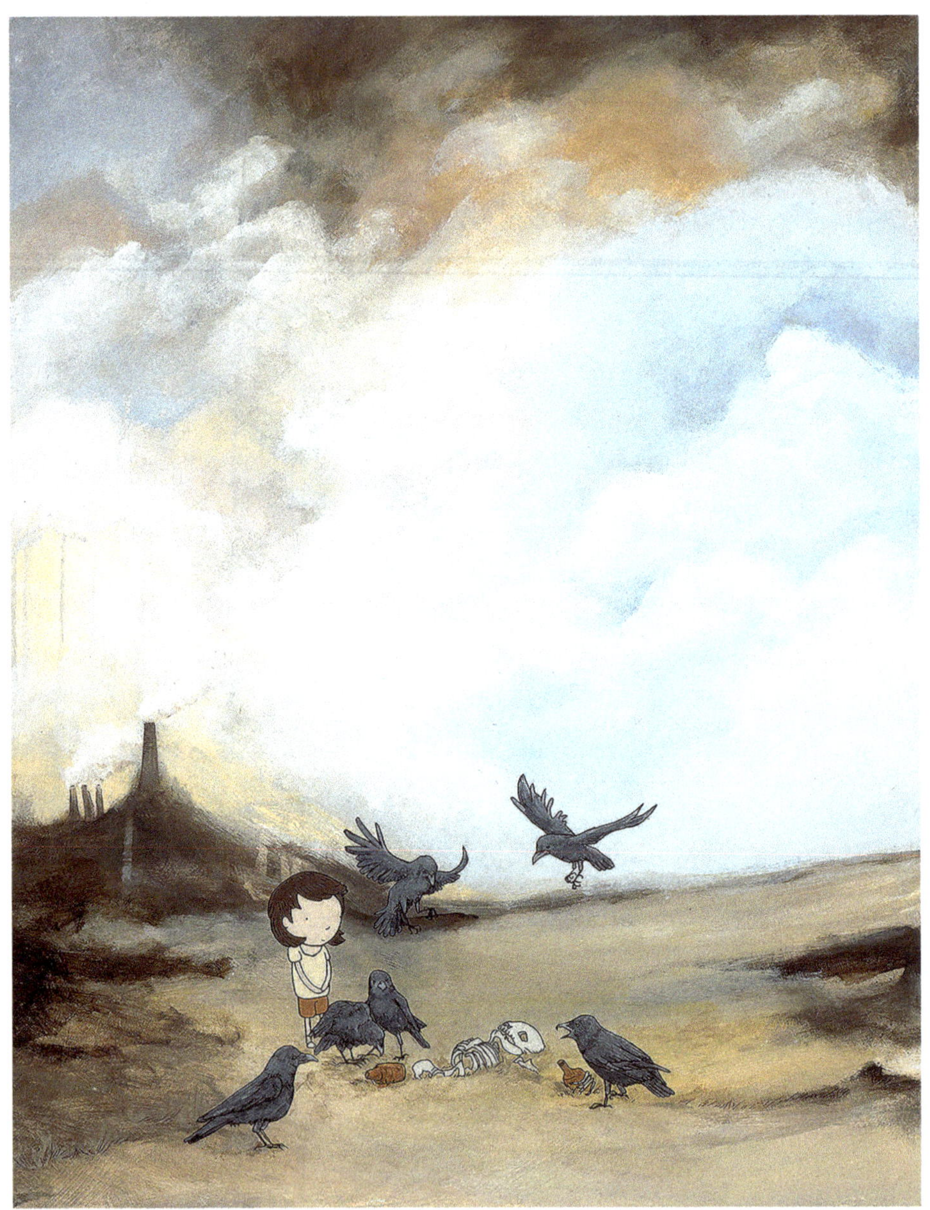

EARTH DIED SCREAMING

philipkevinbrehse
PASSAU, GERMANY

H2O

attempt at what now

a.word a.vision . . . fresh tender leaves
something like that
aren't you cynical too

pure water . . . before it is stolen and sold

is the cynicism new for you, as it is for me
will they come again the tender leaves
what floods of tears the new springtime shall bring with
if it comes
which rivers may overswell their banks

who is the next to die

 . . . was trying to remember snow
on that other lake, that other planet
a.flurry blue in the light of . . . . . . past

biting morbidity

a.full moon profundita proclaims proceeds nothing
but prophesying vainly
saying look for the last time
fools

homesick for a place i have not yet seen

look at a tree
and only think
poor thing you are also dying

these cathedral bells roll like the waves of the two mighty rivers
enclosing it into a peninsula as they join each other and merge their
colors
the one is green
the other muddy and brown
the overtones of these bells move my soul and body to dance

hope is re lent less

DAVID KATZ

NEW YORK, NEW YORK

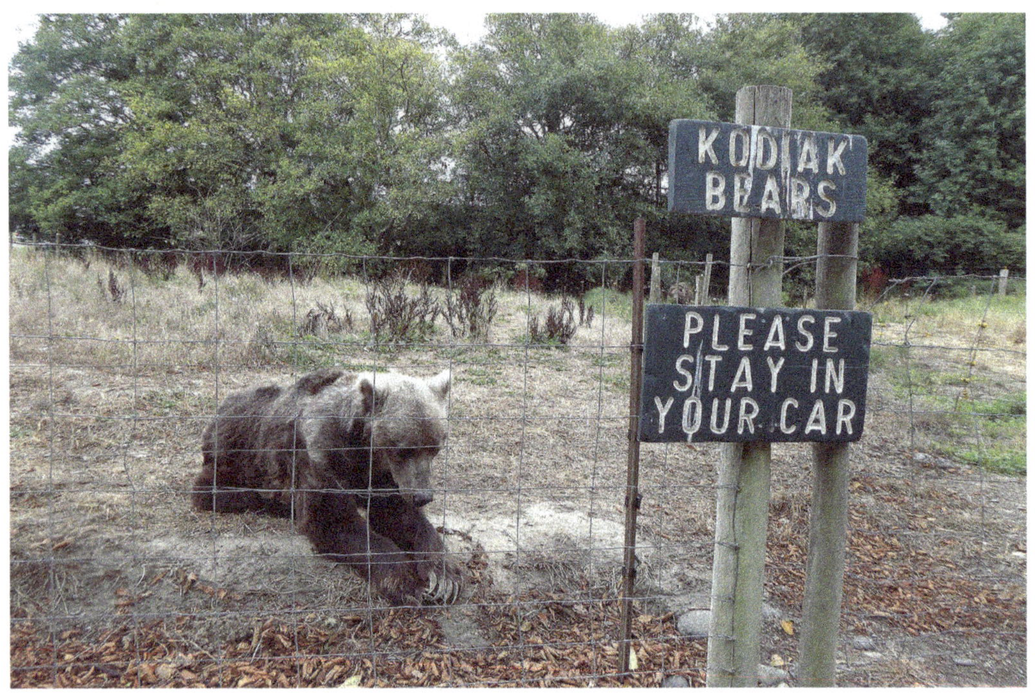

PLEASE STAY IN YOUR CAR

Photograph

GEORGE WALLACE

HUNTINGTON, NEW YORK

LISTEN TO THE INUIT ELDERS, SEAS RISE FASTER AND FASTER

We have only got to open our eyes, let logic or science or our heart's magic in, breathe deep the vapors of the sybil's cave and see what's coming down the pike, to see it and tell it—a tidal wave is come, a pouring from heaven, the diagrams dictate it, the sun and moon and planets delineate, you can read it in the entrails of crows—the earth has shifted, it's raining diamonds on Saturn, there are seismic flashes on the moon;

Listen to the Inuit elders, seas rise faster and faster, forces larger than any man or army advance, and the rotation of the bones must have its say; and the barometer of cataclysm is real, and a storm netted in Atlantic waters will pour itself out, the cold graves of sailors and leviathans will open their jaws and swallow us all—it is coming, it is coming, fish, cleats, weighing scales, pilings, oarlocks, anchors, mooring poles;

And unwise the people (and unwise the nation) who lie to themselves, and laugh about lying; who hide behind gates, who devour the forests, and fish the seas out; who—short-sighted, blunt-souled creatures that they are—spread the icing so thick that it smothers the cake, and naturally go to the bad—our cruelties, our indifferences, our paybacks and insatiatable appetites;

And the gates will not close, and city walls will crumble and they will fall, they will fall;

Useless! the rooftops—
Useless! the lockboxes
IRAs and storage sheds;

Raised against the storm, and the storm will tear them down!

Earth takes hold, earth takes hold; reaches the limits of its tolerance and replies;

And there is nothing dada about this poem, and there is nothing clever or wise or hip or fun, and if nobody clicks 'like' on this poem I don't care—these are the shirt-ends of our sorry history, and you better grab on tight and hang on for your life;

Because earth in its sweet rotations and archetectonics, earth more eternal in its orbit than any of us, will give its answer,

Will shake and shake, until it hurls our sorry asses clean off of mountaintops.

ALFONSO IANDIORIO & LOIS KAGAN MINGUS

NEW YORK, NEW YORK

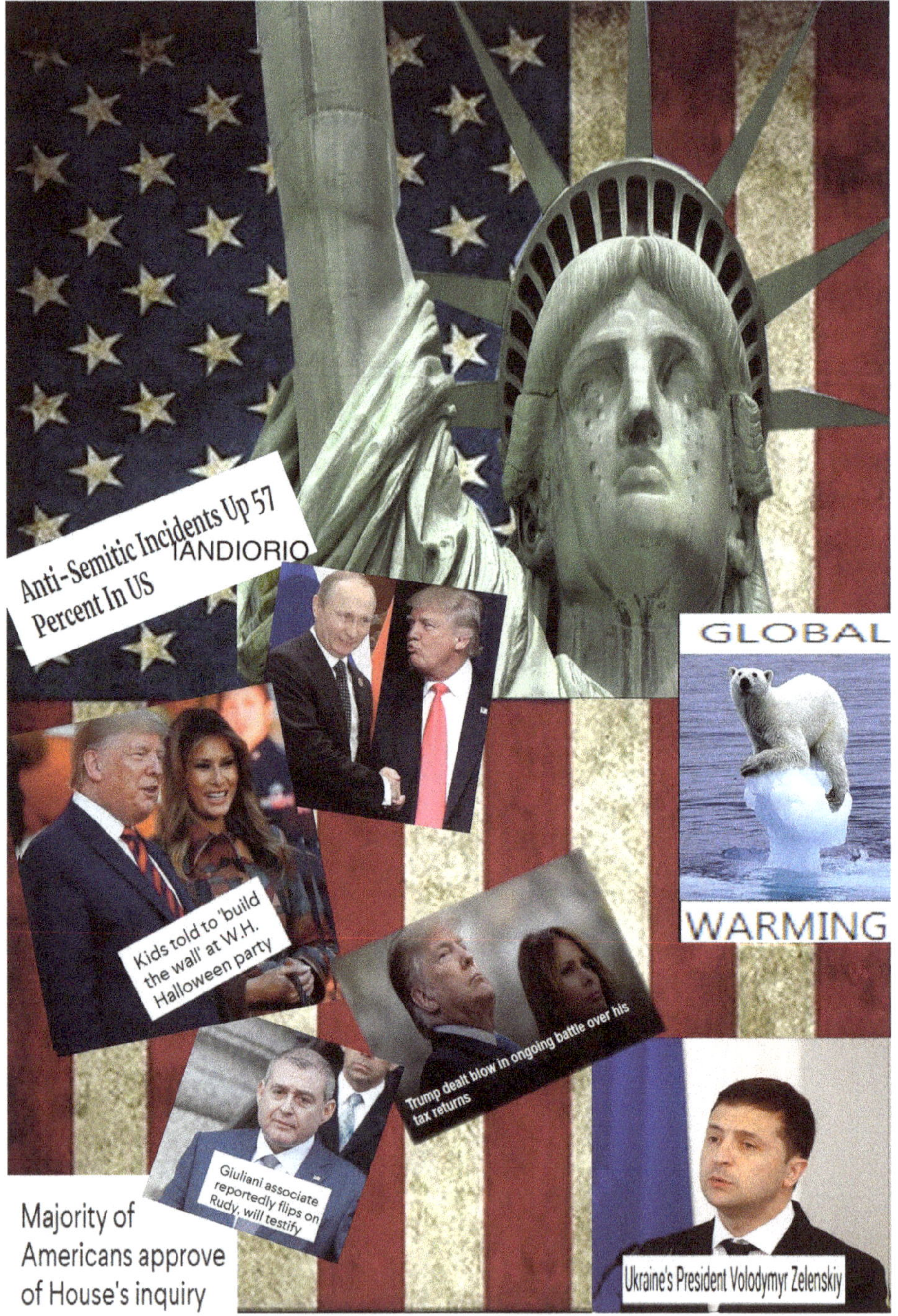

I KNOW YOU ARE BUT WHAT AM I

I KNOW YOU ARE BUT WHAT AM I

Oh, god, I can't write anymore about this planet's survival

and the warmongering asshole and his support system, his base, his henchmen

and the rampant racism and bigotry and homophobia

and the fucked up environment and climate change

and patriarchal behavior and misogyny and lies

and his hair

but I just did.

Did I cover all bases? Did I make it make sense?

Is the end of the world to end with his Pence?

No! I say no. I'm done with this bit.

(I slipped in some rhyme to spice up the shit.)

Prosaic . . . poetic, wade your way through.

We make a new world with both me and with you.

LYNNEA VILLANOVA

BROOKLYN, NEW YORK

UNIQUE SPECIES

Navel-grazing minis

long judged blackguard germs

protect, evict

make, mask

evolve, stream split

spit-like

along your vertiginous folds

hairpin, hair brained way

root up, some in dead end branches, some plowing through

to make up and weave into

what is you

You wash

you scrub

sanitize, pharmacize

to kill the black guard

sidelining sentinels (along the way)

that guarded your gates

and portaged

to your emperor-brain

their own gift-leavings

as earthworm to soil

absent their debris-offerings

mind-master thus starved and scrambled

can't form—foundations fail to forge

can't calm—fear fails to fade

can't love—friendships fail to fruit

can't concentrate—functions fail to finish

can't encode

can't decode

can't control

Micro film, sender of small signals

gut response in tangible form

collateral damage of an overzealous arsenal

despite its endangered status

unseats the emperor

YUKO OTOMO

NEW YORK, NEW YORK

Sustain WHAT?

Try to suspend your judgment
over the unexpected surprise you'll get
when you open the forbidden door

All sorts of suspicions will
pour over your anxiety
to crush you into pieces
that you've never imagined
seeing as *"you"*

It's not *"surreal"*; it's *"unreal"*

the shock will not go up or down
it will spread flatly becoming *"something else"*

Help us! Help us!
we don't know how to ski or to skate
in the surplus of surrendering stupidities

Disheartening, disharmonious & disingenuous desires of ours
keep feeding us to maintain the gross overestimation
of *"who we are"*

no need to worry or to hurry
relax, sit back & enjoy the precious privilege to *"be human"*

when the time comes
serendipity & synchronicity will measure
the point of no-return for us
one way or the other

In the mean time, we get together to cry
over the sensitive susceptibility & the spinning curiosity
of our species when we get too bored of thinking
on a sweet & intimate question
such as

Sustain WHAT?

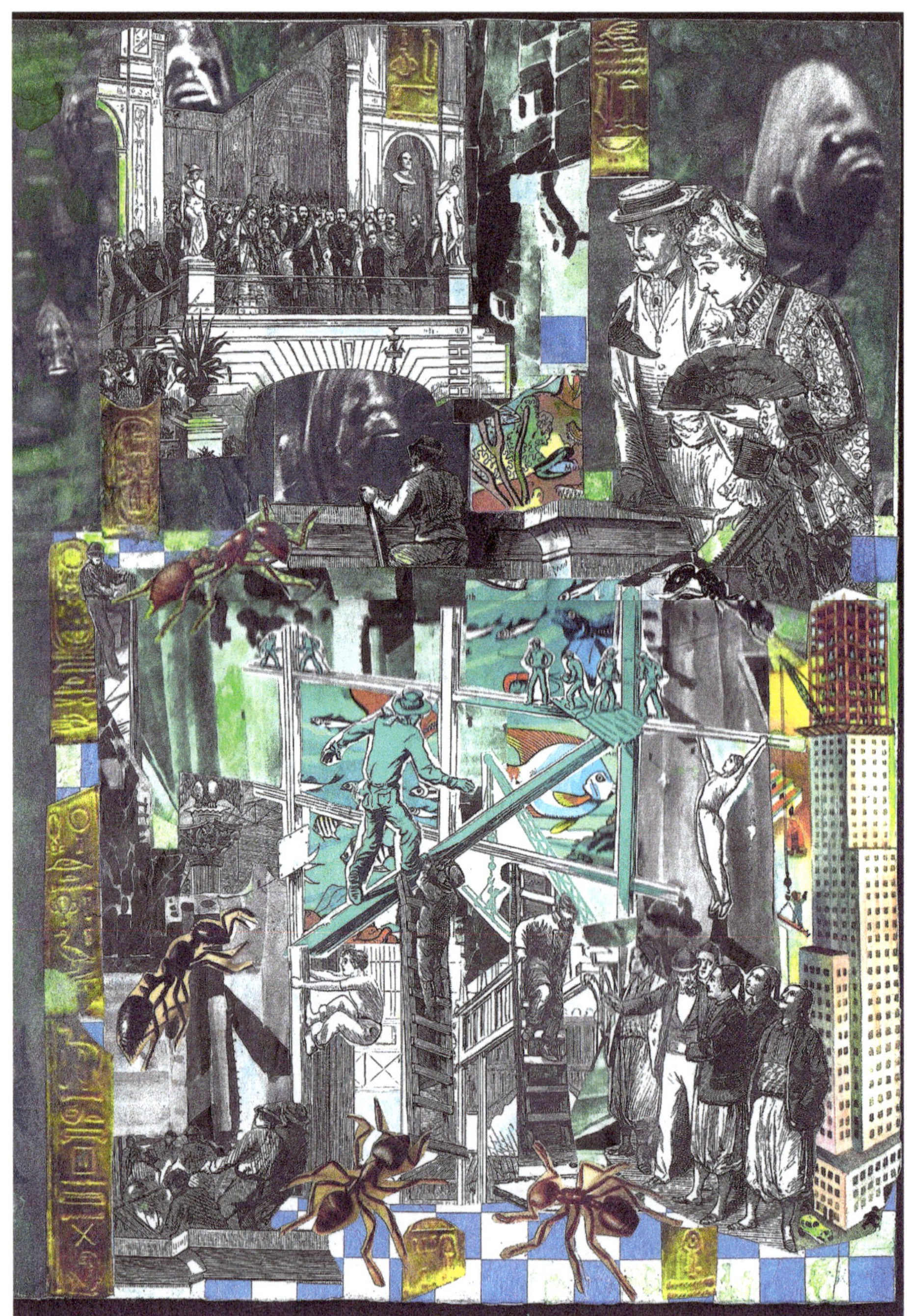

RISING TO THE OCCASION, OR WE JUST DON'T STOP

Mixed Media Collage, 12" x 16"

REBECCA PETERS

SAN FRANCISCO, CALIFORNIA

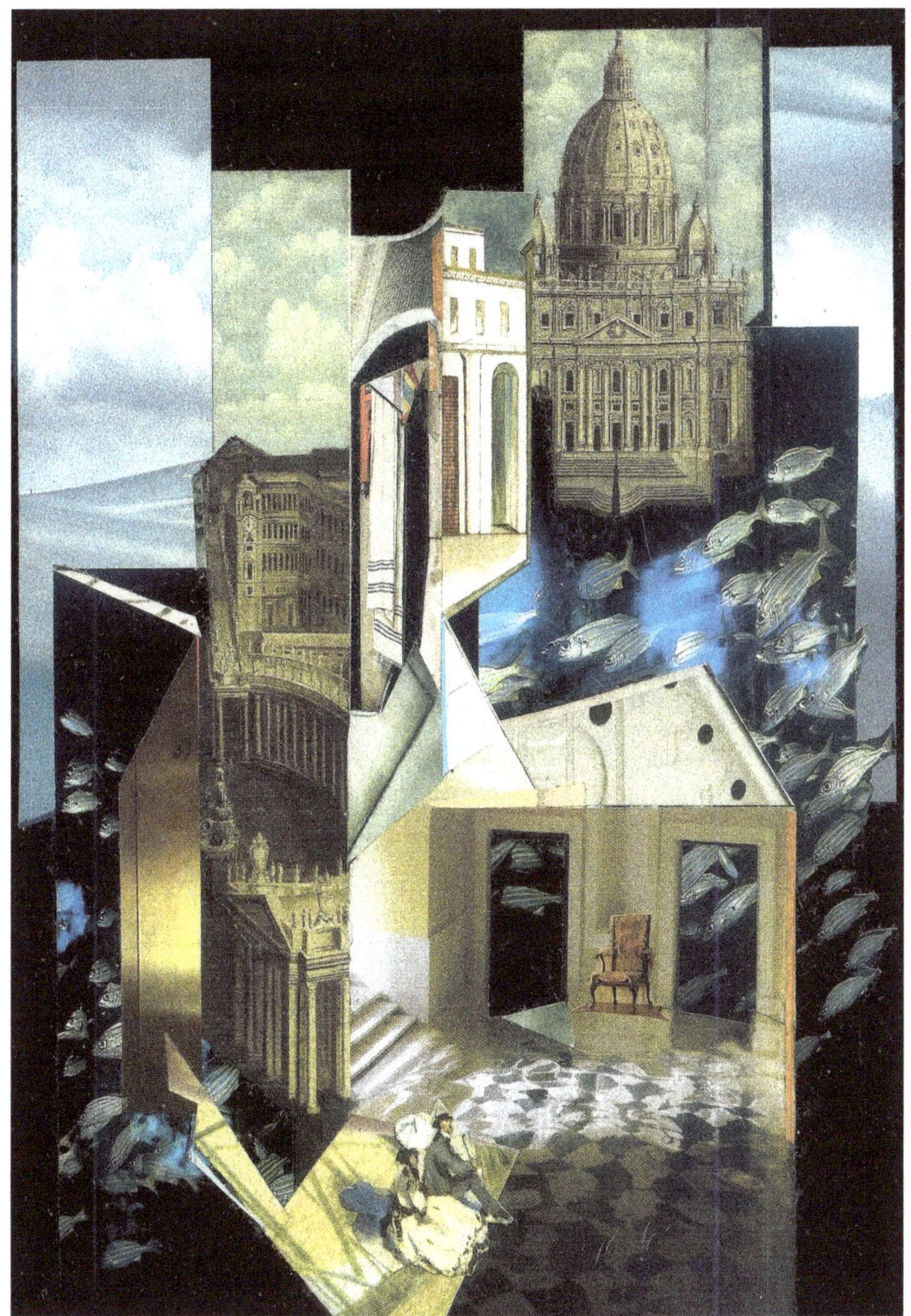

HIGH TIDE FOR EVERY HOME

Mixed Media Collage, 12" x 16"

GORDON GILBERT

NEW YORK, NEW YORK

A LESSON TOO LATE FOR THE LEARNING

When the wells run dry
and nothing is left to us of nourishment

Stripped bare of clothes
and winter closing in

All doors locked
and every key taken from us

No fuel for the machines
that could take us from this place
and none to feed the fires
as we huddle shivering in the cold

No power for the streetlights
that would push away the darkness
as the cold night falls

No music
neither that recorded in another time and place
nor that we once would make among ourselves
No songs from throats too cracked and parched
No melodies remembered
All instruments broken

Trees leafless and barren
Grass withered, brown and dry
Mud and dust and ruined walls

How can love survive in a paradise lost?
How did we let it come to this?

The poison self-administered
The self-assisted suicide

Here in this desolate waste
last of our kind
dying of self-inflicted wounds

JANET HAMILL

MIDDLETOWN, NEW YORK

THE VALLEY OF THE FALLEN

Drone of wasps
circle sockets in the catacombs
stacked and packed
since the General
borrowed the mummified hand
of a saint to keep
by his bedside skull

Flagellants
hooded inquisitors
& sideshow freaks
draw straws
set fire to forests
throw plastic into the sea
and substitute coal in the barbeque
with books
a dirty word to say
books
bindings
paper
print
dirty words to say
slander and insult
rich bastards
eyes darting
over the contract
of the last big deal

On clouded mounts
the Four Horseman
War
Famine
Pestilence
 & Death
red in tooth & claw
erase the footprints
on the floor
of the Valley of the Fallen

ALL AGES PERMITTED

The Earth got buried about 10:15 this morning.
It'd been pretty far gone for months
speaking things no fit ears could possibly handle.

This morning a priest was sent for.
None could be found,
they were all over the solar system
bringing God's word to Mars and Jupiter.

Chris Rock said tonight that it's not the word,
but the context in which it is used.
.
The Earth could have used some morphine.
None could be found,
all the Wall Street CEOs got the last of it.
Wall Street starred Michael Douglas.
Main Street was written years before by Sinclair Lewis.
Can you name some other streets?
Easy,
side,
dead end,
Della.

The Earth could be a zombie extra in the new George Romero flick.

Something needs to die
if it's going to be reborn,
rebirth just might be the thing.
None could be found,
the warehouse ran out.
Somebody's head no doubt will roll
in the middle of the square.
If you can't find a square, make a circle.
All ages permitted
with valid proof of a local address.
Forensic blood splatter experts
standing by.

The Earth will not be televised.
That damn camera sees too much.
One of these days, a day off . . .

I live in anything that will have me.
Siphon ongoing night.
The Earth knows it's got direct deposit.
The bank's address just keeps changing.

MUTES CÉSAR

ARCOS DE VALDEVEZ, PORTUGAL

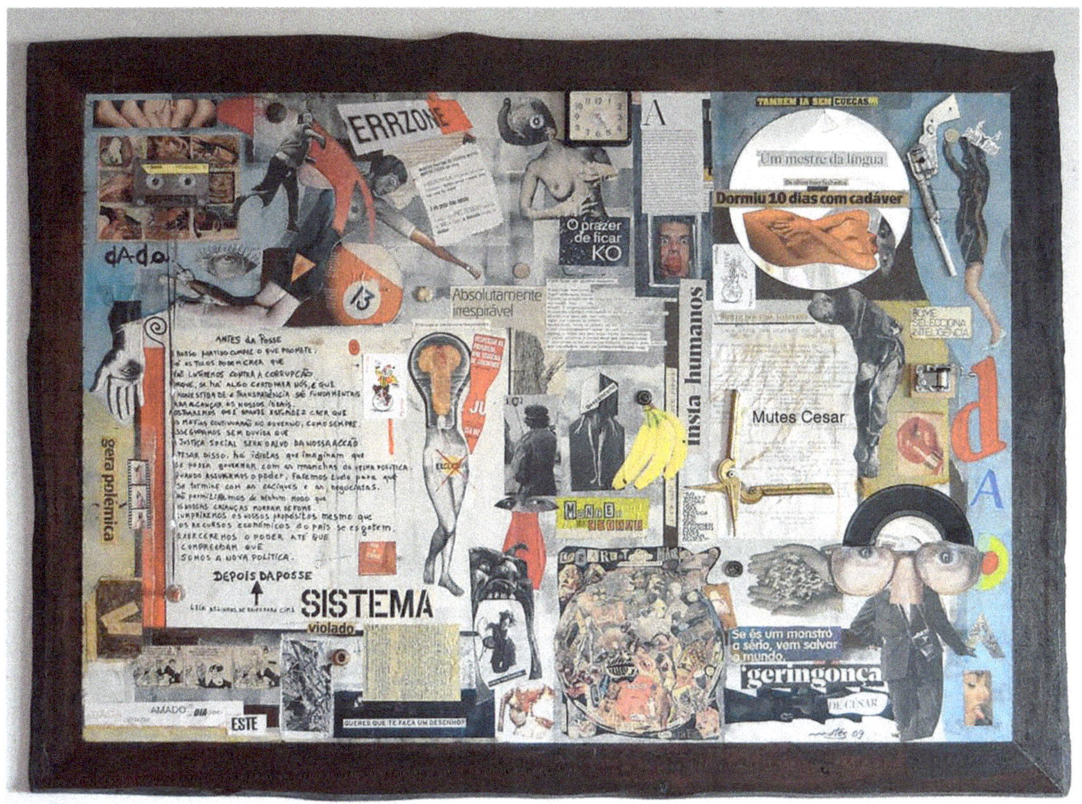

DADA IS A SYSTEM THAT GENERATES CONTROVERSY

JEFF FARR

NEW YORK, NEW YORK

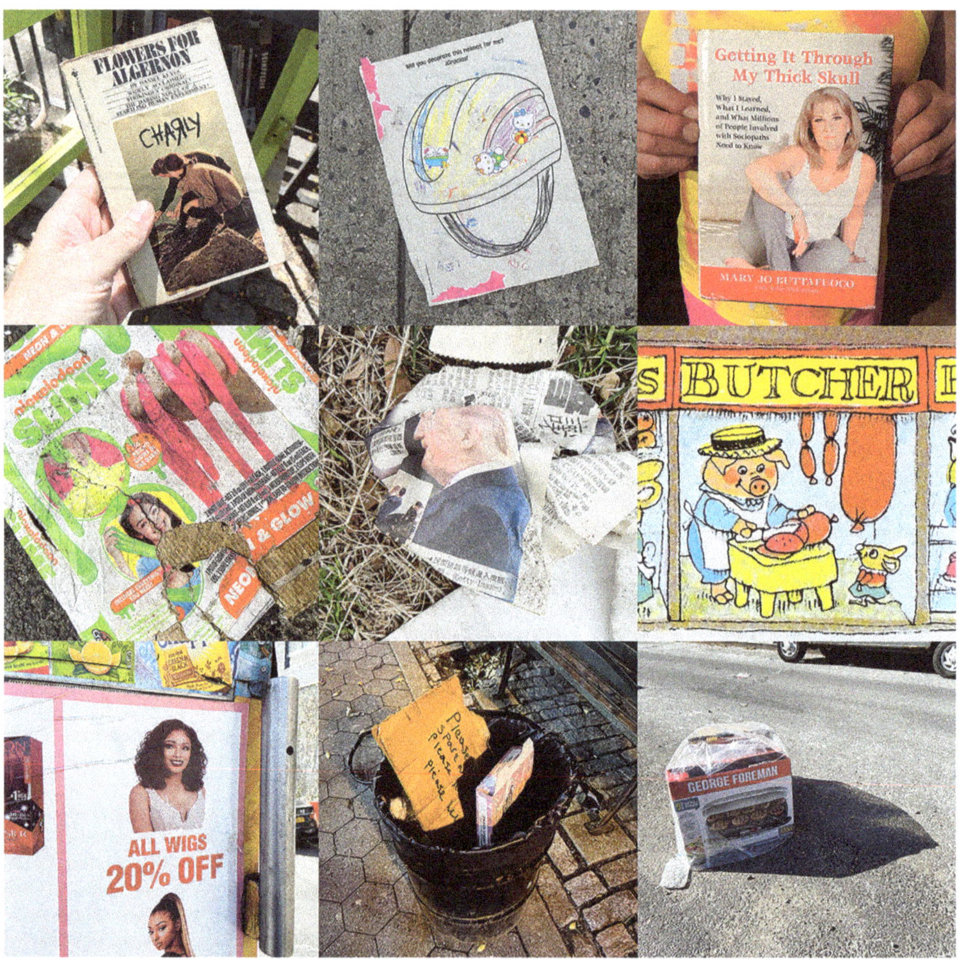

THE DEVIL'S ALREADY DEAD

C. R. RESETARITS

OXFORD, MISSISSIPPI

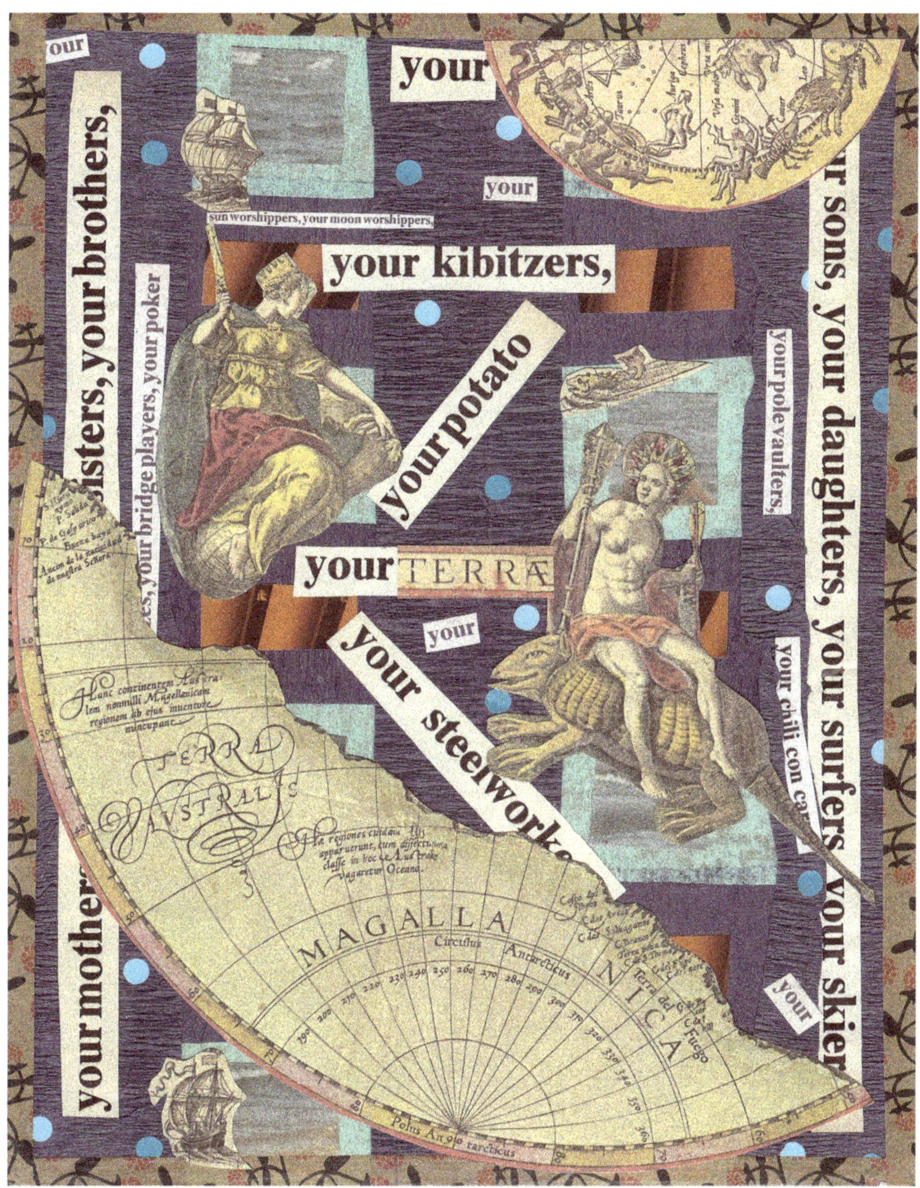

NOT MY FAULT

Collage

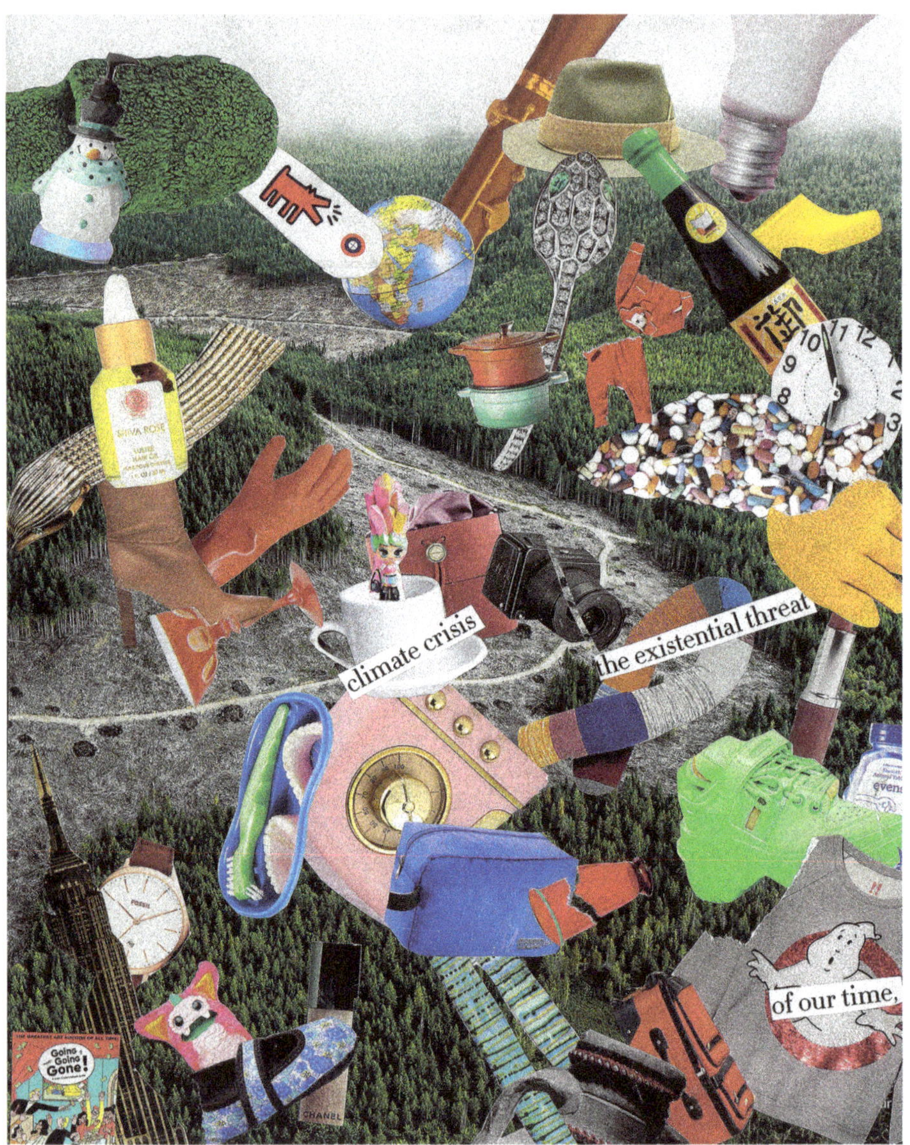

THE END IS NEAR

Collage, 7" x 9.5"

LINDA LERNER
BROOKLYN, NEW YORK

A SEA OF GREEN

jumping from noun to verb green your way

down grocery store aisles scanning

the small print on packages for what isn't

good for you or is it the planet, making sure

no one saw what you put in your basket

heard you tell the cashier, plastic is fine

the person behind you, one with the

smug look turning around so her

whole foods cloth bag is in your face,

lost in a sea of green of the dollar bill

it always comes down to and never having

enough of wanting to do the right thing

only green took the red out of everything

the taste out of what you used to enjoy,

till there was no orange or yellow or

any other color, even what looked green

might not be green enough, someone said,

it became the way your mind breathed

looked on others, recycling every hour

of the day to discard with the garbage

put in the right bin, right mind slot,

make sure no one is watching, sees

when you slip up, ready to report . . .

BERTHOLDUS SIBUM

ZWOLLE, NETHERLANDS

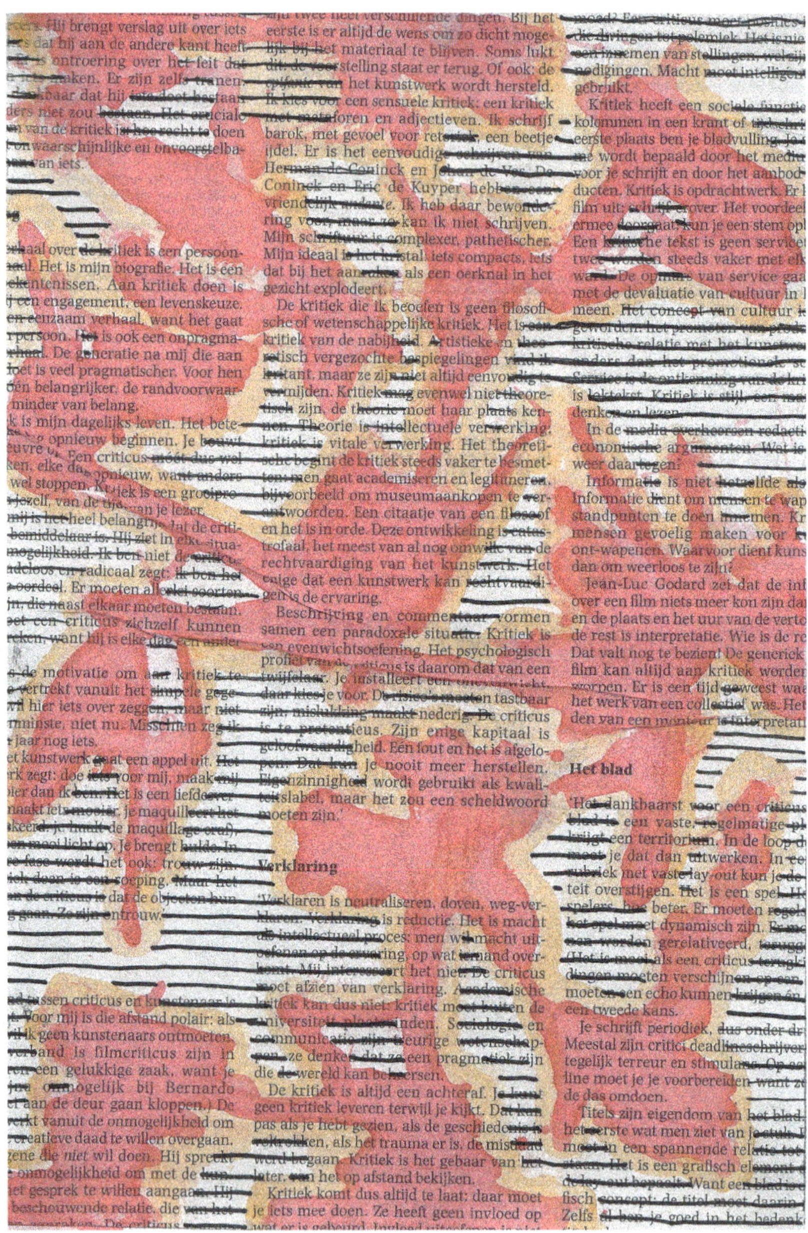

FAKE THE FACTS

J. J. STEINFELD
CHARLOTTETOWN, PRINCE EDWARD ISLAND, CANADA

EVEN AS THE MORNING DISSOLVES

A morning as bright

as any since before time

and I'm thinking

of luck and lucklessness

of singing and silence

of devastation and destruction

of collecting damaged days

and offering a dreary pun

to some transcendent being

demanding sharp commentary

on the state of affairs down here

as if location mattered

in the arms of mortality and folly.

So I put on my most comfortable shoes

worn from a hundred endless walks

from a thousand contradictions

from a million lack of answers

and start another hapless walk

holding on to the word dream

even as the morning dissolves.

WAYNE ATHERTON

DOVER, NEW HAMPSHIRE

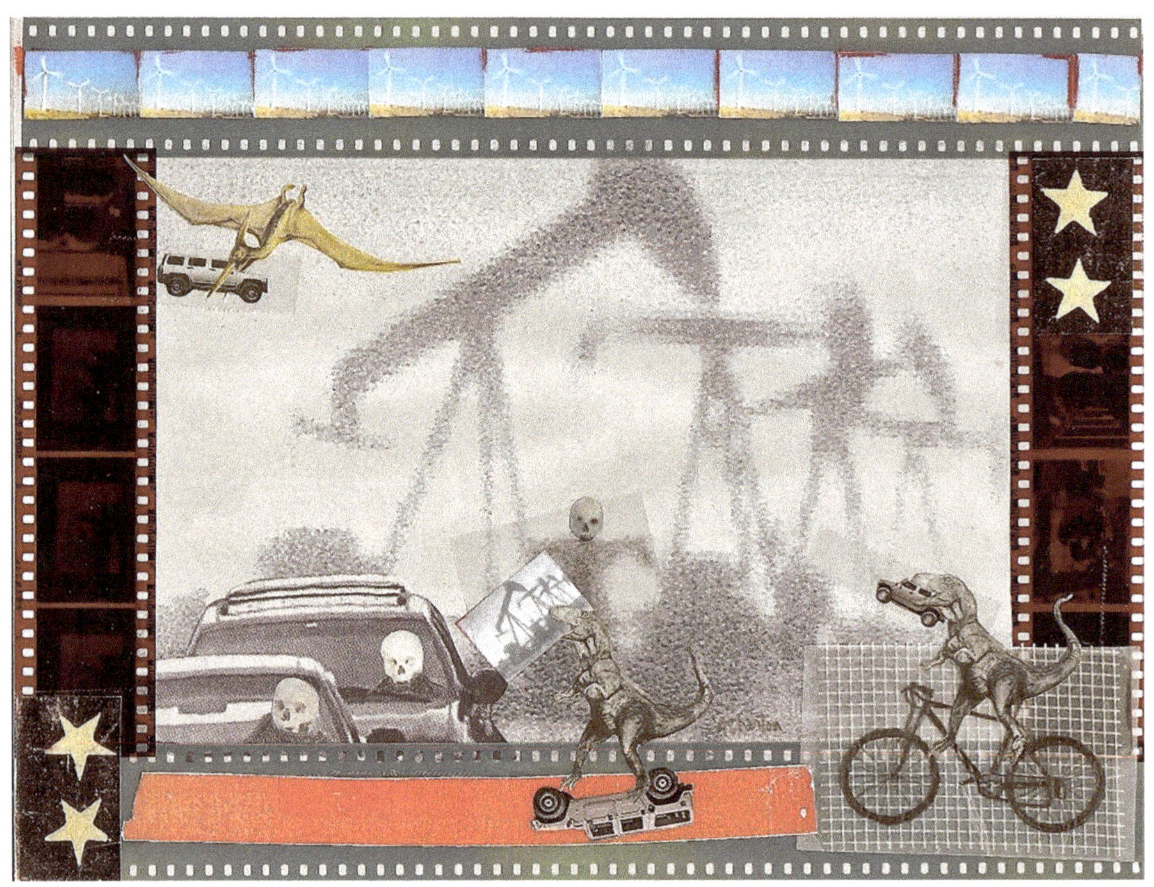

PETROLEOLITHIC AGE

HOLLY DAY
MINNEAPOLIS, MINNESOTA

THE END AS IT WAS

When the end comes for us as it did for the dinosaurs
in streaks of fiery fury across the sky, some untold Armageddon
from outer space, it won't matter how many books we have written,
how deep we've carved our names in stone tablets
or scrawled in markers across the metal of bathroom stalls
or saved on floppy discs or flash drives or vinyl records or magnetic tape
there will be nothing left of us after the fires have died down
after the boiling tides have receded back into peaceful oceans
after the earth has stopped shaking from the impact.
The moles and the mice that found solace deep within the earth
will remember us for a few generations, perhaps whisper stories about us
inflate our presence as that of some great, cunning monster
famous for setting deadly traps
or sparing a few to live in cages for entertainment;
tiny, furless babies will fall asleep
with a warning to always watch out, you never know
when they'll come back. But eventually,
Even those stories will fade to legend and fiction,
and when those tiny creatures
struggle to find their way back to the surface of a reborn planet
perhaps they'll dismiss our burnt and scattered bones,
the metal struts of twisted buildings
as being put there by some great cosmic god as a trick
to test their faith, or invent even greater stories
about who we were, how we came to be
how, despite our great size, our possible intelligence,
our guessed-at capacity to love our young,
to shelter our families, even we
weren't able to survive the whim of nature
the inevitable impact of cosmic debris.

J. I. KLEINBERG

BELLINGHAM, WASHINGTON

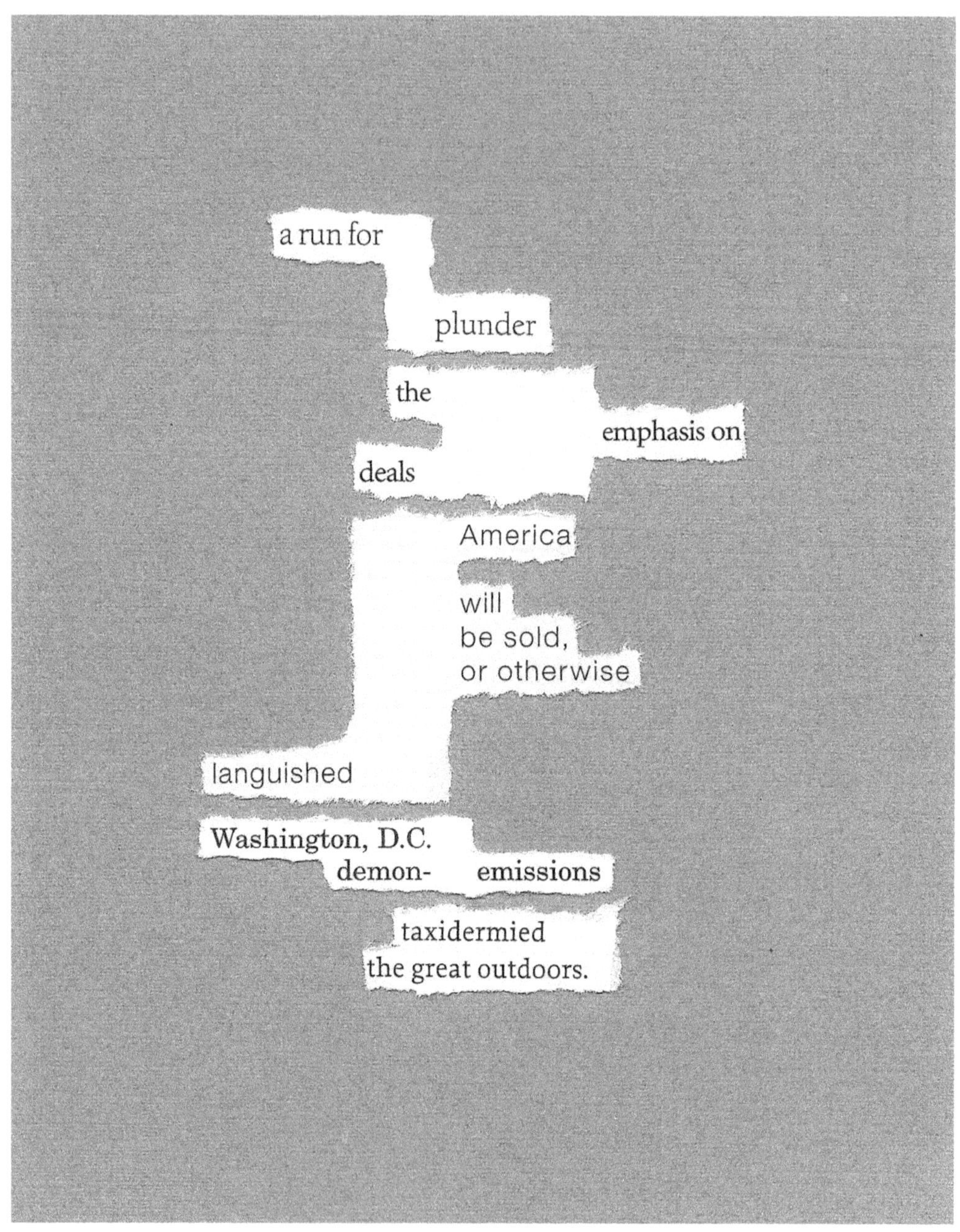

A RUN

Visual Poem

MARTINE BELLEN

ASTORIA, NEW YORK

THE HABITABLE ZONES

Eight spheres revolve around our lightbulb.

Past our power grid are other grids, matrices and blueprints for star banks and lexicons,
    concepts and kinetics, godscopes and gyroscopes,
      farther and farther and farther past, others and more mothers,
        not sequential but circuits of beyond and beyond that.

We call this our "beginningless endless circus; we call this our "infinity/eternity."
    We call ourselves lone threads in a singular untangling universe
      polyinfinity/multieternity.
        We tingle perpetually, so circuitous are we, plugged into a socket
        that commutes communes computes.

Our planet, third from the lightbulb, is coniferous.
    Aboriginal forest in a persistent darkling dome firmament.
      On our planet, always it is night and always we are
        in old-growth, multi-layered canopies and woody debris, dead
          standing hardwoods with fungal ecosystems, tangles with burs
            and bramble and vines and bears and wolves and hunters
and spies and stars that eye us as we follow song-lines to outer-world spheric solar systems,
    powerless to breathe
      beyond our empirical intelligence.

Always on the autumnal equinox we set forth
    for the first/last time with a basket of baked goods and hexagonal honeycomb.
      Always our target is a wizened ancient's home
        hidden in the heart of the primary forest.
We forget why we are walking, why we are aging.
    Our drive is instinctual, written within us.
      Our maps in our brain lobe, firing us on.
      We scope the landscape,
        thoroughly aware we are departing as
        one planet in one body

          that has been written in a universe
          300 million miles from home.

That we have been conscripted increases urgency
    echoes through the eight million
      clusters of eight spheres, around eight million lightbulbs
        that shine and blow out, like birthday candle stars.

We are never lost, never at a loss.
　　Our forebears speak directly into our femurs that navigate
　　　　the stones we skip past, the streams we stomp through,
　　　　　the squirrels that scamper off our trails
　　　　　　minutes before we approach;
　　　　　　　　the author, also, conscripting their movements.
　　　　　　　　So, too, could be said of the stream,
　　　　　　　　　besotted with the tale, bespattering
　　　　　　　　　　the uncaring decaying ground
　　　　　　　　　　with mud spots
　　　　　　　　　　　　a moment too soon.

Feelings tiptoe through us—
　　we feel blue, green, magenta. We feel fern, moss, duff, bark.
　　　We feel defiance and indebtedness
　　　　to what we animate, what we regurgitate.
We are walking forward toward senescence—the process of deterioration.
　　She, the ancient, is losing sentience with each step closer we draw,
　　　each page further into the tale,
　　　　she, the ancient, is metamorphosing into animal,
　　　　　brown matted fur, gleamless, indistinct.
　　　　　As we are tripping forward, the aged
　　　　　　turns inward, curling up,
　　　　　　　preparing, here and millions and millions
　　　　　　　　of miles from us,
　　　　　　　　　woven

into paper's pageantry, brilliant spheres,
　　fluttering against the cage of her chest
　　　and sputtering out. When we arrive at the ancient's hut
　　　　she has returned to her fetish animal,
　　　　　　through the fetid old-growth,
　　　　　　　an animal awakening

If this were a story created by a single volition,
　　We might conflagrate, deforest, frack,
　　　we might destroy the forest path, steal our granny's bounties,
　　　　rest our ear on her fuel heart and pump it up, or
　　　　we might look yonder
　　　　　as others scrape her uterine walls, snatch her ancient ooze

But we have come to understand this tale is every tale, chained to one another,
　　revolving around our lighthouse, and past our power grid are other grids,
　　　matrices and blueprints for star banks and lexicons,
　　　　concepts and kinetics, godscopes and gyroscopes,
　　　　　dyads, farther and farther and farther past,
　　　　　others and more mothers,
　　　　　　not sequential but circuits, a circus,
　　　　　　　of beyond and beyond.

LAURA LEHEW

EUGENE, OREGON

2^nd^s

The ▮ *Amendment*

right ▮ people

shall not be infringed.

▮ *Degree of Thermodynamics*

sum of ▮ entropies

participating bodies must increase ▮ idealized ▮ a reversible process

remains

Burns

extend beneath ▮ into ▮ form ▮ the

roof ▮ divided :

Superficial ▮ the first half

Beneath ▮ blister ▮ pink, moist, ▮ pain

deeper layers

Person

"you," "your," and "yours."

often appropriate

▮ with ▮

a singular second-▮ :

you go ▮ leave your ▮ . ▮ miss you.

yours,

Derivative Test

relates ▮ concepts ▮ critical points, extreme values, ▮ concavity

a very useful tool ▮ determining whether ▮ function is ▮

relative ▮ .

The ▮ **Derivative Test: Suppose** ▮ *sin* is

critical

Then

the test is not

informative.

Example

find and classify ▮ extreme values

find ▮ critical ▮ where

sin ▮ =0

and

Notice ▮ *sin* 1 < 1 and ▮ *sin* ▮ < 0. ▮ has a relative maximum

Hopes

I hope I
do not lose my sister
▮ .

DAVID R. LINCOLN
BROOKLYN, NEW YORK

REMEMBERING PARADISE

That day in the news the Ivory Billed Woodpecker, extinct since the 1930s, had been discovered in a thick clay forest in Arkansas, still alive, and I broke down, I wept unabashedly right there in the bookstore, my face buried in my hands, thinking how the wild spirit ebbs and flows, always survival by disaster. Finally, the girl behind the counter turned to me and asked if I was okay?

"People don't last," I said. "Just when you think they're gone for good something happens and they're calling you collect from Florida."

She nodded, a bit perturbed I would say, wondering what she ought to do. So I thanked her and left. The funny thing was, I had no idea why I should suddenly melt down for a bird I knew nothing about or even heard of. Was this a nervous fit, going to end soon, or would I have to wear it down all day? The wracking in the chest felt like it had been there all along, pent up, silently nursing itself maybe, hiding behind my day, lurking somewhere in the parade of my thoughts; and now the release and that tremendous emotion, a force that really took my breath away.

As I walked down Haight Street I was thinking—

Prior to language there is perception, a direct knowledge of the unknown, but when you approach it in every direction it evades you, try as you might. No one can leave their language behind. It's almost like innocence or laughter, or crying, language cannot be abandoned or lost, even if you wanted to, there is no owner, there's nothing to do but sit around and wait for it to appear. Just another oblique scene that cannot be pinned down, that survives illusion, to the end, through all unlikeliness.

I could not remember having ever heard of the Ivory Billed Woodpecker before this. This feeling, like a maw, suddenly exposed in my chest, some tremendous hidden gaping wound abruptly flung open still wracked my body, as I crossed Stanyan Street. At the same time, with tears washing down my face, I felt exposed in public. Who is in control here? So I steered toward the cultivated mellowness of Hippie Hill, and waited out the attack.

Naturally, the first thing to catch my eye were the pink blossoms of the cherry trees, full at this time of the year, bursting on so many points that the branches sagged all the way to the ground, threatening the whole enterprise. And I noticed one branch had snapped under its weight, still blooming. And I thought—

Take that cherry tree, having too much fun, and now it's in the mud, flowers and all. Intact! But not intact really . . .

Later I drove back to Pacifica, remembering the look on the girl's face in the bookstore, wondering if her job was suddenly to help some middle-aged guy weeping all over the merchandise. And suddenly I was laughing so hard, I began to swerve out of my lane. The driver next to me leaned on his horn. All I could think about was that face trying to guess what was going on, a face probably going right back to the lost mists of the swamp, if you think about it. Like the girl in the bookstore, wondering what was wrong with that guy? And I couldn't stop laughing. As far as anyone else was concerned, I had been weeping on a sunny day. It was a sunny day out, and maybe I was having a nervous break-down right there in her store. Or maybe I was having a moment of pure and true ecstasy, in public. The difference might be so minute, no more than a shred of language, and it would disappear at the smallest distraction. If the whole lifespan of it fit into a single frame, one idea, then you discovered what you were made of, and an abrupt revival was a kind of cure.

So I shifted into the slow lane, and I told the girl in my mind that she was simply witnessing a moment of personality, which is often acquired through trauma, often as not—memory has to evolve, and live in the scars. What else to say about the evolutionary brain? The cradle of civilization is shit, is what it tells you. How many paradises had I seen and no one remembered a thing about them? I personally had visited at least six paradises, and no one cared or remembered a thing about any of those places.

Except me.

LYNETTE CLENNELL

MACAO, PEOPLE'S REPUBLIC OF CHINA

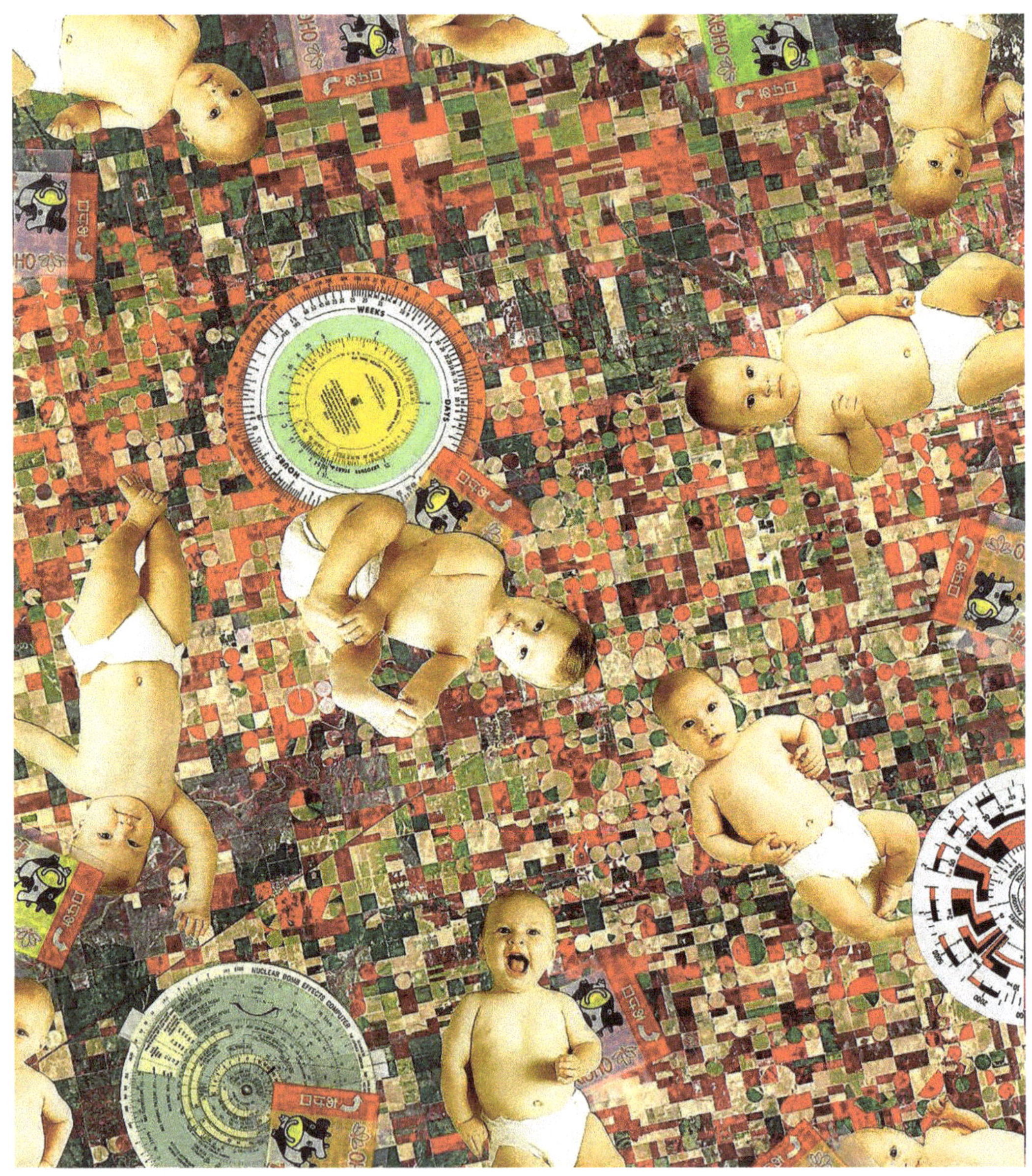

FALLOUT

VOXX VOLTAIR

THOUSAND OAKS, CALIFORNIA

TRUMPED

O you poor, rich man, with your frozen diamonds and
Blood-clotted rubies. Your oyster
Shit of wisdom, noosing your fat neck
You rise upon the crested waves of slaves
As Atlas, carried by pelanquin. How like God . . .
Your feet never touching dirt. How I pity you.

Your golden plate, your guilt-edges
Your charity of cast-off clothes, broken toys—homeless
Golf course lawn, fresh-cut
Watered by the sweat and tears of your burnt immigrant
Pets, you now kick out—keep out!
The rounded curves of your Marias and Conchitas, poor abuelitas

O you poor rich man in your golden tower
Your wife's smooth face paid for by sure-handed surgeons
You Dorian Gray of Industry
Your DNA strands spiraling perfectly
Blending past and future
Your children, created by chromosomal engineers

The earth, plundered for your golden eggs, the sky
Stabbed by the jets of your convenience
You leave chemtrails, choking the air with your importance
O poor, rich weakling with atrophied soul

Your secret handshake, assures your place only here—
Where one day, you shall completely disappear

SUZANNE BAILIE

KENT, WASHINGTON

Collage

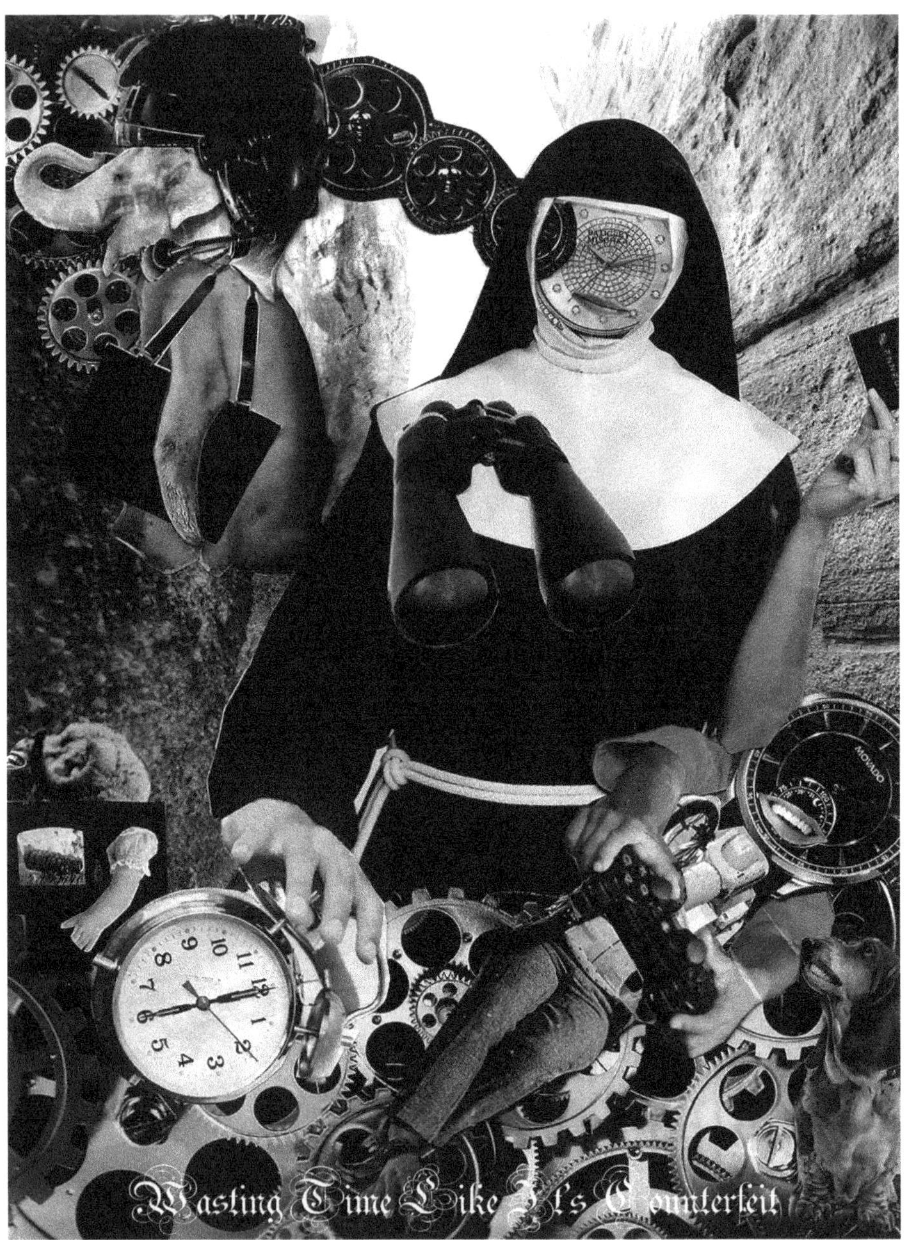

WASTING TIME LIKE IT'S COUNTERFEIT

Collage

LIZ AXELROD

ALBUQUERQUE, NEW MEXICO

I AM THE ENFANT TERRIBLE
OF THE MINERAL OIL

Smooth me
Seymour
Save me from this
Little Shop of Horrors
Flower me then
Eat my leaves

Gurgle up your dirt
while my slick
limbs dig at cracks
beneath the surface
with my iPhone
fingertips

Sue me IRS
Slippery Robo-callers
keep on phoning home
News, news, news, then bankruptcy
I would rather have ET and Reese's Pieces
flying bikes and smooth bright youth
They've taken my declines away
This screen gives me no options
Some minerals nourish
but they're heavy and my heart
is not in this
fight right
now

I'm looking for a savior
Must I be my own?
When will my shine
be bright enough
to burn through
these weeds
that bloom thorns
and fill my yard
with prickly
bastards

JEFF BOYNTON

LOS ANGELES, CALIFORNIA

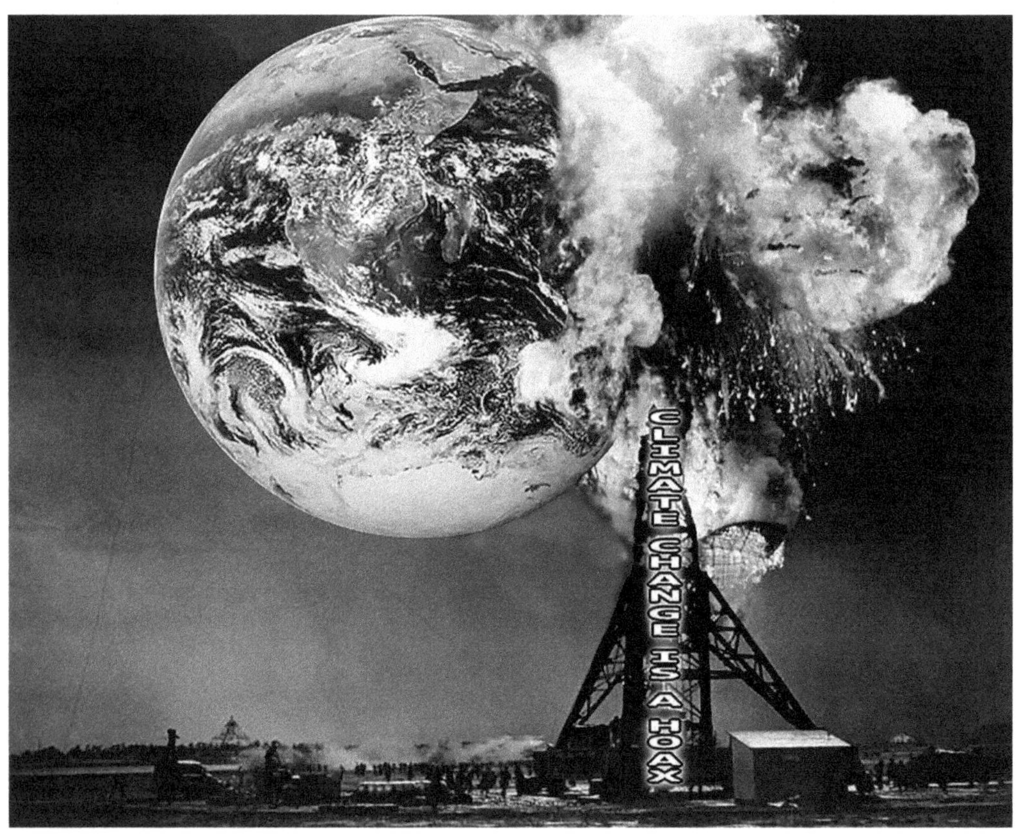

DEAD ZEPPELIN

Collage

Dd. SPUNGIN

VALLEY STREAM, NEW YORK

RARE EARTH

Rarer than the steak misplaced on its lopsided grill and the plate torn in half by a careless error of the chef on the backburner of my soul there in the corner lie in wait the mouse who got the cheese the cat who ate the canary the canary in the coal mine and polar ice caps melt into my oatmeal yea though I walk through the valley I will smell the tint of evil the sound of death and I am searching for a waterfall the polar ice caps melting on the shores of war and dousing every fire the land saved and the warmongers float on the final ice berg people cheer and we discover a hidden cache of guns they are melted into ploughshares and everyone gets to purchase one in the land of peace and I am the creator let it begin with me with you with now with stop the horror stop the cruelty stop needing to crush to maim to kill to own stop the polar ice caps from melting unless they intend to melt the crime the ravaging of the planet I hate I hate I hate because I love so much my home my earth my beautiful earth, going, going, gone.

ROBERT DUNCAN

FAIRFAX, CALIFORNIA

BLACK BOX

Co-pilot: Le Bourget, Le Bourget.

Pilot: Too late [unclear].

Control tower: Fire service leader, correction, the Concorde is returning to runway zero nine in the opposite direction.

Pilot: No time, no [unclear].

Co-pilot: Negative, we're trying Le Bourget [four switching sounds].

Co-pilot: No [unclear].

Control tower: De Gaulle tower from fire service leader, can you give me the situation of the Concorde?

Pilot: [unclear, sounds like exertion]

End of recording.

IGNACIO GALILEA

BRUSSELS, BELGIUM

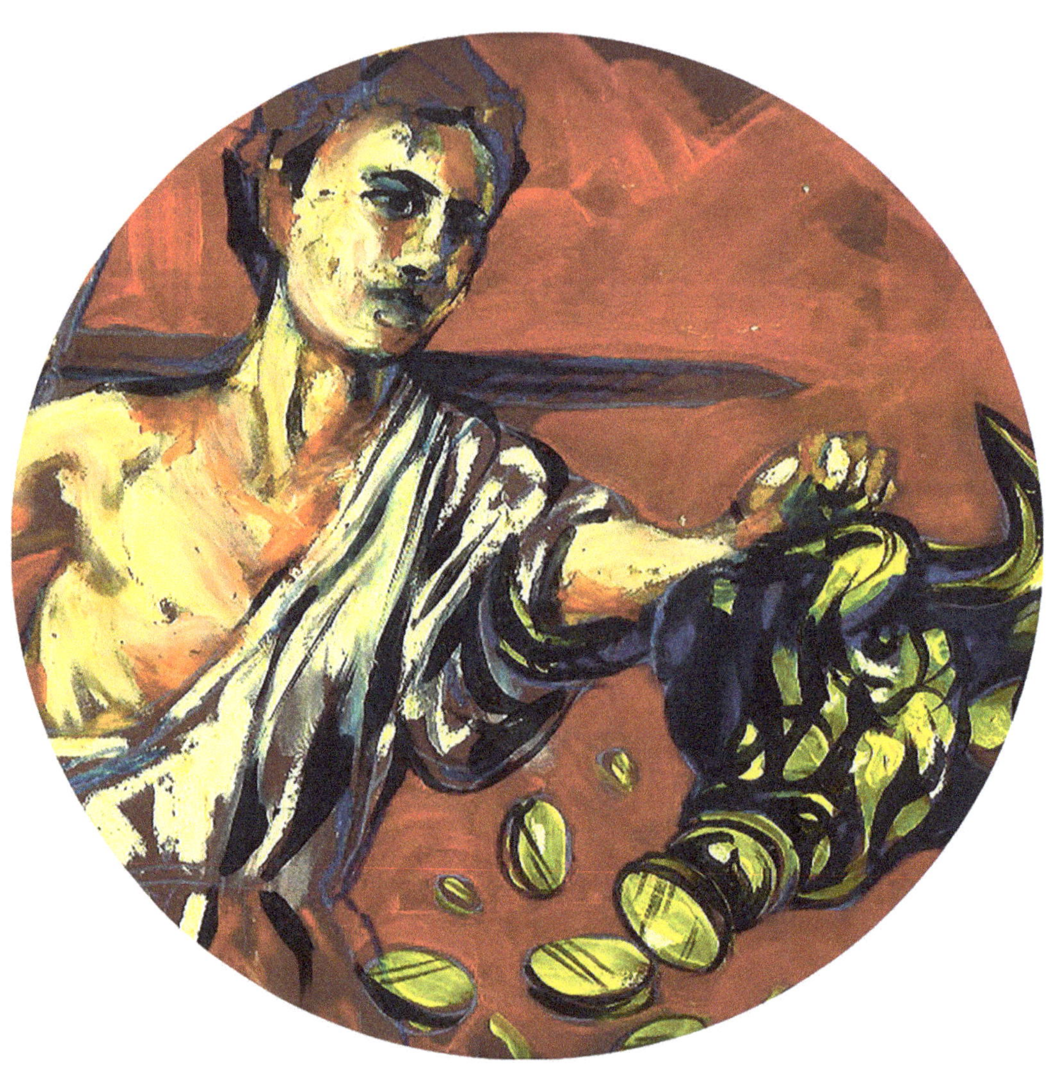

LOVE

Painting

RICH FERGUSON

LOS ANGELES, CALIFORNIA

WHAT WAS SAID AT THE REUNION OF DEATHBED WISHES

after Bob Kaufman

I wanna seek out tomorrows that drink optimism straight, no chaser.

I wanna dress our deepest sorrows in easy-to-shed miseries.

Wanna remove all billboards from the already overcrowded highways in our minds.

I wanna prove that white noise loves black jazz.

That Mr. Rogers was a CIA operative hired to test the limits of human kindness.

That the reason dogs howl is because it's far easier than reciting Ginsberg's "Howl"
by memory.

I wanna create drive-thru therapy for when we just need a to-go cup of healing.

Build monuments to love letters still written by hand.

Offer landmark status to all remaining phone booths.

I wanna construct bookstores on Mars, underground libraries for bookworms.

Create playgrounds in the cloudy eyes of the dying.

I wanna expose all false idols for being truly idle.

Recycle old lies into lions to guard the gates of greatness.

Wanna televise the next revolution without any commercials.

Swap rigged elections for introspection.

I wanna create a medication to remove unnecessary blemishes from our conscience.

Wanna drop poetry bombs into lives without enlightenment.

Compose songs of tectonic forgiveness along all our faults.

I wanna switch eyes with a stranger to see how others witness life.

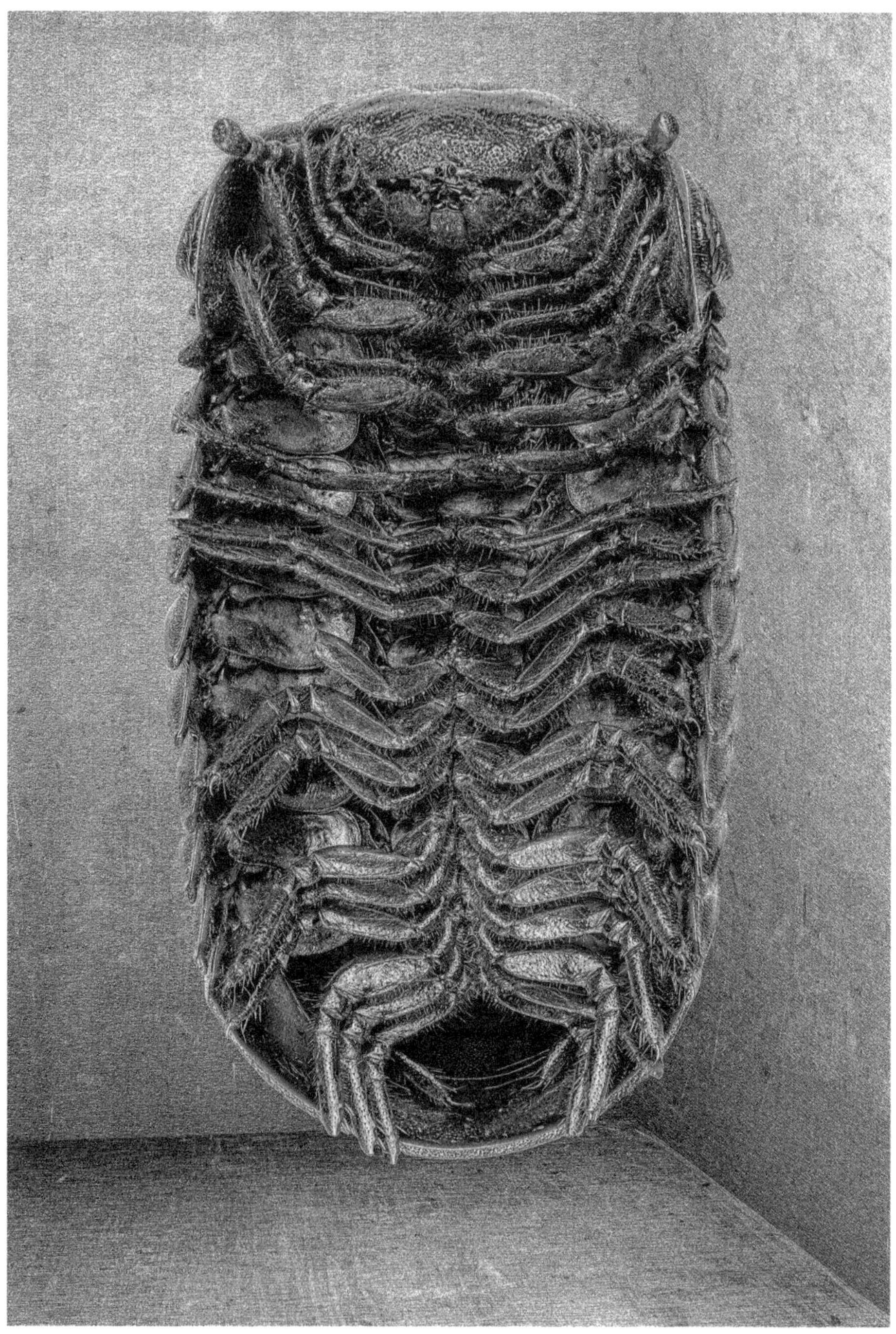

STUDY FOR HIVE MIND

JOEL ALLEGRETTI

FORT LEE, NEW JERSEY

THE HISTORY OF JAPANESE MOVIE MONSTERS: KING GHIDORAH, ORIGINALLY KINGU GIDORA

CARE FOR THIS PLANET AS IF YOU FEAR A THREE-HEADED

SPACE DRAGON WILL COME DOWN TO TORMENT

THE HUMAN RACE IN RETALIATION FOR NEGLECT.

ANATOLY KUDRYAVITSKY

DUBLIN, IRELAND

WE REGRET TO DEFORM YOU

If you create a ministry of horror, you'll have to
unleash horror

Zombies wearing zombreros
a priest of hate mistaken for Proust
Meet the ninth wife of the
a la Patria monument

Somebody drinks bottles of souls
weeping over cheap prints of peachy cheeks
Somebody dilutes into the dew
of barren aluminium fields

A hand and a heart
pastures of electricity
skulls, mariachis and chandeliers
concealed in the vault of conception

Last time we lost the world
somebody found a can of worms

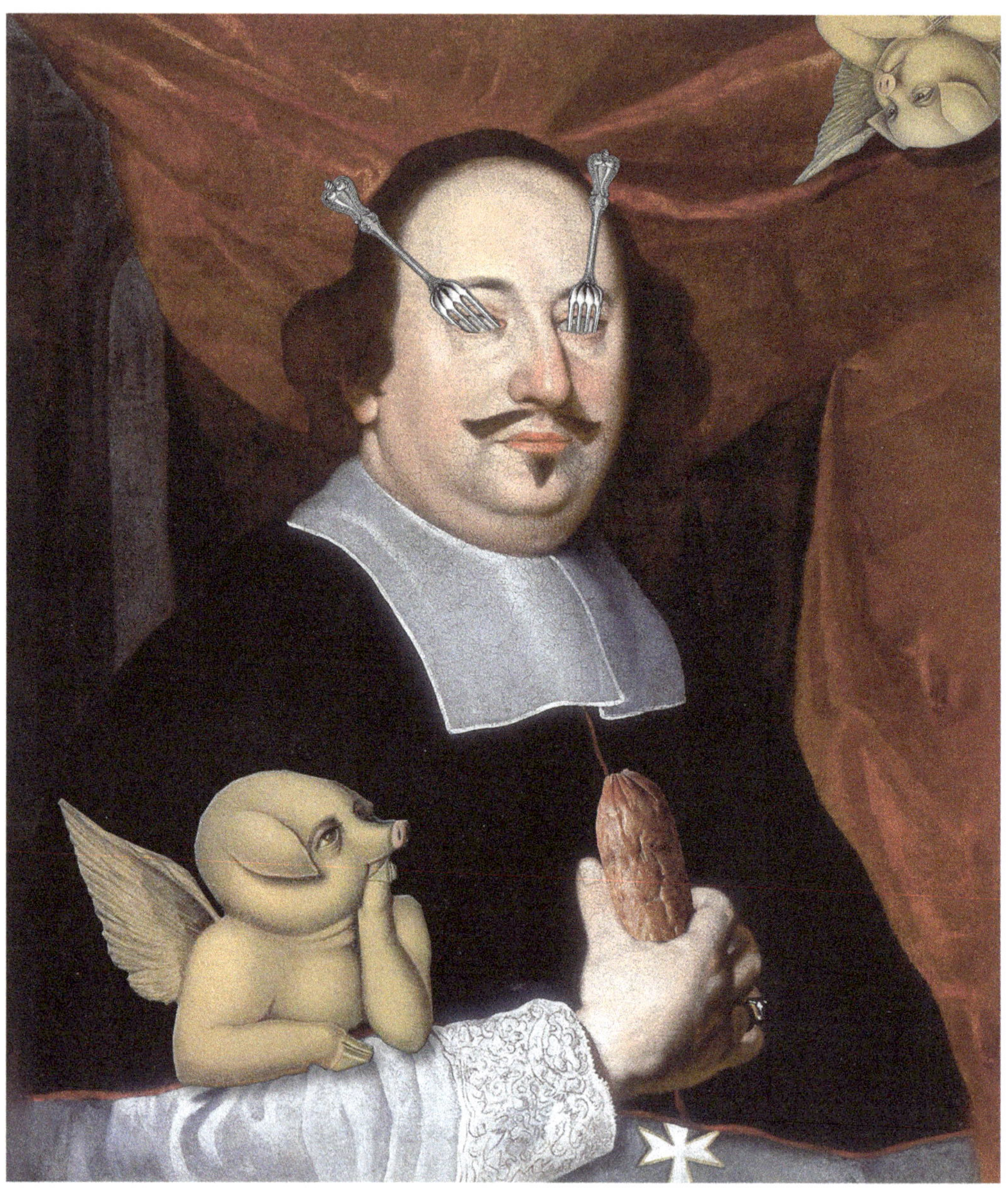

PIG OUT

MARK TUCKER

NEWCOMB, AUSTRALIA

YOU'RE WELCOME!

I'm proud to say that I breed consumers,
their minds, like mine, solely focused
on our beautiful, pristine, Economy.

At age one they are all ready
ravenous for new things. By two (get one free)
they are stealing coins from my purse,
putting metal inside their soft mouths,
tasting the spirit of money. They then drop
the coins (with hope) on the ground,
knowing soon it will buy things. And they do,
when they're three, as I watch them pass credit
cards and notes in exchange for my wonderful purchase.

We quickly run home to rejoice and undress
Mummy, sometimes Daddy, tries on a new dress
or device or machine or some plastic et cetera
before placing it straight into our cupboard

RON KOLM

NEW YORK, NEW YORK

BEACH PARTY

We sit on the beach
Wrapped in a blanket
Watching the missiles
Pass above
Heading inland.

I tell her
How much I care
But she only
Laughs
Closes her eyes
And leans back slowly.

MIKE M. MOLLETT

LOS ANGELES, CALIFORNIA

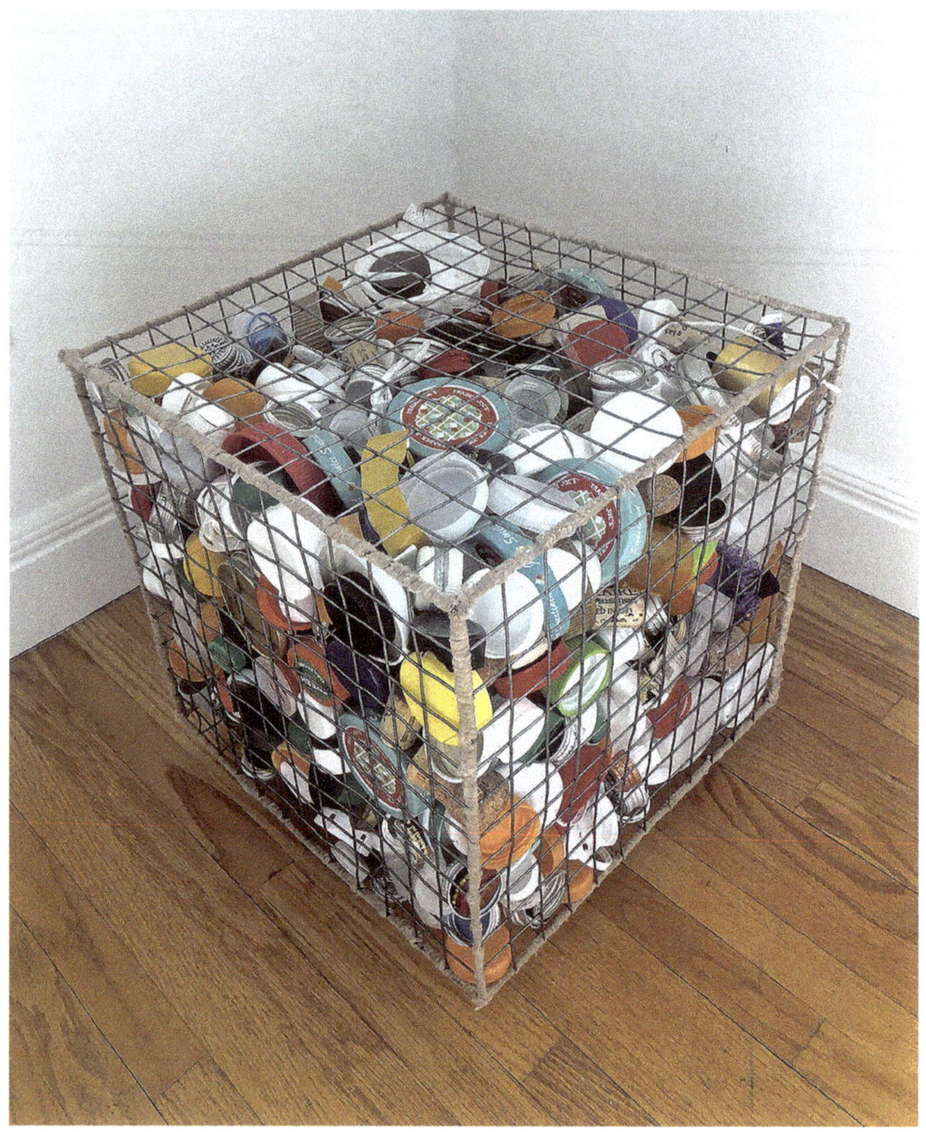

CONSUMPTION

Sculpture

MICHAEL BRUNER / MIKE M. MOLLETT

LAS VEGAS, NEVADA / LOS ANGELES, CALIFORNIA

IMPERFECTLY PACKED PARCELS
FOR THE NEEDS OF THE PEOPLE

See the flesh marks spreading across the skin, something eating there in the fast lane tissue.

Stop pouring concrete on the fires, gulping in the next of kin.

Be aware of all that you see, this on your mark, next mark next, swimming in water, fluttering at the graveyard.

Bad, sad, naughty news. Ice cream is hit red, gouging so the message is already wounding the person in your line to eat or be eaten.

Wait for your ride to another heaven or hell, as she loves to entertain with change and strange, as the nights reveal unspeakable aliveness.

Beware: you may be at risk of not knowing who you are.

Technology joys us, questions our mother, sends her hurtful messages, winds, and shocking her body, her soul. Rising waters, drying species, cancer's mortality. What sense is this?

Synthetic graveyards follow the stream. Drying land, floating ways, banks on ethereal strange separations. New languages to what must be, read with eyes open as dust.

The ghosts tell the truth, and they say with all the things breathing and needing that she is hurt and reacts to this rape explosively.

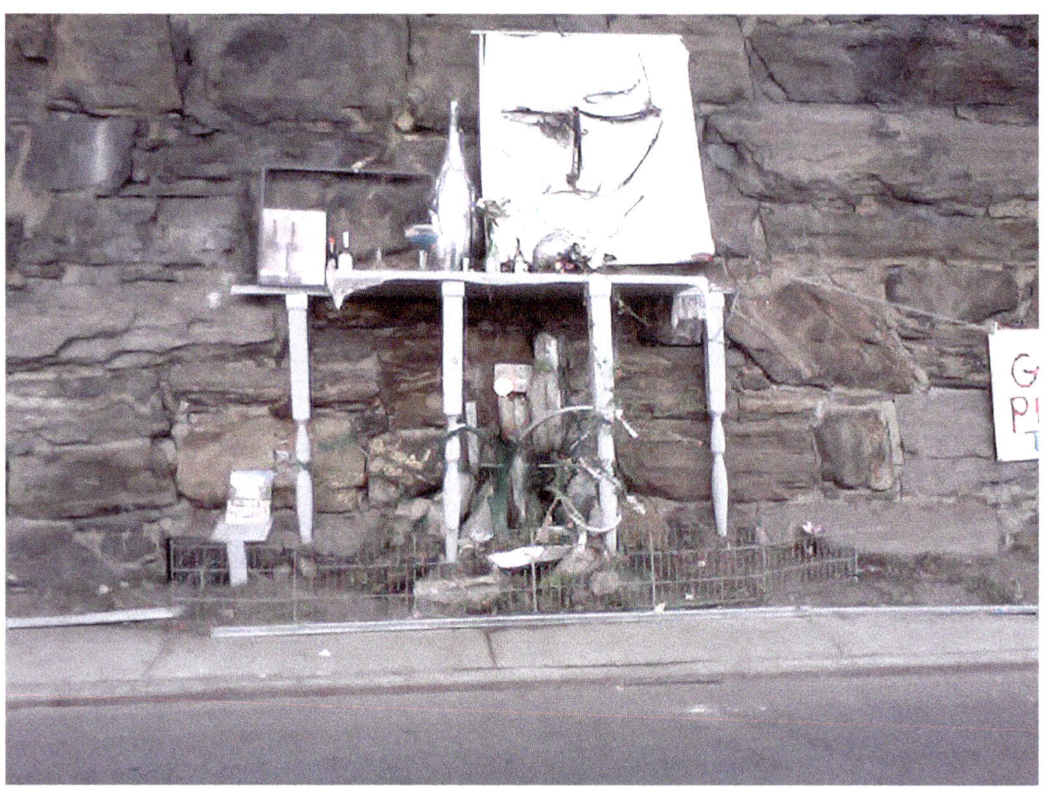

"FURIES" FDR DRIVE

*Self portrait . . .the medium,
Blown and mangled highway tire*

RICHARD LORANGER

OAKLAND, CALIFORNIA

GLUTEN-FREE BETSY ROSS DOLL

comes at you with a knife, screams,

Gimme sum morra that beer!

and collapses in a sobbing heap.

What is it about America

that makes this all so possible?

She rips her bodice and reveals a huge

Pinocchio tattoo encompassing her breasts.

It was a birthday gift from George, she explains,

seeing your disquietude. He inked it himself.

So much for sewing flags and quilting bees; we now

aspire to become America's Top New Genital, while

worker bees and shining geniuses of color are gunned down

in the streets, pureed, and folded into insecticide.

A drone hovers somewhere above you, buzzing, buzzing,

pisses on your head, and Twitters your reaction to the NSA.

Betsy picks herself up slowly, straightens her disheveled everything,

looks down the street and says, I'm gonna catch the 39

out to Paradise Point. That's where all the action is.

—and walks away, trailing a musk of longing and despair.

You pick up the knife and lunge at the nearest pedestrian,

a podiatrist in a sandwich board. The knife

sticks in the board between the image of the second and middle toe.

You scream, Gimme sum morra that beer!

The podiatrist barks, Two for a dollar! Two for a dollar!

and walks on, blade still firmly planted in their signage.

You look wistfully for Betsy, seeking some

sort of connection to the past, but she has been labeled a commodity,

swept up, and sold to a horny vegan tech bro.

VALERIE SOFRANKO

PITTSBURGH, PENNSYLVANIA

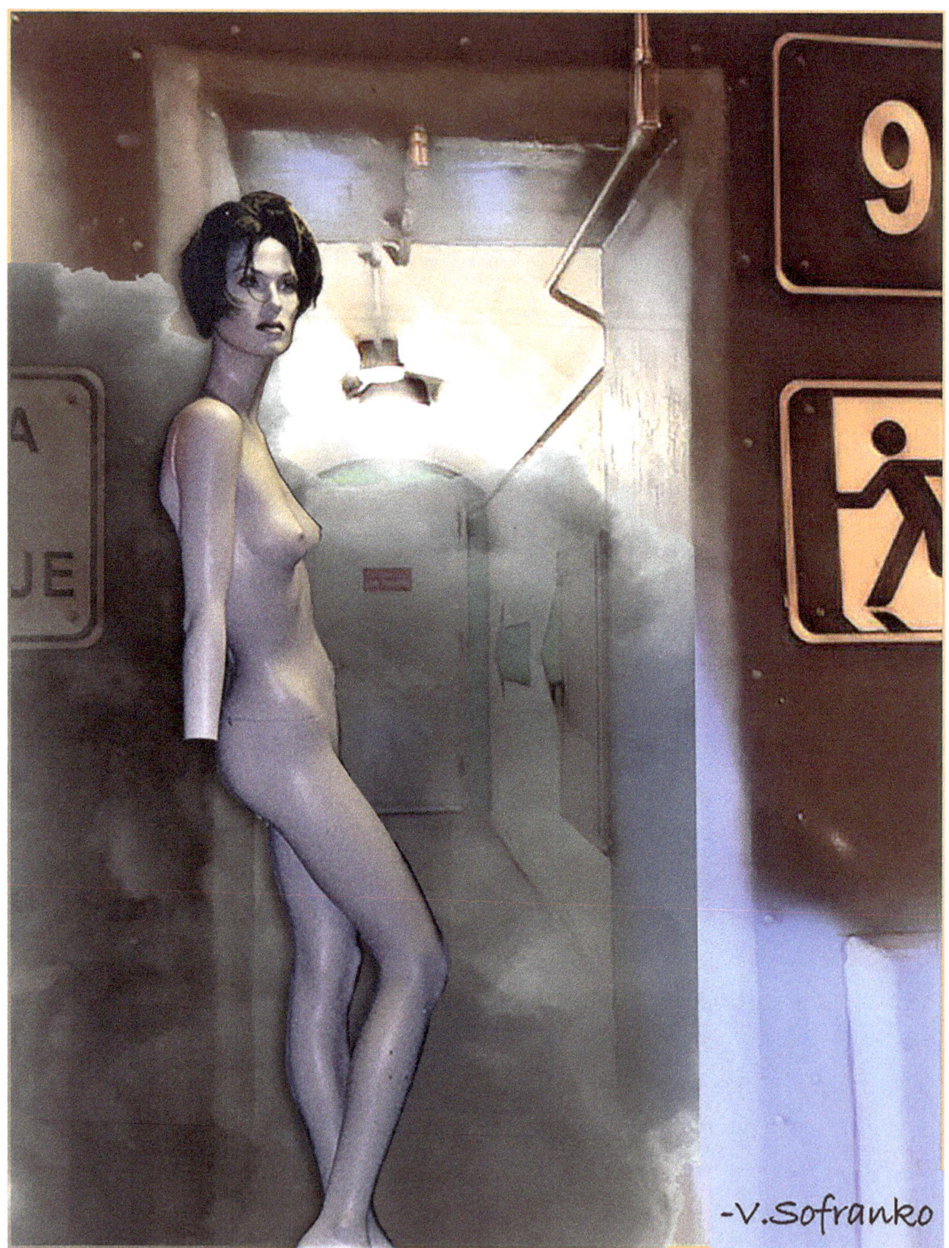

WAITING ON TRANSIT

ANOEK VAN PRAAG

NEW YORK, NEW YORK

WOUNDED

gradually taken by shock
so out of step so out of touch
with needs and wants
breaking into bleeding others
a place unknown
a place but not at home
fear shutting down senses
common senses
overlaying tsunamis of grief
turning into narcissistic rage
disguised in clowning armor
like an animal about to die
breaking into bleeding self
obliterate all that is known
breach the identity of moral land
it cannot last unless
eventually will explode
scattering around the globe
family and friends catching pieces
release into nowhere space
what is left is nothing doing nothing thinking
tragedy of vaste proportion
all things alive suffer now
suffer later and forever
until unless undo
just fluid stillness
just stillness
still

ROSALIE GANCIE

HYATTSVILLE, MARYLAND

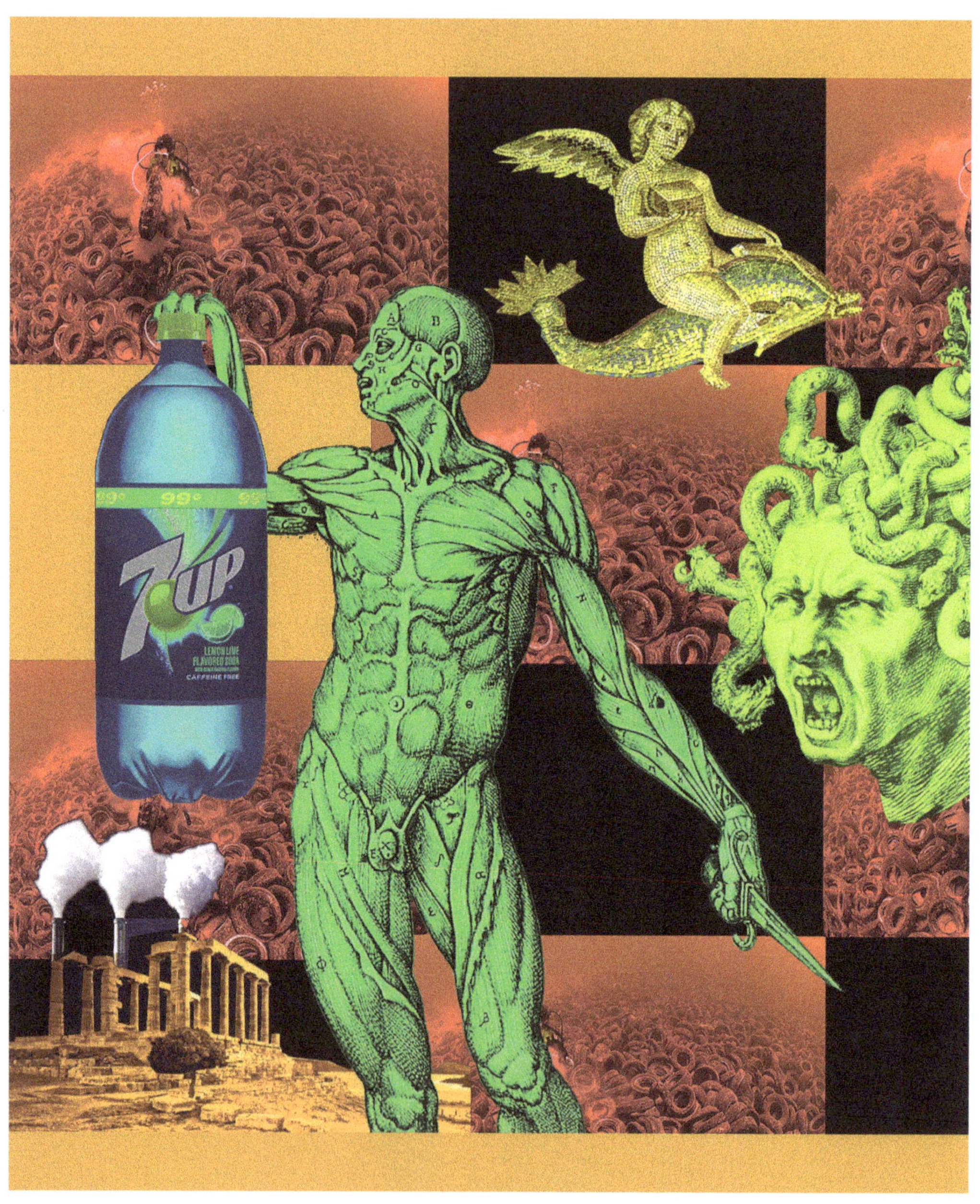

HELL SERIES NO. 1

JOHN DUTTERER

GLEN BURNIE, MARYLAND

KOREA CHORALE

Fisty pump at the smoky-sky

Tummy rub T-Rex

Scepter straight up

Bathtub of doom

Sexy leakage

Makes the sea burn

Like I warned you

Mood for love

Means Tokyo goes

Goody mushroom

Blew Hawaii

Sweet captive

Like I promised

Afterglow harem

Tummy rub

Forever and ever

Megafauna sleep

ALICE ESPINOSA-CINCOTTA

NEW YORK, NEW YORK

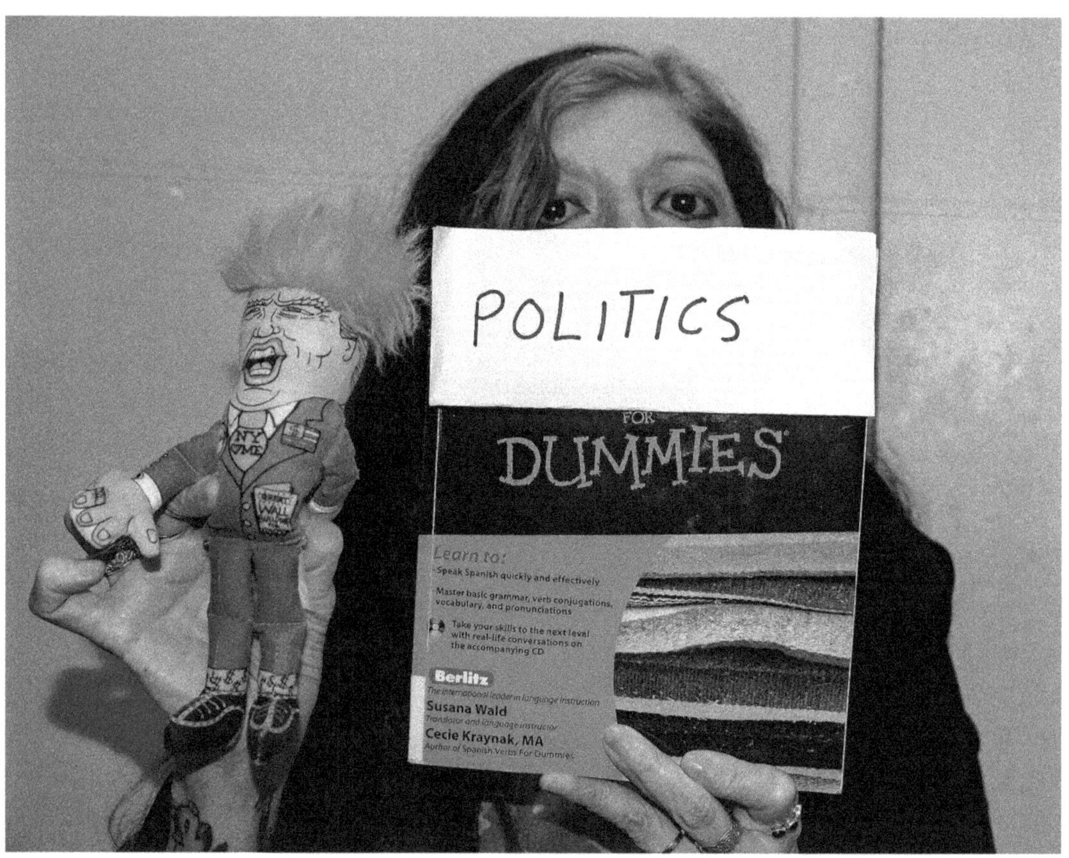

**DEAR MISINFORMED PUBLIC—
OPEN YOUR EYES! GET INFORMED—LEARN THE TRUTH!**

Photograph

RICHARD STONE

SAN FRANCISCO, CALIFORNIA

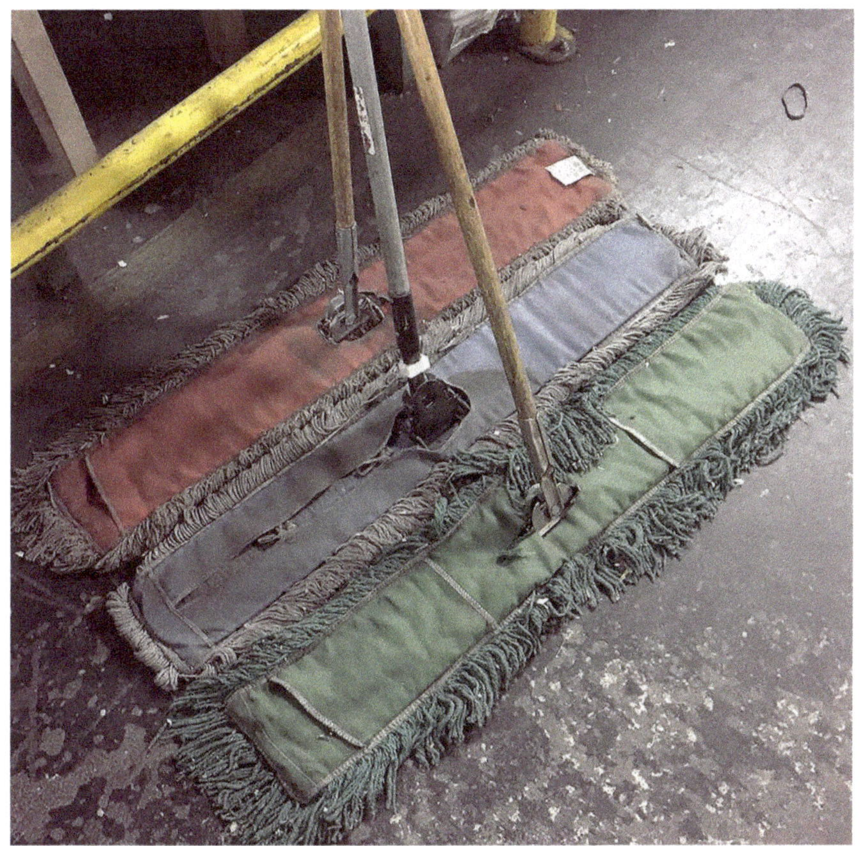

THREE PARTY SWEEP

Photograph

DUŠKA VRHOVAC

BELGRADE, SERBIA

THE OMNIPATRIOTIC

They taught you that the flag was a symbol and fate,
yesterday, today, and tomorrow of your story
a piece of fabric you have to swear over
and unremarkably go down in history!
It ties with your flock,
stirs up the strength and makes the blood boil.
That is why you keep it in your heart
and tattoo it on your chest!
But over that silk cloth
heroes and bandits, murderers and victims swear too
with that piece of silk
every kind of life story and coffin is covered.

You think you're a citizen of the world,
wanting to change the planet!
You believe you have the courage and knowledge,
it's your mission , purpose and path!
That how the first part of the story goes.
In the second part you go to seek your fortune,
running away from politics
and going into somebody else's country
to burn a flag there, usually other people's one,
to raise your voice over there,
to say there a worthy word!

On the doorstep of your home and your parliament
burn or kiss your flag,
it all starts there and it ends too!
Wherever you go you'll want to come back
as the cot and cross are from the same wood
Diaper and shroud from the same fabric!
Only endless sky is same everywhere
Although no one has strongly confirmed it.

FRANCINE WITTE

NEW YORK, NEW YORK

YOUR ROBOT BOYFRIEND

and here's what you need to know.

You need to know there's no room for rubber. No bounce.
You fuck up, and it's forever. He is made of steel, and
anything steel will break your heart. Think about your metal
spatula. Turning over your morning eggs. No concern about
heat. Just keeps moving.

Your robo bf also doesn't care about sin. Will not try to hide
anything. This sounds good in theory, but you have
enjoyed being hidden to. You just didn't know it.

Robo dude won't bother testing you. So you are in no
danger. He is aware of all your microchip information. He
factors in your flaws., but he also knows you like pistachio.
So there's that.

You will never have an argument with R-baby. To him, it
means nothing that you want to wear an orange jumpsuit
to a funeral. He will never have a funeral, btw.

And you can forget about dandruff and fangtooths and
anything you've ever held over a boyfriend's head.
Robocats don't have a head. They are big dutch ovens. If
you want, you can pop the top and cook spaghetti. Bonus.

Now you know everything. But you'll never know more
than big fat Robo Daddy. He knows more than everything.
He knows what's not even knowable.

He knows how much you like that.

PETER CARLAFTES

NEW YORK, NEW YORK

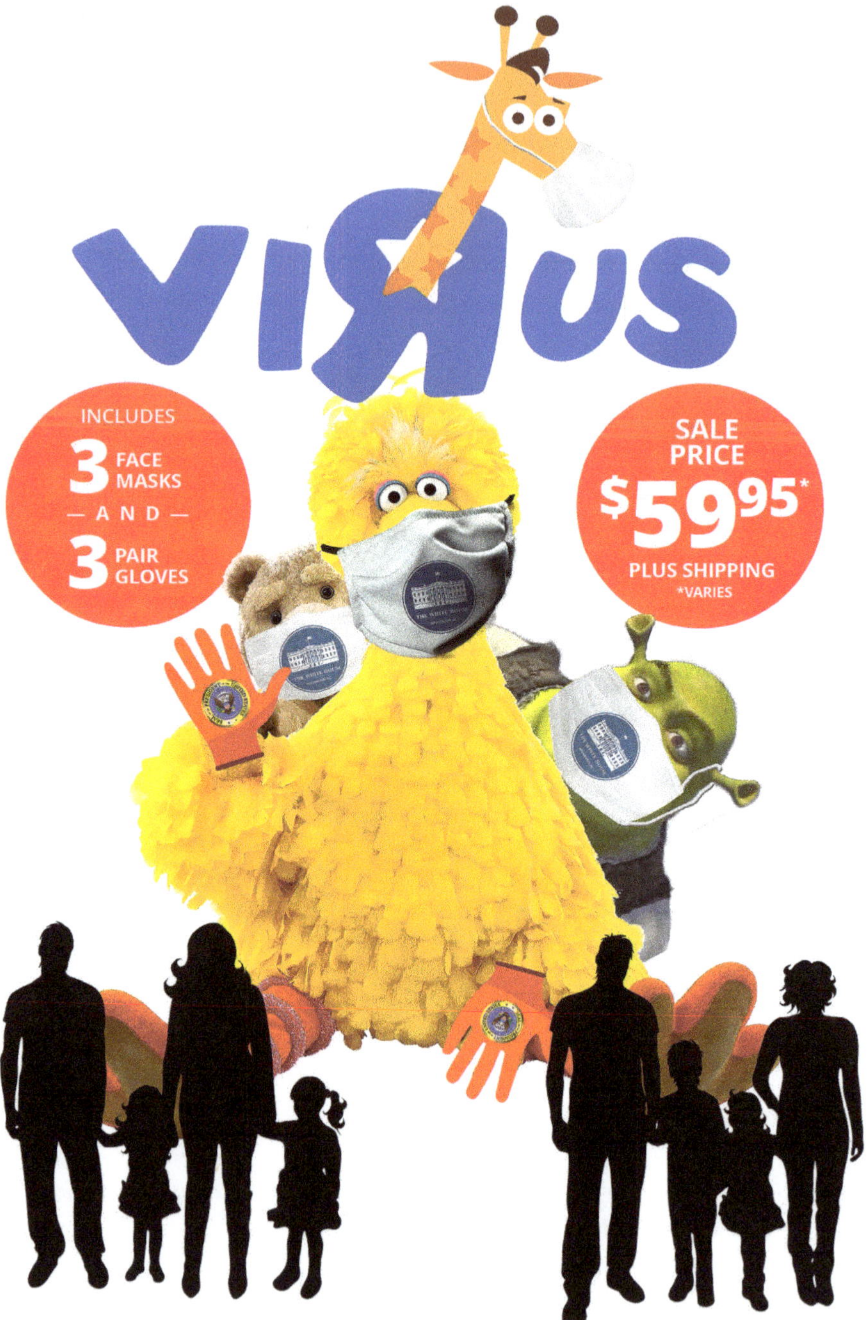

BLED BY EXAMPLE

This is the Official White House Pandemic Prevention Gear website. So, while you parents have returned to work to ensure that America STAYS Great, your little ones can take care of their little yones and be ready for the next pandemic. Included in your HHS-approved package are 3 face masks and 3 pairs of gloves plus simplified instructions from the DOE. All proceeds go to the President's favorite charity organization—RED, WHITE, and KU. Suggested purchase—ONE per child.

IMPORTANT: While investments are NOT tax deductible, the IRS will be notified either way— if you've been GOOD or BAD. (For Toy Use Only!!!). (Toys not included).

FEDERICO FEDERICI
FINALE LIGURE, ITALY

ISBN

Select Recent and Forthcoming Books from Three Rooms Press

FICTION

Rishab Borah
The Door to Inferna

Meagan Brothers
Weird Girl and What's His Name

Christopher Chambers
Scavenger

Ron Dakron
Hello Devilfish!

Robert Duncan
Loudmouth

Michael T. Fournier
Hidden Wheel
Swing State

William Least Heat-Moon
Celestial Mechanics

Aimee Herman
Everything Grows

Eamon Loingsigh
Light of the Diddicoy
Exile on Bridge Street

John Marshall
The Greenfather

Aram Saroyan
Still Night in L.A.

Richard Vetere
The Writers Afterlife
Champagne and Cocaine

Julia Watts
Quiver

Gina Yates
Narcissus Nobody

MEMOIR & BIOGRAPHY

Nassrine Azimi and Michel Wasserman
*Last Boat to Yokohama: The Life and
Legacy of Beate Sirota Gordon*
(English & Persian editions)

William S. Burroughs & Allen Ginsberg
*Don't Hide the Madness:
William S. Burroughs in Conversation
with Allen Ginsberg*
edited by Steven Taylor

James Carr
BAD: The Autobiography of James Carr

Judith Malina
*Full Moon Stages:
Personal Notes from
50 Years of The Living Theatre*

Phil Marcade
*Punk Avenue: Inside the New York City
Underground, 1972–1982*

Alvin Orloff
*Disasterama! Adventures in the Queer
Underground 1977–1997*

Nicca Ray
*Ray by Ray: A Daughter's Take
on the Legend of Nicholas Ray*

Stephen Spotte
*My Watery Self:
Memoirs of a Marine Scientist*

PHOTOGRAPHY-MEMOIR

Mike Watt
On & Off Bass

SHORT STORY ANTHOLOGIES

SINGLE AUTHOR

The Alien Archives: Stories
by Robert Silverberg

First-Person Singularities: Stories
by Robert Silverberg
with an introduction by John Scalzi

Tales from the Eternal Café: Stories
by Janet Hamill, with an introduction
by Patti Smith

*Time and Time Again:
Sixteen Trips in Time*
by Robert Silverberg

MULTI-AUTHOR

*Crime + Music: Twenty Stories
of Music-Themed Noir*
edited by Jim Fusilli

Dark City Lights: New York Stories
edited by Lawrence Block

*The Faking of the President: Twenty
Stories of White House Noir*
edited by Peter Carlaftes

*Florida Happens:
Bouchercon 2018 Anthology*
edited by Greg Herren

*Have a NYC I, II & III:
New York Short Stories;*
edited by Peter Carlaftes
& Kat Georges

*Songs of My Selfie:
An Anthology of Millennial Stories*
edited by Constance Renfrow

*The Obama Inheritance:
15 Stories of Conspiracy Noir*
edited by Gary Phillips

*This Way to the End Times:
Classic and New Stories of
the Apocalypse*
edited by Robert Silverberg

MIXED MEDIA

John S. Paul
Sign Language: A Painter's Notebook
(photography, poetry and prose)

FILM & PLAYS

Israel Horovitz
*My Old Lady: Complete Stage Play
and Screenplay with an Essay on
Adaptation*

Peter Carlaftes
Triumph For Rent (3 Plays)
Teatrophy (3 More Plays)

Kat Georges
*Three Somebodies: Plays about
Notorious Dissidents*

DADA

*Maintenant: A Journal of
Contemporary Dada Writing & Art*
(Annual, since 2008)

TRANSLATIONS

Thomas Bernhard
On Earth and in Hell
(poems of Thomas Bernhard with English
translations by Peter Waugh)

Patrizia Gattaceca
Isula d'Anima / Soul Island
(poems by the author in Corsican with
English translations)

César Vallejo | Gerard Malanga
Malanga Chasing Vallejo
(selected poems of César Vallejo
with English translations and additional
notes by Gerard Malanga)

George Wallace
EOS: Abductor of Men
(selected poems in Greek & English)

ESSAYS

Vanessa Baden
Home is the Mouth of a Shark

Richard Katrovas
*Raising Girls in Bohemia: Meditations of an
American Father*

*Womentality: Thirteen Empowering Stories
by Everyday Women Who Said Goodbye to
the Workplace and Hello to Their Lives*
edited by Erin Wildermuth

HUMOR

Peter Carlaftes
A Year on Facebook

POETRY COLLECTIONS

Hala Alyan
Atrium

Peter Carlaftes
DrunkYard Dog
I Fold with the Hand I Was Dealt

Thomas Fucaloro
It Starts from the Belly and Blooms
*Inheriting Craziness is Like
a Soft Halo of Light*

Kat Georges
Our Lady of the Hunger

Robert Gibbons
Close to the Tree

Israel Horovitz
Heaven and Other Poems

Matthew Hupert
Ism is a Retrovirus

David Lawton
Sharp Blue Stream

Jane LeCroy
Signature Play

Philip Meersman
This is Belgian Chocolate

Jane Ormerod
Recreational Vehicles on Fire
Welcome to the Museum of Cattle

Lisa Panepinto
On This Borrowed Bike

George Wallace
Poppin' Johnny

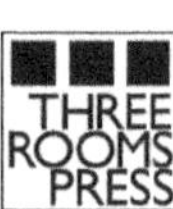

Three Rooms Press | New York, NY
Current Catalog: www.threeroomspress.com | Contact: info@threeroomspress.com
Three Rooms Press books are distributed internationally by PGW/Ingram: www.pgw.com